A Family Business

A Family Business

Kinship and Social Control in Organized Crime

Francis A. J. Ianni
Horace Mann-Lincoln Institute

with Elizabeth Reuss-Ianni
Institute for Social Analysis

RUSSELL SAGE FOUNDATION
NEW YORK

PUBLICATIONS OF RUSSELL SAGE FOUNDATION

Russell Sage Foundation was established in 1907 by Mrs. Russell Sage for the improvement of social and living conditions in the United States. In carrying out its purpose the Foundation conducts research under the direction of members of the staff or in close collaboration with other institutions, and supports programs designed to develop and demonstrate productive working relations between social scientists and other professional groups. As an integral part of its operation, the Foundation from time to time publishes books or pamphlets resulting from these activities. Publication under the imprint of the Foundation does not necessarily imply agreement by the Foundation, its Trustees, or its staff with the interpretations or conclusions of the authors.

Russell Sage Foundation
230 Park Avenue, New York, N.Y. 10017

La Famiglia "Lupollo":

> *Lu mortu è mortu,*
> *pinsamu a lu vivu.*

Contents

List of Illustrations

Foreword

In *A Family Business,* Francis Ianni presents an eloquent demonstration of the value of the field methods of the social anthropologist for the discovery of social processes in a field of human activity that is completely closed against other research methods commonly used by social scientists.

Many years ago when I began the field work leading to *Street Corner Society,* I hoped to gain an inside view of what were known locally as the rackets and racketeering. A precarious relationship with a "50 percent man" (the second level from the bottom of the organization) represented my farthest penetration into the world of organized crime. Thus, while I express my admiration for Ianni's achievement, I must seek to explain how he was able to do it.

As Ianni says, being of Italian extraction facilitated his entree, but I would not be inclined to put too much weight on this factor. In the North End of Boston, a friend of mine once lost a five dollar bet when it turned out that I was *not* of Italian extraction. Apparently he had assumed that since I fitted into the local scene, I must share the ethnic background of the other fellows on the corner.

Clearly Ianni has exceptional skills as a participant observer. He also is a man of great patience, being content to be on the scene repeatedly, over a period of many months, to let the story unfold before him. To be sure, he did a good deal of informal interviewing, but he adjusted the depth and range of the topics covered to the closeness of his relations with the informant and was careful not to "press" with the kind of questions that might have jeopardized his position in the social system.

Beyond personal skills, Ianni was able to recognize the difference between the outsider's and the insider's view of the scene he was studying. To the outsider, whose knowledge is limited to what he picks up from the mass media, the world of organized crime appears to be peopled by monsters engaged in a highly secret conspiracy against society. It is hard then to imagine any member of the conspiracy being willing to talk frankly with any non-member.

Ianni proceeded on a different set of assumptions. Distorted and fragmentary though they may be, reports in the mass media make frequent reference to "crime families." It occurred to Ianni that it could be useful to set out to study the family in this social context just as the anthropologist might study a family system in other settings. He could then expect to encounter recognizable human beings participating in a network of interpersonal relations and engaged in activities which seemed quite ordinary and defensible to them. Ianni followed that network where it led him. It did not lead him into intimate contact with illegal activities, for he found a degree of specialization and division of labor within the family, and his relations were closest among those largely engaged in "legitimate" activities. However, he did learn enough of the dynamics of the family system to provide an important new perspective on organized crime.

Ianni also places his study in a context of social processes having their roots in Sicily and goes on to show how successive generations of his family make different adaptations to American society. We see how illegal activities have served as a base from which later generations have become "respectable" business men and professionals, in some cases being cut off entirely from illegal activities. With changes in ethnic distribution in the central city, we also see new groups of organizers from the Black and Puerto Rican communities moving in on terrain once held by this Italian-American family, while its members in turn shift toward new lines of business activities.

For anyone who wishes to see beyond the headlines regarding organized crime, this is an essential guide book. It is also necessary reading for serious students of urban life.

William Foote Whyte

February 1972

Acknowledgments

Parts of Chapter 2, Chapter 3, and Chapter 8 appeared in slightly different form in an article entitled "The Mafia and the Web of Kinship" in *The Public Interest,* Winter 1971. Parts of Chapters 6 and 7 were originally published in "Formal and Social Organization in an Organized Crime 'Family': A Case Study," *University of Florida Law Review* (Vol. XXIV, No. 1, Fall 1971.)

While I am solely responsible for the data on the Lupollo and De Maio families described in this book, my colleagues Francesco Cerase of the *Instituto di Statistica e Ricerca Sociale* at the University of Rome and Elizabeth Reuss-Ianni of the Institute for Social Analysis each had responsibility for particular areas of the field work. Cerase reviewed the extensive Italian literature on criminal secret societies and, working with Donatella Torzo, developed the ethnographic and demographic materials on Corleone. Ms. Reuss-Ianni did the literature search in this country and also interviewed government law enforcement personnel at the federal and local level, and relatives and neighbors of the Lupollos.

I am greatly indebted to a number of colleagues and friends for help, encouragement, and criticism. First thanks must go to Russell Sage Foundation for the financial assistance which made the study possible and to three members of the Foundation staff who were particularly helpful. David Goslin helped conceptualize the study and turned me toward the Foundation, and Orville G. Brim, Jr., president of the Foundation accepted the notion of this rather unusual proposal with understanding, and I think, courage. Hugh F. Cline, incumbent president of the Foundation, was the program officer who monitored the project and also monitored me with impartial doses of criticism and encouragement when each was needed. Not a few of the ideas in this book resulted from long conversations in which his insight helped resolve any number of conceptual problems.

Frank Jennings, Dwight Smith, Daniel Bell, Lawrence Cremin, Pietro Russo, Harold Laswell, and Spenser Jameson read sections of the manuscript in various stages of development and offered ideas and suggestions. Ralph Salerno, Franco Ferracuti, and William Foote Whyte read the manuscript in its entirety and their criticisms reshaped portions of it. Luigi Barzini and Giovanni Schiavo offered suggestions after reading "Mafia and the Web of Kinship" which were incorporated into this book. Helen Hardy, my administrative assistant, organized a number of typists and editors to complete the manuscript.

Finally, I wish to thank my students in the Seminar on Social Organization and Robert Schaefer and John Fischer (my dean and president) for understanding that some notions about social organization are common to both secret societies and to education.

1 / Introduction

On March 14, 1891, Italians throughout the world celebrated the birthday of Umberto I, then in his thirteenth year as king of the newly unified Italy. The Italians in New Orleans were no exception, and Umberto's royal banner fluttered throughout the city's "Little Italy." But the festivities were short-lived. Ironically, the flags flying in the Italian sector helped provoke a mob of citizens to violence which climaxed with the killing of eleven imprisoned Italians.

Many Italians had settled early in New Orleans. At first they worked as day laborers or as fishermen, but by 1890 they had made economic advances. They owned more than three thousand small businesses in New Orleans, controlled much of the wholesaling and retailing of fruits and vegetables, and were struggling with the Irish for control of the docks. As the Italians displaced the Irish on the docks, however, rival gangs of Sicilian and Neapolitan stevedores found themselves in competition for business.

The rivalry between the Neapolitans Joe and George Provenzano, and the newly arrived Sicilian Charles Matranga finally broke into violence. New Orleans police chief David Hennessey charged that the *Mafia,* a secret criminal society imported by Sicilian immigrants, was responsible. He claimed they were conspiring with other Sicilians to organize crime throughout the United States. He announced that he had written to Rome for the criminal records of some *Mafia* members, and would publicize the records when they arrived. Hennessey never got a chance to carry out his threat. As he returned home on the evening of October 15, 1890, he was ambushed and shot. Nine hours later, Hennessey died, but not before he reputedly identified his assassins as "Dagos."

The killing outraged New Orleans. Hennessey had threatened to expose the *Mafia,* and he had been assassinated. The link was quickly made, and hundreds of Italians were arrested. Fourteen were eventually indicted, and finally nine, including a young boy accused of running ahead of Hennessey to whistle a signal to the assassins, were tried. The jury deliberated for nine hours, found six defendants not guilty, and failed to decide on the other three. All the defendants were then remanded to the Parish Jail on Bienville Street to await trial on other charges.

The verdicts shocked the citizenry; they had expected a quick trial and

1

immediate justice. Public feeling ran high. It was rumored that quantities of gold had been seen and sinister threats heard in the courtroom as the *Mafia* attempted simultaneously to bribe and threaten the jury. The furor came to a head on Umberto's birthday. Angry citizens, misinterpreting the Italian flags as an audacious celebration of the prisoners' acquittal, decided to take action. A group of twenty entered the Parish Jail by a side door, and while several thousand men, women and children milled outside, massacred the nine accused assassins and two other Italian prisoners as well.

The massacre stirred the world. American editorial opinion condemned the mob, but also expressed fears that criminals spewed from southern European prisons were invading the country. The Italian government protested and recalled its minister from Washington. It was even rumored that Italy's then-powerful fleet might attack. Eventually, the United States agreed to pay an indemnity of $25,000 to the families of the three victims who were Italian citizens, and the incident passed quietly into history.

But many questions about the killings remain unanswered. Were the nine men innocent or guilty? What were the slain police chief's motives? Did anyone tamper with the jury? Were the lynch mob's leaders moved by outrage or by prejudice? These questions, although interesting to the social historian, have little present importance. One major question, however, still concerns Americans today: is there a secret nationwide society of Italian immigrants—a *Mafia* which controls crime in America?

Americans have long assumed that there is. In 1890, one of the two grand juries investigating the Hennessey assassination reported:

> The range of our researches has developed the existence of the secret organization styled *Mafia.* The evidence comes from several sources fully competent in themselves to attest to its truth, while the fact is supported by the long record of blood-curdling crimes, it being almost impossible to discover the perpetrators or to secure witnesses.[1]

Nor was the *Mafia* conspiracy found only in New Orleans. The New York *Tribune,* in editorial reaction to the worldwide condemnation of the New Orleans massacre declared that:

> . . . not only in New Orleans but generally in large cities throughout the country, Italians of criminal antecedents and propensities are more or less closely affiliated for the purpose of requiting injuries and gratifying animosities by secret vengeance. These organizations, in common speech and belief are connected with the *Mafia,* and that designation fairly indicates their character and motives. Through their agency the most infernal crimes have been committed and have gone unpunished. They have succeeded in keeping their existence

---

[1] Quoted in Giovanni Schiavo, *The Truth about the Mafia and Organized Crime in America,* El Paso: Vigo Press, 1962, p. 146.

and doings wrapped in mystery and darkness, and in the opinion of thousands who condemn the New Orleans Mob, a branch of the order is immediately responsible for the crime which the mob avenged.[2]

As the furor over the New Orleans lynchings subsided, the public lost interest in the *Mafia;* only a few law-enforcement officials remained concerned. The wave of Italian immigration during the first years of this century reawakened public fears about the importation of crime, but the First World War ended both immigration and concern. During Prohibition, public interest in crime was raised again, but this time included Irish and Jewish crime as well as Italian. In the late 1930's and early 1940's, District Attorneys Thomas E. Dewey and William O'Dwyer exposed "Murder Incorporated," a reputedly nationwide ring of Jewish and Italian extortionists and murderers, bringing the issue of a national conspiracy of crime to public attention once again. But the Second World War intervened, and the public had other things to think about. Not until 1951, when Senator Estes Kefauver's Senate Crime Committee concluded that "there is a nationwide crime syndicate known as the *Mafia* [whose] leaders are usually found in control of the most lucrative rackets in their cities," did the specter of a *Mafia* in the United States reappear.

Even after the Kefauver Committee's investigations, the existence of a national organization of Italian-American criminals—whether *Mafia* or something else—remained a plausible but unproved contention of some law-enforcement agencies and federal investigative bodies. In the early 1950's, even the Federal Bureau of Investigation doubted the existence of a *Mafia* or any other national crime syndicate in the United States.

In November 1957, however, police broke up a large meeting of Italian-Americans in the village of Apalachin, New York. Between sixty and one hundred men had gathered at the house of Joseph Barbara, a reputed *Mafia* leader. Barbara and some of his guests claimed they were just old friends meeting to have a steak roast. The newspapers and the police insisted that it was a meeting of *Mafia* bosses. Whatever the purpose of the meeting, it had two main effects: it seemed to substantiate the belief in a centrally organized confederation of Italian-American criminals, and it sparked more thorough attempts to investigate and uncover the nationwide criminal apparatus.

Investigators were still limited, however. No one had ever publicly admitted membership in the *Mafia* or any other Italian-American criminal confederation. Evidence was second-hand, gathered through police intelligence, observation of suspected members, and electronic eavesdropping. In 1963, however, Joseph Valachi testified before the Permanent Subcommittee on Investigations of the Committee on Government Operation ("the McClel-

---

[2] New York *Tribune,* March 23, 1891.

lan committee") of the U. S. Senate. He claimed he was a member of a nationwide criminal organization called the *Cosa Nostra*. Valachi was serving a twenty-year term in Atlanta's federal penitentiary, and he had killed another prisoner because (Valachi said) he had mistaken the man for a *Cosa Nostra* assassin chosen to kill him for informing. He reported that he still feared for his life, since his former associates were even more determined to get him, and that his only hope was to destroy them first. The testimony received wide public attention, but produced little information that had not already been made public in government reports on the *Mafia*—a name that Valachi insisted he had never heard used.

After Valachi testified, *Mafia* and *Cosa Nostra* began to be used interchangeably as generic terms for organized crime. It should be pointed out that they are not the same. *Cosa Nostra,* if it exists, is native to America; a nationwide *Mafia* organization, if it exists, is an American adaptation of a form of organization that originated in Sicily. In itself, Valachi's testimony has one disturbing characteristic from the scholar's point of view. The *Cosa Nostra* he describes is very similar to the national criminal syndicate that the government law-enforcement agencies had been maintaining was in existence.

More information emerged in 1969. The government suddenly released partial transcripts of tapes made by electronic surveillance of *Cosa Nostra* suspects. The segments and summaries which were made public (as the "De Cavalcante tapes") pointed to the existence of an Italian-American criminal organization (at least in the New York–New Jersey–Pennsylvania area) and suggested that it was overseen by some type of commission. Unfortunately, the tapes themselves were not released.

Late in 1969, the "strike forces"—massive concentrations of federal, state, and local law enforcement agencies organized by the Department of Justice to apply continuous pressuré on suspected members of the *Cosa Nostra* —began to produce a large number of indictments and some convictions. Partly as a reaction to such pressure on the family of Joseph Colombo, a reputed member of the *Cosa Nostra,* a series of demonstrations and protests against harassment of Italian-Americans broke out in New York in the spring and summer of 1970. Shortly thereafter, the Department of Justice dropped the terms *Mafia* and *Cosa Nostra* as generic for organized crime. Spokesmen for President Nixon's administration insisted that the decision was in no way related to the demonstrations, which were of course attributed to the *Mafia* itself, but was the result of sensitivity to the argument that large segments of organized crime are not Italian-dominated.

Whether or not the Nixon administration is sensitive to it, such an argument gains little ground in American law-enforcement agencies. Their officials paint a compelling portrait of a carefully organized and powerful nationwide confederation of Italian-Americans which, they claim, is also a portrait of organized crime. They picture a secret organization of ruthless and violent men bound by a common interest in illicit gain, ordered by a rigid code of rules, rights, and obligations, and maintained by the constant threat of death to informers or defectors. They describe an intricate national and even international network ruled by a council of overlords which maintains exacting discipline. Members of this vast criminal conspiracy are alleged to have influence in all levels of government and to control numbers of politicians at all levels. With the money gained from illicit enterprises, the syndicate members are now reputedly moving into and corrupting legitimate business. FBI Director J. Edgar Hoover, for example, made the following statement before an appropriations subcommittee of the House of Representatives:

> *La Cosa Nostra* is the largest organization of the criminal underworld in this country, very closely organized and strictly disciplined. They have committed almost every crime under the sun . . . *La Cosa Nostra* is a criminal fraternity whose membership is Italian either by birth or national origin, and it has been found to control major racket activities in many of our larger metropolitan areas, often working in concert with criminals representing other ethnic backgrounds. It operates on a nationwide basis, with international implications and until recent years it carried on its activities with almost complete secrecy. It functions as a criminal cartel, adhering to its own body of "law" and "justice" and, in so doing, thwarts and usurps the authority of legally constituted judicial bodies. . . .[3]

Recent books and articles by government officials and social scientists support this view. One supporter is Donald Cressey, the criminologist who worked with the task force on organized crime which was part of President Johnson's Commission on Law Enforcement and Administration of Justice. Another is Ralph Salerno, a former head of the organized crime intelligence squad in New York City.[4]

Cressey, who had access to the files of a number of law enforcement agencies, states that

- There is a nationwide alliance of at least twenty-four tightly knit Mafia "families" which control organized crime in the United States.
- All of the members of these twenty-four "families" are Italians and Sicilians or of Italian or Sicilian descent.

---

[3] Cited in the President's Commission on Law Enforcement and Administration of Justice, *The Challenge of Crime in a Free Society,* Washington, D.C.: Government Printing Office, 1967, p. 192.

[4] See Donald R. Cressey, *Theft of the Nation,* New York: Harper and Row, 1969, pp. 21–23; Ralph Salerno and J. S. Tompkins, *The Crime Confederation,* New York: Doubleday and Co., 1969; and Harry Anslinger and Will Oussler, *The Murderers,* New York: Farrar, Strauss and Cudahy, 1961.

- Each "family" has a hierarchical structure of positions which regulates power in that family.
- These "families" are linked together by "understandings, agreements, and obedience to a nine member commission."
- The names of at least 2,000 members of these twenty-four "families" are known to law-enforcement officials (others place the figure as high as 5,000).
- Members of these "families" control: (*a*) all but a tiny part of illegal gambling in the United States (now estimated at $50 billion per year with $15 billion in profit). (*b*) Virtually all of the loan-shark operations in the United States. (*c*) The importation of narcotics. (*d*) Most of Las Vegas as actual owners or behind-the-scenes owners.
- In addition, they have infiltrated labor unions, made liaisons which give them power over state and federal legislators, and other officials in the legislative, executive, and judicial branches at local, state and federal levels of government, and have complete control of a number of legal business enterprises (said to be worth tens of billions of dollars).[5]

Popular culture and the public press have also given prominence to this view of the involvement of Italian-Americans in organized crime. The names and activities of Italian-American mobsters are as well known to the public as they are to the police, and even their street names—"Sam the Plumber" or "Joe Bananas"—are instantly recognized. Terms such as *Mafia* and *mafioso* and the more recent *Cosa Nostra* are used without explanation by the mass media, and even the most prestigious newspapers, including the *New York Times,* use the terms freely in headlines. Public interest in Italian-American mobsters and how they organize themselves has been constant since the Kefauver hearings, and each new government disclosure—the Valachi confessions, the De Cavalcante tapes—is quickly followed by books, articles, and films presenting fictional or "documentary" accounts based upon the data supplied by government sources. Most large urban newspapers have a staff reporter who specializes in organized crime; several have written popular books based on these same government data.[6]

---

[5] Paraphrased from Donald R. Cressey, "The Structure and Function of Criminal Syndicates," in *Task Force Report: Organized Crime,* The President's Commission on Law Enforcement and Administration of Justice, Washington, D.C.: Government Printing Office, 1967, Appendix A, pp. 25–60. The data within parentheses are later estimates from various newspaper accounts.

[6] Edward J. Allen, *Merchants of Menace—The Mafia: A Study of Organized Crime,* Springfield, Ill.: Charles C. Thomas, 1962; Peter Maas, *The Valachi Papers,* New York: Bantam Books, 1969; Ed Reid, *The Grim Reapers, the Anatomy of Organized Crime in America,* Chicago: Henry Regnery Co., 1969; Frederic Sondern, Jr., *Brotherhood of Evil: The Mafia,* New York: Farrar, Strauss and Cudahy, 1959; Nicholas Gage, *The Mafia Is Not An Equal Opportunity Employer,* New York: McGraw-Hill, 1971.

As always, where there is a conspirational theme, there is a lunatic fringe which sees even greater plots. At various times, it has been reported that the *Mafia* was approached by the Ghanaian government to get rid of the embarrassing exiled Nkrumah; that the *Cosa Nostra* was issuing guns to black nationalists in Chicago as middlemen for a southern white extremist seeking to stir racial wars in the North; that the New Orleans *Mafia* engineered the assassination of John F. Kennedy for Lyndon Johnson and his associates;[7] that the *Mafia* was using Italian-supplied guns and ships in Haiti to protect the regime of the late President Duvalier and their gambling interests against rebels backed by the CIA; and, most recently, that the *Cosa Nostra* organized attacks on pacifist students by "hard-hat" construction workers in New York. But not everyone agrees that all of this is so.

Despite all the evidence cited by the government, there are still law-enforcement officials and social scientists who do not accept the existence of an Italian-American *Mafia,* and those who maintain that there is still insufficient evidence to support such a contention. For example, Burton B. Turkus, the Brooklyn prosecutor who was instrumental in the "Murder Incorporated" trial convictions, reacted to the report of the Kefauver Committee as follows:

> If one such unit had all crime in this country under its power, is it not reasonable to assume that somewhere along the line, some law agency—federal, state, county, or municipal—would have tripped it up long before this? No single man or group ever was so clever, so completely genius, as to foil all of them forever. . . .[8]

Among the most skeptical are social scientists. Sociologist Daniel Bell has commented on what he calls the "Myth of the Mafia":

> Unfortunately for a good story—and the existence of the Mafia would be a whale of a story—neither the Senate Crime Committee in its testimony, nor Kefauver in his book, presented any real evidence that the Mafia exists as a functioning organization. One finds public officials asserting before the Kefauver committee their belief in the Mafia; the Narcotics Bureau thinks that a world-wide dope ring allegedly run by Luciano is part of the Mafia: but the only other "evidence" presented—aside from the incredulous responses both of Senator Kefauver and Randolph Halley when nearly all the Italian gangsters asserted that they didn't know about the Mafia—is that certain crimes bear "the earmarks of the Mafia."[9]

---

[7] Ed Reid, a journalist who specializes in organized crime, offers yet another assassination theory; Carlos Marcello, reputed head of the "Mafia" in New Orleans, was angry at Attorney General Robert Kennedy who was trying to have him deported and "knew that he would have to remove the President." Reid, 1969, p. 158.

[8] Burton B. Turkus and Sid Feder, *Murder, Inc.: The Story of "The Syndicate"* New York: Farrar, Strauss and Young, 1951, p. 87.

[9] Daniel Bell, "Crime as an American Way of Life," *The Antioch Review,* Vol. 13, Summer 1953, pp. 131–154.

While Bell has been the chief critic, other social scientists and writers such as Norval Morris of the University of Chicago Law School and his colleague, criminologist Gordon Hawkins, while readily admitting the presence of Italian-Americans in crime, are skeptical of the existence of a national crime syndicate or cartel.[10] Eric Hobsbawm, the British social historian who has studied the *Mafia* in the south of Italy as a generic form of social banditry, sees the belief in an American *Mafia* that conspires to infiltrate business and distort government as a "myth enshrined in the official and public view."[11]

These contrasting conceptions about the *Mafia* have persisted for more than two decades, in one of the most extraordinary sociological puzzles of the times. There has seemed to be no way of resolving the almost diametrically divergent conclusions. William James once said that whenever there is a contradiction it is the result of the fact that the parties to the dispute have failed to make relevant distinctions. Perhaps that is the case here: perhaps we have asked the wrong questions about the *Mafia* and the role of Italian-Americans in organized crime in America, so that we have searched for answers which were inevitably misleading. Virtually all research on organized crime has been conducted by social scientists serving as consultants to law-enforcement agencies, and is based on those agencies' files. These files are unavailable to the ordinary social scientist, for a maze of security checks intentionally discourages anyone not a consultant or employee of the agency. As a result, most of the evidence pointing to a national confederation of Italian-American criminals cannot be put to the test of independent examination, since it comes from data disseminated by law-enforcement agencies which are themselves party to the controversy. Even if their files were opened, however, they would probably not help us to determine the nature and functioning of organized-crime syndicates or "families." The focus of the agency studies has been on criminal activity rather than on the nature of the organization through which the activity occurs. For this reason, they failed to ask the kinds of questions about organized-crime groups among Italian-Americans that lead to an understanding of how and why they exist and persist. The place to frame questions and to seek answers is in the field among crime families themselves, not in the files.

In 1967, Francesco Cerase, a sociologist at the *Istituto di Statistica e Ricerca Sociale* in the University of Rome; Elizabeth Reuss, an anthropologist now with the Institute for Social Analysis; and I decided to do just that, and began a comparative field study of criminal syndicates in the United States and Italy. We were interested in looking at them as secret societies rather than simply criminal organizations, and in seeing whether there is a common model

---

[10] See, e.g., Gordon Hawkins, "God and the Mafia," *The Public Interest,* No. 14, Winter 1969, pp. 24–51; and Norval Morris and Gordon Hawkins, *The Honest Politicians Guide to Crime Control,* Chicago: University of Chicago Press, 1970.

[11] Eric J. Hobsbawm, "The American Mafia," *The Listener,* Vol. 82: No. 2121, November 20, 1969. See also Schiavo, 1962.

—some system of order or code of rules—which describes social controls within all criminal secret societies. We hoped to find the system of implicit rules shared by the members of Italian-American criminal families—if such a system existed—by observing how members of such groups apply these rules.

Our approach determined the questions we asked, and must be understood if our answers are to be assessed properly. Criminal syndicates have generally been viewed as a type of formal organization—that is, a social unit deliberately designed and constructed to achieve specific illicit goals. In this view criminal organizations are similar to business or government bureaucracies: rationally designed and constructed formal organizations with personnel arranged in a hierarchy which can be diagrammed and then changed by recasting the organization charts. As a result, Italian-American criminal syndicates have been studied with the concepts and techniques of organizational analysis usually applied to the study of business or government. Our approach, on the other hand, was to view Italian-American criminal families as a form of social organization patterned by tradition and responsive to culture. We see the relationships within secret societies such as the *Mafia* as being much like kinship and much unlike the relationships within a formal organization. Since we studied these groups as social systems, we used the techniques of kinship or social-network analysis.

This means that our research focused on the kinds and qualities of social relationships which existed. We looked at pieces of social behavior to try to find the norms and rules which regulated relationships, and asked how they functioned as mechanisms of social control within the organization. Our search was for regularity rather than idiosyncrasy, and this required observing people in day-to-day interaction over a long period of time and with few preconceived notions about how they would or should behave.

Looking at Italian-American crime families as social systems naturally leads us to assume that members share a common culture, and organize their universe and respond to it in ways which are considered culturally appropriate. This shared culture is internalized as a code of implicit rules of behavior which they learn to use as members of these systems. The code of rules is manifested in their behavior, since it defines the equation through which they perceive the objective world and make culturally acceptable decisions about how to behave. Since we believe that the code of rules is the key to understanding how social systems operate in organized crime, the central question of our research was: what is the code of rules that makes a criminal syndicate a social system, and how do its members apply it? We attempted to learn that code by observing the family members in day-to-day life.

If criminal syndicates are viable, persisting social systems—and they are—then they must function as integral parts of the surrounding society. The view that criminal social systems are functionally related to the larger societies in which they operate led us to look for the ways in which behaviors in these secret societies are related to the value orientation of the larger society. In our view, to begin by asking whether an Italian-American criminal "syndicate" or "corporate organization" exists is to miss the most salient cultural facts about Italian-American life and its roots in the south of Italy, and thus to misperceive the nature of the ties which do exist among Italian-American gangsters and which shape the modes of their activity. If organized crime is, as Daniel Bell once put it, an "American way of life," then one must look at the *Mafia* not as a specific organization, but as an aspect of an "Italian way of life," and then see if both these perspectives can clarify the role of Italian-Americans in organized crime in America. Thus, as a first step in studying Italian-American crime families, we studied secret criminal societies in the south of Italy. We examined secret societies as a generic form of social organization and considered the way in which that form of organization emerged in the south of Italy. Only then did we turn our attention to the Italian-American crime family.

While the *Mafia* is the best known in Italy as well as in the United States, secret societies have been formed throughout history in most parts of the world. Where sufficient evidence allows comparative study, they are found to be quite similar in form and function. Initiation rites and oaths, origin myths and heroic legends, codes of behavior with prescribed punishments for violations, and the general exclusion of women are common features of secret societies wherever and whenever they are found. The *Mafia* and other secret criminal societies in the south of Italy have followed this same pattern. More important, however, is the characteristic relationship of secret societies with the surrounding society: all have emerged in periods of social disorganization or political upheaval. The reformist Chinese Boxers at the turn of the twentieth century, ritual brotherhoods like the Freemasons in seventeenth century England, racist groups such as our own Ku Klux Klan, and criminal associations such as India's Thugees in the early nineteenth century are all examples. Any particular secret society is probably an attempt to cling to a threatened social, economic, or political order.

In Italy, the early nineteenth century was just such a period of upheaval. The brief respite from growing anarchy and chaos which Napoleon's imposed unity (1800–1830) had provided was coming to an end. Freemasonry had come to Italy, and the Masonic lodges were producing a political awakening among a growing middle class. Nationalist secret societies sprang up in many parts of the country. The most famous, the *Carbonari,* seems to have been founded in northern Italy around 1810 by a group of republican Italian army officers serving the French forces.[12] In every sense a classical political secret society, the *Carbonari* spread to many parts of Europe. Its original aim

---

[12] The *Carbonari* took its name and much of its ritual from the mutual aid societies established among Italian charcoal-burners in the Middle Ages and later heavily influenced

was to drive Bonapartism out of Europe. After the defeat of Napoleon in 1815, its members turned their libertarian attentions to the Holy Alliance. They won new constitutions in Spain and in a few of the Italian states, and were instrumental in winning independence for Greece. Their victories were short-lived, however, and the unsuccessful Decembrist rising against Nicholas I of Russia in 1825 marked their last serious threat to the reactionary powers in Europe.

While the *Carbonari* spread north, east, and west from its point of origin, this middle-class, quasi-Masonic secret society was unable to engender any national or even nationalistic movement in southern Italy and Sicily. There were, indeed, indigenous secret societies throughout southern Italy and Sicily during this period, but unlike the *Carbonari,* their vision was local rather than national, and their aims were nativistic, not nationalistic. Thus when lodges were founded on the basis of Carbonarism in Sicily, they were primarily aimed towards local issues—they were more interested in securing the roads against the many independent bandits than they were in national unity. This difference between the secret societies in the north and those in the south resulted from the fact that there have been, and continue to be, not one but two Italies, with distinct histories and culture. Since the vast majority of Italian-American immigrants have come from the south, it seemed to me that this was a perspective on Italian-American crime that should be considered.

Italy's rich and plentiful literature on secret organizations establishes three major facts. First, secret societies developed primarily in the south, where poverty and political oppression kept the popular reformist and social protest movements focused on local issues. Second, the *Mafia* is only one of a number of secret societies in the south of Italy. And third, the *Mafia* is not a single organization, but a generic model throughout the south. Power is distributed throughout a network of local gangs (*Mafie*) which operate parallel to the law.

Similarities between conditions in the south of Italy and in the Italian-American ghetto lead one to speculate on a possible relationship. Cultures have often preserved, almost unnoticed for long periods, some traditional pattern of response to particular kinds of stress. It is possible that southern Italian immigrants in America resurrected the *Mafia* model, under the stress of ghetto poverty and lawlessness, to organize their movement out of the slum and into crime. This seemed an interesting and researchable question.

In late 1968, Francesco Cerase, Elizabeth Reuss, and I received an appro-

---

by Freemasonry. For more information on the *Carbonari* and/or this intriguing period of history, see: Charles William Heckethorn, *The Secret Societies of All Ages and Countries,* Vol. 2, New Hyde Park, N.Y.: University Books, 1965; Thomas MacKenzie (ed.), *Secret Societies,* New York: Holt Rinehart and Winston, 1967; Herbert R. Marraro (trans.), *The Fate of the Carbonari: Memoirs of Felice Foresti,* New York: Italian Historical Society, 1932.

priation from Russell Sage Foundation for this study. Cerase was to conduct research in Italy, examining the essential themes in the southern culture and seeing how they related to the secret criminal societies which had formed there. Elizabeth Reuss was to examine the American literature and assist me in the field. I would conduct field work in western Sicily, but my major task was to observe the behavior of Italian-American crime families and to learn from these observations:

- Who is related to whom within Italian-American crime families and to whom outside;
- The nature of these relationships—their rights and obligations, their patterns of association, dominance and submission, their patterns of giving and receiving protection, and so on;
- The norms and rules that regulate these relationships, and the way they function as mechanisms of social control in the organization;
- How members of these families describe the organization and its functions.

I had already spent two years in fairly close association with a New York–based crime family to which I have given the pseudonym of "Lupollo." My contact with this family began through personal friendship with one of the members. In a sense, then, I had been observing family behavior patterns before the study formally began. Now, however, I began to record the data I observed, and to discipline my techniques in accordance with the procedures of anthropological field work. Over the two years of the study, I was able to observe behavior in settings which varied from large-scale family events such as weddings and christenings, to more intimate situations such as dinners with one or more family members at home or in social clubs or restaurants. I should add that members of the family were aware of my role as an anthropologist.

In addition to the Lupollo family, to which I already had access, we planned to observe a second family in New York City where I had some contacts and, hopefully, to find a third family either in New York or in northern New Jersey. We also hoped to expand on some contacts in Utica and Niagara Falls in upstate New York and in Philadelphia, Pennsylvania. Unfortunately, release of the De Cavalcante tapes in the spring of 1969 and the resultant publicity made it impossible for us to establish any real contacts outside the New York City area. We were able to continue some field work with two other families, the De Maio family of East Harlem and the Passalaqua family of Bayonne, New Jersey, but our data on these families are not as rich as those we gathered from the Lupollos. Still, they do allow for some comparisons and have extended our knowledge into some areas of business activity which do not concern the Lupollo family. These two families are discussed in Chapter 8.

This book reports our findings on the nature of *Mafia* in Italy and how the south Italian culture, which produced it, came to the early Italian-American ghettos; it tells how one crime family in the United States organizes and controls itself to achieve the goals shared by its members; and it analyzes the relationship between the organization and control of this family and the *Mafia* code of behavior.

Chapters 2 and 3 review the history and present status of secret criminal societies such as the *Mafia* in the south of Italy and discusses the mass migrations to the United States, into the "Little Italies" which grew in every major urban center.

Then we describe the Lupollo family and its internal and external relationships. Two issues arise here which should be dealt with at the beginning. The first has to do with objectivity. We have tried to present the data as we saw and heard it. We have wanted neither to expose or destroy any group nor to preserve or protect it. We have tried instead to understand how this particular Italian-American family operates and how it relates to the world around it.

The second issue is one which any anthropologist faces in reporting on field work, but in this case, because of the nature of the group we were studying, the problem is more difficult. The problem, stated simply, is how to present an authentic record of people and events while at the same time preserving the anonymity and confidence of the people we studied, particularly those who spoke with me at some length. First of all this involves the question of invasion of privacy. Second, this group has a real and compelling need to maintain secrecy: people's reputations, safety, and perhaps even their lives are at stake. In carrying out the study, I never sought to hide the fact that I was studying the social organization of Italian-American crime families. All who asked were told the truth. But still, I saw and heard things which were not intended to be seen and heard, and certainly were not intended to be reported. We have not done so, except where the data were critical to the purpose of the study, and even then every attempt has been made to maintain anonymity for those involved. We used our own criterion of scientific utility: we have reported only those data which we believe will further an understanding of how such groups operate. We have tried to make the chapters on the Lupollos an honest ethnographic report and, since our interest is in social organization, we have presented the data in terms of appropriate concepts such as roles, norms and values. Criminal activity is described only where it is pertinent to these topics or where it helps to organize or direct social behavior.

In our final chapters we attempt to draw some inferences from what we learned. We make no sweeping generalizations about organized crime and the role of Italian-Americans in it. Before any generalizations can be made, more field studies must be carried out. We have enough data from our work here and in Italy, however, to attempt some preliminary answers to such questions as how Italian-American crime families are organized, what holds them together and relates them to each other, what their future is, and who is likely to replace them as they move out. But these are matters for later chapters.

2 / Mafia in the South of Italy

One must understand the culture of the south of Italy and its values if one is to appreciate the distinct character of the Italian-American entry into organized crime. Moreover, much of the behavior and many of the attitudes of the Lupollo family refer back to the values which Giuseppe Lupollo—the founder of the family empire—and other immigrant members of the family brought with them, and which have mixed in varying proportions with American values to shape belief and action in succeeding generations of Lupollos.

Every government committee investigating organized crime in America has pointed to some organizational link between Italian-American crime syndicates and the Sicilian *Mafia*. But anyone searching for the link finds problems on both sides of the Atlantic. In the first place, by no means all of the reputed members of *Cosa Nostra* are Sicilians. Many, like Vito Genovese, came from Naples; some, like Frank Costello, are from Calabria. True, all are from the south of Italy. But the second problem is that while the Sicilian *Mafia* is well known to Americans, each of the other two southern provinces—Calabria and the Campania (Naples and its environs)—also produced its own distinctive secret criminal society, and there is no evidence of any organizational linkage among the three. These two facts, long known but largely ignored in studies of Italian-Americans in organized crime, are of fundamental importance. They are the bases for our answer to the question of whether or not there is or ever was a *Mafia* in the United States.

Our field work in the south of Italy convinced us that *Mafia* is a generic form of social organization which developed in the south of Italy under some very particular social and cultural conditions. It is impossible to understand the Lupollo family as an organized crime group unless you first understand what "family" and *Mafia* really mean to them. So we must look at the south of Italy and the culture which the immigrants brought with them to understand what *Mafia* is, before looking for it here.

The Culture of the Mezzogiorno

There are, as almost everyone knows, two Italies—the urbane and economically advanced north and the rural, still semi-feudal south, the *Mez-*

zogiorno. As one travels south, however, a subtler distinction appears which, at least to the Italian, explains far better than geography or economy why the south has lagged behind the north. The northern Italian is a European; the spirit of capitalism and the attainment of the good life through the acquisition of wealth motivate him as surely if not as singlemindedly as they do the Swiss or the German. And the northern Italian is likely to feel a stronger colleague-ship with other Europeans than with his southern countrymen.

The southern Italian, on the other hand, is a Mediterranean rather than a European. Perhaps his historical ties with Greek and Albanian, and his sub-jection to Saracen and Spaniard, help to explain this affinity. Political progress and economic schemes for the acquisition of material goods are secondary to him; people and the power to influence them are his primary concern. The northerner is a modern capitalist who seeks wealth as a means of acquiring material objects he wants; the southerner seeks wealth as a means of com-manding obedience and respect from others. While the north has accepted the modern ethic that power follows wealth, the south clings to the medieval tradition that wealth comes from power. These differences are not superficial; they mold the behavior of the child as he grows and shape adult roles and all social relations. While beginning to change, these values are still obvious in the three imperatives which shape southern Italian culture—the primacy of the family, the juxtaposition of church and state, and the ascendancy of per-sonal honor over the statutory law. It is these three imperatives which explain why the *Mafia* and other secret societies developed in the south.

Italy is a nation of families, not of individuals. Throughout Italy the family is the chief architect of the social structure, commanding allegiance above all else. In the south, however, the family *is* the social structure. Nei-ther the state nor the church has ever successfully challenged its supremacy. In the north as in the south, the family is inextricably interwoven in business and government. But there are differences in the way this is done. The north-ern businessman surrounds himself with relatives, but he insists that they work for him in businesslike fashion to produce more goods and profits. The south-ern Italian runs *his* business as he does his family, and respect, fear, and affec-tion, not just profits, are his preferred rewards. The civil servant in Milan may win his position through blatant nepotism, but he works first and foremost for his bureau or department and its goals. The *prefetto* in the small Sicilian provincial capital, however, owes his first allegiance to his family, and the prestige and glory as well as the more tangible rewards associated with his position fall on all of his extended family. In the south, the family does not intrude into business and politics, it *includes* them as sub-systems of an all-pervasive system of kindred.

Luigi Barzini, the Italian journalist who has distilled the Italian character

Figure 1

THE SOUTHERN PROVINCES OF ITALY
AS OF 1915

Ancona

Roma

COMPANIA

APULIA

Napoli

LUCANIA

CALABRIA

Palermo

Reggio Calabria

Corleone

SICILY

Sciacca

into his book, *The Italians,* marks the family as the "first source of power" among Italians. He continues:

> The family extracts everybody's first loyalty. It must be defended, enriched, made powerful, respected, and feared by the use of whatever means are necessary, legitimate means, if at all possible, or illegitimate. Nobody should defy it with impunity. Its honour must not be tarnished. All wrongs done to it must be avenged. All enemies must be kept at bay and the dangerous ones deprived of power or destroyed. Every member is duty bound to do all he can for its welfare, give his property, if needed, and sometimes, when it is absolutely inevitable, sacrifice his life. Men have spent their last penny to save a relative

from bankruptcy. The family should by every means be safeguarded from runs of bad luck, the disastrous effects of political mutations, and economic crisis. For this, at least one representative must be a member of the party in power and another of the opposition. A well-run family must split in all civil wars. It must be made to prosper for generations, possibly till the end of time. There must be children, of course, lots of children, especially sons who can carry on the name. . . . One fundamental point which escapes most foreigners must be understood and remembered. Most Italians still obey a double standard. There is one code valid within the family circle, with relatives and honorary relatives, intimate friends and close associates, and there is another relating life outside. Within, they assiduously demonstrate all the qualities which are not usually attributed to them by superficial observers; they are relatively reliable, honest, truthful, just, obedient, generous, disciplined, brave, and capable of self sacrifices. They practice what virtues other men usually dedicate to the welfare of their country at large; the Italians' family loyalty is their true patriotism. In the outside world, amidst the chaos and the disorder of society they often feel compelled to employ the wiles of underground fighters in enemy-occupied territory. All officials and legal authority are considered hostile by them until proved friendly or harmless: if it cannot be ignored, it should be neutralized or deceived if need be.[1]

The pattern of roles within the southern Italian family mirrors the divine family in Catholicism. The stern, authoritarian father is a patriarch who commands immediate obedience. The true *paterfamilias,* he represents the family's power and status in the community. The mother is subservient to the father; her humility, fidelity, and willingness to bear all burdens enshrine the honor of the family and win the respect of her children. Daughters, like mothers, are humble, and their chastity is a matter of great moment: in Italy wars have been waged over a daughter's honor. The son is Christlike in his obedience to his father and in his respect for his mother.

The pattern of relationship extends beyond the nuclear family into a network of related families. While the economic realities of peasant life in the south make a true extended-family pattern impossible, the extension of the family to include all cognates (blood relatives) and affines (relatives by marriage) is a paramount feature of the culture. If they cannot live together because land is so scarce and life so difficult, the relatives can and do still identify with a larger collectivity, an identifiable clan of all persons related by blood or marriage—*i parenti*—who share responsibility for the honor of the clan. Though a newly married couple is seldom able to live with parents or relatives, their marriage does serve to affiliate families, since there is no distinction between the rights and obligations of cognates and affines.

This kin-centered network of cognates and affines is further extended

---

[1] Luigi Barzini, *The Italians,* New York: Atheneum, 1964, pp. 193–194.

by *compareggio,* the practice of establishing fictitious kin roles in conjunction with rites of passage.[2] At baptism each child is given two sponsors, whom he calls *madrina* (little mother) and *padrino* (little father), and who in turn use the complementary terms *figlioccia* (little daughter) or *figlioccio* (little son) towards the godchild. The parents of the child and the godparents become *comare* (co-mother) and *compare* (co-father) to one another, and all adult members of both families partake of the relationship. Similar relationships are established at confirmation, and among newly married couples and their ceremonial sponsors. The *comare–compare* relationship is also established informally between good friends of the same sex. All these relationships are blessed by San Giovanni, the patron saint of *compareggio.* They are products of ritual kinship, but the mutual rights and obligations established are real and binding.

One of the reasons why the southern Italian family has primacy in bestowing status and security is that no other institutional system has challenged the family. The southern Italian treats government at any level with skepticism and diffidence. He surrenders everything to the family, but nothing to the state. What little potency the state might have salvaged, it has relinquished to the church. Yet Italians, even those of the south who are deeply religious, do not really *trust* their church as an institution. They have always seen the church as an independent *temporal* power as well as a religious institution, and distrust it just as much as any form of government. It is this juxtaposition of church and state—a unified church to which all Italians belong but most distrust, and a weakly united state which few Italians serve—which has kept any strong political or religious authority structure from forming. Even today, when church and state are to some extent merged in the ruling Christian Democratic Party, the southern Italian still sees the central government as powerless because he knows the limits of their mandate in local issues. In a very real sense, southern Italy has always been a land of anarchists, but not of anarchy, for the rule of law is replaced by a familial social order invisibly and spontaneously regulated.

This social order is internalized in a code of rustic chivalry which exhorts each man, regardless of his age or rank, to protect the family's honor and to avenge with his own life, if need be, any breach of that honor. The code is actually an integrative behavioral system which reaches outward to embrace all members of the extended family and inward into the man's own self-image, so that he knows he must defend his honor at all costs and never allow the smallest slights or insults to go unavenged. It binds families to each other throughout each village and town in a ritualistic web difficult for the southern

---

[2] We use the term *compareggio* rather than the more modern *comparatico* because it was in use when the Lupollos left Sicily and they still use it.

Italian to escape and just as difficult for the non-Italian to understand. When the American (or the Englishman or the German, for that matter) explains his killing of someone who has wronged him or his family, he says "I had to kill him," in what is essentially a psychological reasoning. When the Sicilian explains such an act, he says "it had to be done," giving a social reason. In the first case, the man may show some contrition for having broken the law. The Sicilian would be incredulous if his act were considered wrong.

The code of honor finds expression in a variety of ways. Obviously it is the basis for *vendetta,* the interfamily feuds which often continue until every male member, regardless of age, has been wiped out. It is also the basis for the southern Italian—particularly the Sicilian—belief that a man's rank and worth are to be measured by the fear and respect he can generate in other men. A man who is feared will not receive challenges to his honor, and this shield of fear will reach out to cover all those who are close to him. Thus, the Sicilian defends his honor and prestige (and that of his family, for the two are inseparable) with his life. He and his male kindred will give their lives or take anyone else's for the honor of the family. The same loyalty and sacrifice is seldom shown in defense of the state and even less frequently for the church.

These major themes which shape the culture of the *Mezzogiorno*—a strong family, a weak political structure further weakened by a dominant religion, and a primitive sense of honor which takes precedence over the law —are at the heart of southern Italian culture. Although they reach their highest expression in Sicily, they are true of the entire south. Not only do they distinguish the southern Italian from his northern countrymen, they also explain how and why secret criminal societies formed in the south but not the north.

Criminal Secret Societies in Calabria and Naples

There have been numerous secret societies in southern Italian and Sicilian history.[3] They have served every function—political, religious, nativistic— that such societies serve elsewhere, but always with the cultural flavor we

---

[3] For more information on these societies see Francis M. Crawford, *Rulers of the South: Sicily, Calabria, Malta,* New York: The Macmillan Co., 1900; Francis M. Crawford, *Southern Italy and Sicily, and The Rulers Of The South* (late edition), New York: The Macmillan Co., 1905; Thomas Frost, *The Secret Societies of the European Revolution, 1776–1876,* Vol. 1, London: Tinsley Brothers, 1876; Charles W. Heckethorn, *The Secret Societies Of All Ages and Countries,* Vol. 2, Rev. ed., New Hyde Park, N.Y.: University Books, 1965; Robert M. Johnston, *Napoleonic Empire in Southern Italy and the Rise of Secret Societies,* Vols. 1 and 2, New York: The Macmillan Co., 1904; John H. Lepper, *Famous Secret Societies,* London: S. Low, Marston & Co., 1932.

have described. Three societies have particular relevance in the history and organization of organized crime in the United States: Calabria's *Onorata Società,* the *Camorra,* and the Sicilian *Mafia.*

While the Sicilian *Mafia* is the best known of the Italian criminal societies, the weakness of the central government and the oppression of alien governments have produced numerous and widespread bands of brigands throughout the *Mezzogiorno,* with aims ranging from profit to blood revenge, to reform and social justice. The function of these bandits, if only at the outset, has usually been to fight oppression by the state, the police, or the rich. Although he did well for himself, the social bandit was also often the only champion and protector of the peasants. These bands, however, do not really qualify as secret societies; they were *ad hoc* associations with no past and a doubtful future. But they spring from the same cultural sources which produced the *Mafia* and other criminal secret societies and are in many ways ancestral to them.

In Calabria, the mountainous and remote province at the southernmost tip of mainland Italy, an organization somewhere between social banditry and a criminal secret society existed almost unknown to the outside world throughout the eighteenth century. Known colloquially as *fibbia* ("clasp" or "buckle") or *'ndranghita* ("brotherhood" in Calabrian dialect), it is also called the "Honorable Society" (*Onorata Società*). Like the *Carbonari,* the *Onorata Società* seems to have been influenced by Masonic forebears, for its structure and ritual resemble those of Freemasonry.[4] Unlike the *Carbonari,* but typical of other south-Italian secret societies, it was nativistic rather than nationalistic, and conservative in defense of the "Calabrian way of life." The *Società* appears to have declined since its zenith in the mid-nineteenth century, but as recently as the late 1950's there were small isolated bands operative in the provincial capital of Reggio Calabria, as well as in the isolated mountain villages.

The functions, organization, and code of the *Società* are remarkably similar to those of the Sicilian *Mafia.* Its activities follow the classical *Mafia* pattern of selling and bartering protection and influence, and for some time it managed to maintain a parallel system of government and law in southern Calabria. The *Società* was not, however, internalized in the culture and character of Calabrians to the same degree as the *Mafia* was in Sicily. This is probably why it has not continued to flourish. The close similarity between the two societies—the parochial and conservative aims, the kinship-like social organization, and the central importance of being a man who has won respect —results from the cultural and social similarity of the two regions.

---

[4] Cf. C. Guarino, "dai Mafiosi ai Camorrisi," *Nord e Sud,* Vol. 13, 1965, pp. 76–107, and C. Cervigni, "Antologia della 'fibbia,' " *Nord e Sud,* Vol. 18, 1956.

While the differences are more difficult to account for, they are significant. As we shall see later, the genius of the *Mafia* has been its ability to adapt to changing social conditions, so that it can persist as an organizational form, even when it must change its function. The *Società,* on the other hand, was unbending and non-adaptive in its heyday. Italians might attribute this to the difference in character of the two groups: Calabrians are famous for their stubbornness, while Sicilians are noted for their superb ability to adapt in chameleon fashion to changing laws and lawmakers. Moreover, the Calabrians enjoyed centuries of relative stability as part of the Kingdom of Naples, whereas the Sicilians have had to adjust to centuries of rule and misrule from Greeks, Romans, Carthaginians, Saracens, Normans, French and Spanish (and now, the Sicilians would add, the Italians).

While the *Onorata Società* developed in the isolated mountain villages of Calabria, another criminal secret society, the *Camorra,* was born in the city of Naples.[5] While the origin of the *Camorra* remains obscure, two things seem certain: the organization began in the prisons of Naples and first reached public notice in 1820. The name itself is a mystery, since it is not of Italian origin. Most authorities trace the term to the Spanish word *chamarra* or "cloak"; the excessively cruel prison wardens were agents of the Spanish Bourbon kings. The history of the *Camorra* before 1820 is unknown.

In 1820, the *Camorra* existed only in the prisons of Naples. At that time the prisons were controlled as much by the *camorristi* as by their wardens, with the organization levying taxes on the prisoners, maintaining order, and finding privileges for its members. Such arrangements are not unknown in American prisons today; what distinguishes the *Camorra* is that it spread outside the prisons into the city of Naples, and eventually throughout the surrounding province. Discharged criminals formed the nuclei of the "external *Camorra,*" and from 1820 to 1860, *camorristi* organized for robbery, blackmail, kidnapping, and smuggling. As their influence spread, so did their membership and sphere of activity. After 1830 they were more efficiently organized than the police, and set up a parallel system of law in typical southern Italian style. The organization had become so powerful that members openly flaunted their affiliation with the "secret" society and wore a characteristic sash, a red neckerchief with the ends thrown over each shoulder, and large numbers of finger rings. One hundred years later, Al Capone, a Neapolitan-

----

[5] Giuseppe Alongi, *La Camorra, studio di sociologia criminale,* Torino: Bocca, 1890; Heckethorn, 1965; Marco Monnier, *La Camorra: Notizie Storiche Raccolte e Documentate,* Napoli: Arturo Berisio Editore, 1965; John Lepper, *Famous Secret Societies,* London: S. Low, Marston & Co., 1932; F. Russo and E. Serao, *La Camorra: Origini, usi, costumi e riti dell' "annorata soggieta,"* Napoli: Edizioni Bideri, 1971; Arthur Train, *Courts, Criminals and Camorra,* New York: Charles Scribner's Sons, 1912; Herbert Vivian, *Secret Societies, Old and New,* London: Thornton Butterworth, 1927.

American, epitomized the showy bravado of the *camorrista* in his sharply tailored suits and wide-brimmed hats.

The *Camorra* followed the kinship-like structure of other southern criminal secret societies. In Naples, there were twelve "centers" or geographical areas controlled by *camorristi*. Each center was broken down into its component nuclear "families" or gangs, called *paranze*—the local word for "boat." A *capo paranza* headed each "boat," assisted by a "treasurer" who handled the financial affairs. The leaders of the twelve centers met from time to time to discuss matters of mutual interest, but each center maintained its autonomy as an independent extended family of gangs.

Recruitment was initially from the criminal class but, as the society gained power and prestige, others sought membership. A person first entered into an apprentice-like grade where he worked as servant or errand boy for more experienced members. When he had given proof of his courage and zeal—traditionally, by killing or disfiguring someone—he was elevated to the next rank, in which he served a novitiate of six to ten years. The *capo paranza* was the gang member who commanded the most fear and respect.

Ritual and legend were important threads which tied *camorristi* together. There are several accounts of the initiation ceremony available, and the one we heard while in Naples agrees with these other accounts. The candidate, who had to be of an "honorable family"—no sister in prostitution and he himself never convicted of passive pederasty—was proposed for membership by two active members. Oath-taking was an important part of the initiation ceremony, and the candidate was sworn to secrecy, obedience, and unquestioning willingness to come to the aid of his fellows and to respect womanhood. The candidate and the members then gathered around a table bearing a dagger, a gun, and a tumbler of poisoned wine. After holding the gun to his head, the dagger to his heart, and then the poisoned glass to his lips, to signify his willingness to lay down his life for the society, his arm was pierced with a lancet and he was smeared with his own blood. He kissed every member on the lips once and the *capo* twice to indicate that he was now a member of the "family." The importance of the ritual and myth as external indicators of solidarity is obvious. Even the knives used as weapons were symbolic and bore ritual terms. There was an elaborate system of secret symbols and signs using the cries of animals and a special slang which was known only to members. Despite its origin as a mutual assistance association among convicts, the *Camorra* developed all of the paraphernalia—and so all of the cohesion and persistence—of a secret society.

By 1860 the *Camorra* had broken into a "lower" society which was the continuation of the "old" criminal gangs, while the "upper" *Camorra* was the expression of the status and prestige of a newer political orientation. The "uppers" still used the "lowers" to wrest political control and shared in their profits, but they had attained a new respectability. Neapolitans will tell you that even Garibaldi and his King, Victor Emmanuel I, were unable to overcome the *camorristi*. In 1877 the King did try to wipe out both the *Camorra* and the Sicilian *Mafia* but without success. The *Camorra* seems to have reached its peak in the decades after Victor Emmanuel's death in 1880; lawyers, magistrates, army officers, professors, and even a cabinet minister were known to be members.

Is there a *Camorra* in Naples today? While the *Camorra* was far more centrally and hierarchically organized than the Calabrian *Onorata Società* or the Sicilian *Mafia,* it is nonetheless true that there were *Camorre*—a number of individual bands—not one single *Camorra.* Not only were there the "upper" and "lower" branches, there was a *Camorra* which extorted from businessmen, a *Camorra* which regulated the sale of fruits and vegetables, and even one which arranged for the kidnapping of reluctant maidens for anxious swains. Today, particularly in Naples, there are gangs and gangsters who smuggle or steal cigarettes and gasoline, extort money, and operate the full range of familiar rackets. They are often known to Italians as *camorristi,* but they retain little more than the aura of the old *Camorra.* The real *Camorra,* which required a weak government and social disorganization to flourish, did not survive the first decade of fascism in Italy. If nothing else, Mussolini did bring strong (in an authoritarian sense) government to Naples, and the *Camorra* was forced to go underground, where it seems to have died. At least it did not re-emerge after fascism.

The Mafia in Sicily

Mafia is a word which has at least two distinct meanings to the Sicilians.[6] When the word is used as an adjective, it describes a state of mind, a sense of pride, a philosophy of life, and a style of behavior which Sicilians recognize immediately. It is *bravura,* but not *braggadocio.* It bespeaks the man who is known and respected because of his ability to get things done. It suggests that he is unwilling to allow the merest hint of an insult or slight, and it insinuates that he has means at his disposal to punish it. He is a "man of respect" who

---

[6] The dual meaning of *"mafia"* is well known and accepted in Italy and, in fact, Gaetano Mosca in *"Mafia"* in the *Encyclopedia of the Social Sciences* (London: The Macmillan Company, 1933, Vol. 10, p. 36) says: "The word is employed by Sicilians in two different although related senses; on the one hand, it is used to denote an attitude which until recently has been fairly widespread among certain classes of Sicilians; on the other hand, it signifies a number of small criminal bands." Luigi Barzini distinguishes between the attitude *"mafia"* (lower case) and the organization *"Mafia"* (upper case) and I have adopted this useful means of showing the distinction. See Barzini, 1964, pp. 253–254, and his *From Caesar to the Mafia,* New York: The Library Press, 1971, p. 326.

has "friends." In Palermo, even the style of dress, with the hat cocked to one side, the walk which we would call a self-assured strut, the manner of speech and the general air of self-reliance can mark a man as *mafioso* (the Sicilians actually say *mafiusu*). Such a man may or may not be a member of a formal organization in which he has a clearly defined role. Yet even in Sicily, the word *Mafia* when used as a noun, clearly denotes such an organization *as well as* such a state of mind.

An Italian scholar or journalist will say "*mafia* is an attitude, not an organization," and to the non-Italian, this seems to mean that "there is no *Mafia*." He is, of course, saying nothing of the kind. Rather, he is suggesting that *Mafia* exists as a pattern in Sicilian culture regardless of the persistence of the *Mafia* as an organizational form and that the organization would be impossible without the pattern. A Sicilian will say "*che cavallo mafioso*" when he sees a prancing stallion, well proportioned and proud. The horse is obviously not a member of the *Mafia*, but he carries himself with pride. The distinction is real, but subtle. To a Sicilian, the (lower-case) state of *mafia* and the (upper-case) powerful secret organization, *Mafia*, are two sides of the same coin.

The origins of the word *mafia* are lost in history. Some of the theories of its origin are patently absurd; one suggests that it is an acronym for the sentence "*Morte alla Francia Italia Anela*" ("Italy desires death to France"), supposedly a battle cry of the revolutionary Sicilian Vespers of 1282;[7] another that it stands for "*Mazzini Autorizza Furti, Incendi, Avvelenamenti*" ("Mazzini authorizes theft, arson, and poisoning"), the oath of a Sicilian terrorist society established by Mazzini in 1860.[8] More reasonable theorists claim that the word derives from the Arabic for "place of refuge" or "cave," in which the earliest Sicilian *mafiosi* sought escape from Saracen oppression. But perhaps the most reasonable explanation is that the term simply derives from the Sicilian adjective *mafiusu*, which has been used since the eighteenth century to describe people and objects as "beautiful" and "excellent." Whatever its origins, the word first gained currency throughout Italy in 1863, when a Sicilian playwright, Giuseppe Rizzotto, described a criminal organization in his play, "*I Mafiusi di la Vicaria*." (La Vicaria is Palermo's jail.)

The origins of the spirit of *mafia*—the *mafia* state of mind—are easier to find. The spirit of *mafia* is essentially the quintessence of south Italian culture—family and honor, in juxtaposition to a weak state, require that every man seek protection for himself and his loved ones in his own way. Every Sicilian knows that his rank is determined by how much fear and respect he commands, and he must defend that rank with his life. He must aid those

---

[7] Ed Reid, *The Grim Reapers,* Chicago: Henry Regnery Co., 1969, p. 4.
[8] Heckethorn, 1965, p. 279.

who are his friends, because they will support his rights and his dignity even when he is wrong. It is his friends and the friends of his friends who will aid him, not the state, and so he must never give information or trust to anyone who is not a friend or a friend of a friend. The net of friendship is cast wide to describe a pattern of social relations which has more permanence than religion and more legitimacy than law. Each man and each family know what they owe to others and what is due to them from others. Favors become obligations, and wrongs become debts which demand redress: *"Si moru mi voricu; si campu t'allampu"* ("If you kill me they will bury me; if I live, I will kill you"). The spirit of *mafia* persists because it is born of the culture. It is, in turn, the progenitor of the secret organizations, the *Mafie*.

There are numerous theories about the origin of the secret organizations known as *Mafie*. The most romantic trace their origins to pre-civilization and tribal periods. Some Italian scholars think they began in secret sects of avengers (*Vendicatori*) during the Spanish occupation, and some in attempts to throw off external occupation by Saracens, Spaniards, or Normans. Certainly political movements to counter government oppression, and to gain independence from various invaders (and the mainland Italians), are part of the heritage of the *Mafia*.

A more immediate portion of this heritage, however, is to be found in the private armies maintained by landowners for centuries to protect their lands and families from bandits and other Sicilians. Like private armies everywhere, these *compagnie d'armi* operated with the vigilante spirit of swift and direct justice. There were no courts and no prisons, so death was the most common punishment for any wrongdoing. Degrees of guilt and nuances in behavior were not recognized. Nor were specific laws enforced. The *compagnie d'armi* became the defenders of order, and in the process, defined a rigid code of conduct. Man instinctly knew right from wrong; wrongs were righted, the weak defended, robbers punished, and outraged virgins married off to their seducers in a rough peasant version of the code of chivalry imported by Norman invaders in 1070.

In the eighteenth and nineteenth centuries, the *compagnie d'armi* grew in power in direct proportion to the increasing absenteeism of the landowners. In time they became a law unto themselves. More and more their sphere of concern spread beyond the needs and wishes of their masters, to cover every aspect of life on the estates which they protected. In time, they recruited members from among the very bandits they were supposed to repel. Like the marshals and sheriffs of our own western frontier, they learned that the outlaws were more willing to take risks and knew the countryside far better than the ambitious serfs who saw the *compagnie* as a means of escape from serfdom. Soon the *compagnie* and the bandits developed a system of coexistence which permitted the bandits to plunder others' territories and then find sanctuary with their own *compagnia*. So long as they preyed only on neighboring or distant fiefs, they posed no problem to the *compagnie,* and in fact represented a source of additional revenue.

The absentee landowner in Palermo or Naples knew little of this, and if he did, could do nothing about it. After all, what power could he resort to, other than the *compagnia* itself? Furthermore, as long as they protected his land from bandits, what did he care if the troops caused trouble for his neighbors? In return for their services he gave them a share of the crops and defended their interests in Palermo. He soon found himself more and more dependent upon them. As a result, they often accumulated enough money to buy land from the same landlord (often managing to set their own prices). The *compagnie d'armi* formed the basis of an emergent middle-class in feudal Sicily.

Then, in 1812, the Napoleonic victory was followed by the collapse of the feudal system. This date more certainly than any other marks the emergence of the *Mafia.* Before this time there was certainly *mafia;* for centuries the peasant in Sicily, as elsewhere, had had to respond to and cope with a remote, impersonal central government, and a local regime made up of landlords and their agents, and had developed his own defensive customs and institutions. But only after 1812 did the *Mafia* emerge, embodying this spirit of *mafia.* With the collapse of feudalism, the old aristocracy, clinging to its ancient feudal prerogatives, came into open conflict with the mass of peasants unable to capitalize on the abolition of the feudal system. There were no established norms or roles to define and regulate their new relationship. The central government was too weak and too unconcerned to establish any new political order, and in the ensuing chaos the *compagnie d'armi,* with their well-established social structure, emerged as the one organized social network capable of maintaining order. The members of the *compagnie d'armi* and other entrepreneurs paid absentee landlords a lump-sum rent for their estates and then re-rented them to the peasants. It is in this group of middlemen—the *gabellotti,* who became a new rural ruling class—that the *Mafia* had its origin.

Essentially, the *Mafie* became the mediator between two social strata which otherwise could not have interacted without violent conflicts resulting in ultimate destruction for one or the other. At first, the *Mafie* sold the landowners protection against the resentful masses. In this role the *Mafie* served the aristocracy through the organized use of violence and intimidation. They became more feared than the police and more powerful than the law, and enacted and enforced their own code of conduct. In time the peasant class also sought out the *Mafie* to protect itself against the landowners and to act as "judges" in interpersonal conflicts. The *Mafie* rose to power because there was a vacuum between the social strata in Sicily and dissonance between the political and socio-economic systems. They became the source of order within the Sicilian social system.

Because the *Mafie* grew with the rural bourgeoisie, their range of influence spilled over the boundaries of the local fiefdoms. They were at once localized societies and influential elsewhere. The *Mafie* were local in the sense that they were based on territoriality and did not operate outside certain boundaries; but they had a community of interest with other *Mafie* and required the services of their colleagues in various ways. Since most of the absentee landlords lived in Palermo, the *gabellotti–mafiosi* came together there in power linkages if not in actual contact. In this way, the loose structure of the *Mafia* as a formal organization grew; it was interconnected with common purpose and concern, rather than any fusion of individual *Mafie* into a tightly knit organization. The system of coercion which the *Mafie* imposed on the island was equally shapeless and decentralized but, nonetheless, powerful.

Until approximately 1860, the *Mafie* continued their primary role of mediator between the fossilized aristocracy, with its feudal conception of social organization, and the masses unable and unwilling to look beyond their own poverty, immediate sense of social injustice, and misery. After unification in 1860 the *Mafie* became a political force in themselves. In many ways the period from 1860 until the First World War represents both the finest hour and the height of power of the classical *Mafie*. *Mafia* "families" had already emerged as local power networks as peasants and miners, bandits and bullies, former members of the *compagnie d'armi* and others, surrounding a strong man who became their *capo* or chief. The *capi,* who were property owners and agrarian capitalists, had no interest in crime and saw their *Mafia* "families" essentially as armed retainers who protected them and their land from bandits. On the other hand, they saw the necessity of allowing their followers to use their coercive powers for private gain in much the same way that big-city political machines in America have been known to countenance police shakedowns of merchants. But the *mafioso* "families" were not all bad. Certainly they helped Garibaldi far more than he or later Italian historians have been willing to admit.

The history of the *Mafie* from 1860 to the First World War is as much, if not more, the history of politics as it is the history of crime. Not only did the *Mafie* work to win victory for the Garibaldian troops against the Bourbons, but the *squadre della mafia,* largely the *Mafia* "families" re-formed into military companies, and fought on the side of the liberal forces in Palermo. Then, when the new Kingdom of Italy appeared to be just as foreign and almost as oppressive as the other foreign rulers, the *Mafie* were at the forefront of rebellion *against* the Italians. They had much to rebel against. The predominantly northern Italian government in Rome imposed military conscription, which even the Bourbons had avoided, and blatantly chose to build up the north of Italy at the expense of the south. It is this early political orientation which explains two of the more puzzling features of the history and growth of the *Mafie*. First, it helps to explain why *Mafia* occurs only in eastern Sicily and, even there, is at its greatest concentration in the region of Palermo. While ethnic and economic differences between eastern and western Sicily have been cited as explanations, they are not very convincing to one who knows the island and its history. Palermo is the key to understanding; and the political activism of the *Mafie* is the keyhole. Palermo, more than Messina or any other Sicilian city, has always been the center of Sicilian political activity and intrigue. It is here that regimes have been established and overthrown, governments formed, and revolutions hatched. It was the home of the aristocracy and the landowners as well as the conspirators against them. In the late nineteenth century, the newly powerful *gabelloti–mafiosi* controlled the surrounding countryside and could deliver the votes of their *square* and eventually of their regions as well. Thus, Palermo was the center where all elements in the emerging political struggle came together. It was here that the symbiotic relationship between politics and *mafia* could be formed. This fortuitous confluence also explains why the *Mafie* came to embrace killers and jurists in one grouping of "men of respect"—the power brokers in the new politics.

This period of open political activism on the part of the *Mafie* did not last for very long. The popular labor movements that were emerging among the rural peasants and miserable city dwellers took the rebellious reformist role away from the *Mafia,* and by 1894's great peasant uprising known as the *Fasci Siciliani,* the *Mafie* were on the side of reaction. At the same time, the new ruling class in rural Sicily, the union of *gabellotti* and Palermitan politicians, had learned to accommodate itself to the "Piedmontese" government in Rome (so called by Sicilians because King Victor Emmanuel was of the Piedmontese House of Savoia). When the central government extended the franchise, the *Mafie* found a new power base in the vote. The central government needed and was willing to pay—covertly—for large popular majorities in elections. The *Mafie* were able to deliver that vote at will, because the great masses of Sicilian peasants and urban poor still viewed it as part, if no longer the totality, of the popular movement. Thus, by the late nineteenth century, the *Mafie* became both the visible and invisible government in Sicily. The tacit partnership between Rome and the *Mafie* gave them control over patronage, and they held local hegemony because they offered the only alternative to the law.

While the *Mafie* were establishing themselves as the dominant political power in Sicily, they were also consolidating and elaborating the extra-legal activities and organization which persist to this day. By 1900, a loose confederation of the local gangs had begun to emerge, bound together by a complex policy of infiltration into all spheres of activity. There was a dual organization. First there was the local *Mafia* family which was, and continues to be, the basic organizational unit. Modeled after the extended family which is the ideal

of Sicilian social organization, the *Mafia* family at first was always made up
of relatives by blood or marriage, but as it grew in size and strength, *amici*—
friends—became associated with it. The rank and power of the family was
determined by the fearlessness and cunning of its members, particularly the
capo, who was always the most authoritative member. But gradually, as the
family grew in power, its connections outside the family and the village, became important. Several *Mafia* families could exist in the same village as long
as their spheres of activity did not conflict. Each family worked in its particular activity but, like colleagues everywhere, united whenever there was a
common threat.

Sometimes groups of families concerned with the same activity—the sale
of cattle or control over water rights—joined together to form a *cosca* in
which one family usually dominated. The word *cosca* comes from the Sicilian
word for artichoke—a number of leaves functionally joined into one solid
unit. Numbers of *cosche* with similar or related interests formed *consorterie,*
with one *cosca* dominant in each because it was more powerful and could do
most to help the other *cosche.* One *consorteria* controlled pasture lands, another fruit and vegetable wholesaling. *Consorterie* did not always get along
with one another. Michele Panteleone, one of the most careful students of the
Mafie in Sicily, has described one such feud:

> A famous example of such a feud was that between the so-called *stoppag-
> lieri* of Monreale and the *fratuzzi* of Bagheria. It lasted from 1872 to 1878 and
> there were dozens of victims on both sides. The association of the *stoppaglieri*
> of Monreale had been founded with the praiseworthy aim of combating the
> delinquency which, abetted by the police, was infesting the rural districts
> around Palermo, Monreale, Altofonte, Boccadifalco and as far afield as
> Brancaccio. To do their job the *stoppaglieri* considered they had the right to
> cross the boundary of the Bagheria plain which was the centre of operations
> of the great *fratuzzi cosca,* whose criminal activities prospered. . . .
>
> The two *consorterie,* though differing even in their political allegiance, did
> their utmost to keep clear of each other and so maintained the *Mafia* tradi-
> tion of friendly relationships between all the various *cosche* and *consorterie.*
> But whenever there were strong divergences of opinion between the two politi-
> cal groups, trouble and frequent clashes occurred. In one particularly violent
> clash the *compare* Giuseppe Lipari was murdered. He was associated with the
> *fratuzzi* and was therefore hated by the *stoppaglieri;* moreover he had been
> guilty of the serious offence of *"infamita,"* (treachery), having got one of the
> leading *stoppaglieri* arrested.
>
> *Infamita* by one member of a *cosca* against a member of his own or another
> *cosca* is looked on as the worst act of cowardice, and is punishable by death
> at the hands of the offender's own *cosca.* In this particular case Lipari de-
> served "punishment" not only to prevent his bad example from spreading but
> also, and perhaps especially to give satisfaction to the rival *cosca.* However,

the *fratuzzi* chose to ignore this rigid tradition and consequently Lipari was killed by the *stoppaglieri* who also tried to shoot the non-commissioned police officer who had corrupted him. There followed a long string of murders on both sides, the victims including two non-commissioned police officers thought to have been friendly to the *stoppaglieri.*

In fear of their lives, dozens of families from both sides left Monreale and Bagheria. One or two *Mafiosi* even turned to the police for help and others tried to collaborate with the authorities, but woe betided them, for in the end they were done away with. One man, Salvatore D'Amico, whose relatives had all been murdered, told everything he knew about the *stoppaglieri* to the investigating judge, and finished with the words: "I shall be killed by the *Mafia* without a shadow of a doubt, and neither you with all your authority, nor all the police in Italy can save me." Eleven days later his body was found, riddled with *lupara* shot and with a cork stopper (*stuppagghiu*) the symbol of the *stoppaglieri,* in his mouth; his eyes were covered with a cloth phylactery with the image of the Madonna of the Carmine, which the *fratuzzi* wore round their necks as a talisman and identity disc. The two *Mafia* groups had thus temporarily joined hands to punish the traitor, even though they went on destroying each other for many years thereafter.[9]

All of the *consorterie* in Sicily form "the *Mafia*" but no one there calls it that. There it has always been called the *Onorata Società,* the honorable society, and is often known by names such as *gli uomini qualificati* ("the qualified men" or "the specialists"). Members do not call themselves *mafiosi,* nor does anyone else call them that. They are known simply as *gli amici* ("the friends") or *gli amici degli amici* ("the friends of friends"). After the turn of the present century, the *Onorata Società* controlled most of the economic life of western Sicily. It had some difficulty with fascism, but after the Second World War it made a spectacular recovery—thanks to the Allied Forces— and today has returned to its old prominence in much the same form, in its own miracle of postwar recovery.

All of this success did not just happen. Much of it is attributed by Sicilians to the genius of one man. In this case he was Don Vito Cascio Ferro, the first and the greatest *capo di tutti* in Sicily. Born of illiterate peasant parents in Bisaquino, near Palermo, he reigned over the *società* as its informal "top dog" from the end of the last century until he was imprisoned by Mussolini and died in the late 1920's. Under Don Vito, all crimes became organized and the *società* controlled them all either directly or through licensing arrangements.[10] He devised the Mafia system of demanding tribute—of *fari vagnari a*

---

[9] Michele Panteleone, *The Mafia and Politics,* New York: Coward-McCann, 1966, p. 35.

[10] The title *Don* is a title of respect in Italy and, despite its common association with *Mafia* in this country is not a title bestowed by the *società.* In Italy, priests, as well as *Mafia* leaders are commonly called *"Don."*

pizzu ("wetting the beak") by dipping into every business venture. He also maintained rigid discipline. In fact, if popular legend is to be believed, it was the strength of his discipline which led to Mussolini's determination to wipe out the *Mafie,* and so resulted in Don Vito's own undoing. While he was visiting Sicily in 1924, Mussolini decided to visit Piana dei Greci, a picturesque village near Palermo which retained much of its Greek heritage. The village was, however, a *Mafia* stronghold, and *Il Duce*'s police escort was stunned by his spontaneous request. Like the good Sicilians they were, they realized that only one man could arrange for a visit without an "incident." They got in touch with Don Vito, an easy matter for he held court every day, and he graciously agreed. Mussolini was, after all, certainly an *uomo rispettato.* As legend has it, Don Vito simply had the *mafioso* mayor of Piana dei Greci, Don Ciccio Cuccia, ride in the car with *Il Duce.*[11] Don Ciccio openly indicated that Mussolini was under his protection. When Mussolini discovered this, he finally came to realize the power of the *Mafia* and determined to destroy it. Or so the story goes.

Don Vito's control was exercised through influence and respect as well as fear, and he established a kind of peace throughout western Sicily. He admitted having killed one man in his life, Sergeant Giuseppe Petrosino, the head of the "Italian squad" of the New York Police Department who had come to Sicily in 1909 to study the relationship between the *società* and the criminal gangs then springing up in New York City. Petrosino was a Neapolitan by birth who had emigrated as a boy; he did not know Sicily or Sicilians and assumed that he was safe, since no one but the New York police knew he was going to Sicily. But Don Vito knew; just a few hours after he arrived, Petrosino was shot to death in front of Palermo's courthouse. Don Vito was, of course, never tried for the killing.[12] When he was finally sent to prison in 1928 it was on the trumped-up charge of smuggling—the one crime, he said contemptuously, he had never committed. He died in Ucciardone Prison, and prisoners long after his death read the words a friend carved for him on the wall: *Vicari malalia e nicisitati, si vidi lu cori di l'amicu*—"prison, sickness, and necessity reveal the heart of a friend."

While Don Vito's leadership built the *Mafie* to a high level of organizational efficiency, he also was present at their temporary demise. As always, there were internal disputes within the *società.* The *"old Mafie,"* the more parochial and family-oriented *gabellotti,* were challenged by the next generation during and after the First World War. Young toughs who saw the spheres

---

[11] *Il Duce* did not fare as well the year before in eastern Sicily where his hat—and a bowler hat at that—was stolen. Since there was no *Mafia* there, no one was able to arrange its return.

[12] Sicilian legendry has it that Don Vito did the shooting himself, but the evidence suggests that two underlings actually carried out the assignment.

of activity of the *"old Mafiosi"* as the one sure way to wealth and power did not view the more ritualistic and fraternal features of the *società* as either attractive or necessary. But the generational clash occurred within biological *Mafia* families as well, as sons entered non-*Mafia* professions and daughters achieved acceptable non-*Mafia* marriages. In both cases, the conflicts were resolved only after internecine quarrels.

More directly, however, the golden years of the *Mafie* were brought to an end by the advent of fascism. At first the *gabellotti* and their aristocratic colleagues in Palermo welcomed fascism because Mussolini was a conservative and seemed to offer the prospect of a return to the good old days. But the fascists also did away with elections, and so robbed the *Mafie* of their primary source of power. Moreover, police powers were increased, an authoritarian police state emerged, and the period of government acceptance came to an end. The fascists applied unrelenting pressure on the *società* and Mussolini's special appointee Cesare Mori, who was given unhindered police power, refused any accommodation. The "law and order" policy of the police state was impressively and immediately effective, but the fascist success in driving the *Mafie* underground was not primarily the result of police action. Certainly Mori arrested thousands of suspected *mafiosi* along with thousands of other political prisoners. What really brought the *Mafie* to their knees, however, was the reintegration of the political and economic systems. The general tightening of the normative structure—albeit in authoritarian terms—removed the interstices in which the *Mafie* had operated. The police and so the state were reestablished as feared and powerful agents, and the courts were no longer responsive to *Mafia* pressure. There was nothing left to mediate, and there were no more deals in which the *mafioso* could dip his beak.

The Allied conquest of Sicily during the Second World War resulted in significant changes in the Sicilian social and political structure. Because of the peculiar way in which that conquest took place, and in particular because of the role that the *Mafie* are reputed to have played in bringing about that conquest, the *società* reemerged after the war as a legitimate, quasi-legal power. The use of Sicilian-American crime figures such as "Lucky" Luciano is still only conjectured in the American press. In Sicily, however, numerous "eyewitnesses" will tell of American tanks dispatched to bring *Mafia* chieftains to meetings with Allied officers. When the liberating troops released the political prisoners from fascist prisons, the *mafiosi* prisoners gained their freedom too. Throughout western Sicily, well-known *mafiosi* were elected to key political and administrative positions, largely, many Sicilians say, through the efforts of the Allied forces. Later, the *Mafie* joined forces with the ruling Christian Democratic party in Italy, at first to eliminate the Separatist movement which would have made Sicily independent (or a part of the United States!) and then to deliver the vote as they had always done before fascism.

Despite renewed—if feeble—attempts on the part of the Italian government to rid Sicily of the *Mafie,* there is little question that they remain the dominant social and political force in the west of the island. As one old prefect observed, when asked if *Mafia* was at last doomed,

> See those willows in the wind? Follow the newspaper reports during the next few weeks, and you will read of many arrests. These are the hands and brains of the *Mafia,* you will be told. Yes—scarecrow hands and brains, paraded by spirits behind the scenes. When the storm passes, the willows will rise again.

This rather romantic description illustrates how deeply rooted the concept of *mafia* is in Sicilian culture and points to the psychological determinants which have allowed the *società* to operate as a "state within a state."

Are there *Mafie* in Sicily today? There are, but they are undergoing change. Part of the change results from general cultural and social changes which affect the spirit of *mafia.* For example, the basic code of the *mafiosi* centers on the concepts of *omertà.* The word denotes the code of silence which requires a man to endure any pain or temptation rather than divulge information to the authorities. *Omertà* means much more than that, however. It is derived from the Sicilian dialect *omu* or man, and to the Sicilian it connotes the impossibility of separating an individual's humanity from his honor.[13] The rules of *omertà* are nowhere written; they are part of the culture, and learned from childhood. But his agreement to give mutual assistance to any fellow member, to avenge any offense against a member, to obey the *capo,* and to refuse to divulge any secrets is binding with greater force than any oath. A Sicilian legend describes one member of the *società* who, apprehended by the police, feigned dumbness for five years to prevent any possibility that he would compromise his fellows.

The importance of *omertà* reaches beyond the *Mafia* into *mafia* itself. Not only will members of the *società* not divulge any secrets, neither will any other Sicilian, man or woman, child or adult. Some of this reticence is based on fear, but much more of it stems from the sociocultural forces characteristic of the area. Today, however, the code of silence is breaking down. People *do* tell the police what they have seen. They may not do so often, but it does happen.

The familial basis of the *Mafia* is also beginning to change. The *"old Mafia,"* where everyone was a blood relative or a *compare,* and where the *capo* achieved his greatest respect when he was called *zu* ("uncle"), is giving way to the *"new Mafia."* The new generation still maintains the structure of

---

[13] Giuseppe Alongi sees the word as derived from *umilta* (humility), given the Sicilian pronunciation which is *umirta.* In this sense *omertà* would not refer to a proud affirmation of one's honor in "being a man," but to a sense of obedience and resignation to the will of the powerful. Regardless of the derivation, the resulting behavior is the same.

the old secret organizations, but they are changing their function. The old men of the *Mafie* steadfastly refused to be involved in "unmanly" crimes such as prostitution or drugs. Not so their successors, who have come to be called the *"Mafia Gansteristica"* because, say the Sicilians sadly, they have been corrupted by the American example.

Early in the summer of 1971, following the assassination of the chief prosecutor of Palermo, fifteen reputed *capi Mafia* were exiled to the small Sicilian island of Filicudi as part of a crackdown by the Italian authorities. The residents of the island fled and the *capi,* whose average age was 50, were left alone with their guards, a score of *Carabinieri,* the paramilitary Italian federal police. Eventually, the natives of Filicudi prevailed on the government and the *capi* were transferred elsewhere. Later other suspected *mafiosi,* including the late Joe Adonis (Doto), one-time big shot in the New York underworld who fled to Italy to escape impending deportation, were picked up by the *Carabinieri* in other parts of Italy.

The culture is changing and *mafia* is responding; *Mafia* is also changing, both because there is no longer unequivocal support from the culture and because its own internal mechanisms are in a state of disequilibrium.

It is still possible, however, to find *"old Mafie"* in the mountain villages around Palermo. They exist today somewhat anachronistically side-by-side with the *"new Mafie."* Probably the best way to understand *Mafia* and *mafia* is to see the operation of the organization and the sustaining role of the culture as we saw it in Corleone, the town from which the Lupollos—Giuseppe, his wife, and his two young sons—emigrated in the early part of this century.

Mafia and Mafie in a Sicilian Town

Corleone is located about 56 kilometers from Palermo, in a hilly area about 1,500 feet above sea level. The town clings to barren rocks in a countryside of yellowish fields and dried-up stone pits. Not far off rises the highest mountain in the area, the ominous Rocca Busambra, a famous hideout for bandits and outlaws, which is reputed to be the favorite spot for *Mafia* executions.

Probably of Byzantine origin, the town underwent a considerable expansion and renovation in the eighteenth century which eliminated all traces of the medieval period. It numbered almost 20,000 inhabitants fifty years ago, but is now in decline. Heavy emigration has taken its toll of the productive younger men, leaving Corleone with a high proportion of elderly people. Between the censuses of 1951 and 1961, Corleone lost 12 per cent of its population, declining to 14,682 inhabitants.

Even compared to surrounding areas of Sicily, the percentage of Corleone's labor force employed on the land is very high—65 per cent in 1961, as compared to 42 per cent in the province of Palermo and 28 per cent in Italy in general. As a result of the Land Reform Estate Partitions of 1950 and 1954, most holdings are very small; 40 per cent of the farms are smaller than two and a half acres. The poverty of the soil, old-fashioned agricultural methods, and the smallness of the plots (which makes machinery difficult to use) result in a low natural yield. Accordingly, many farmers cannot live on the produce of their farms and must work as day laborers on large farms or in the area's few small mills and factories. Locally, industrial work is largely seasonal and irregular, and there appears to be a marked tendency to leave the land and seek permanent employment in industry in northern Italy, Switzerland, and other western European nations. In part, the movement reflects a desire for more stable and continuous work; in part, it reflects the higher social status of the industrial worker. As Alongi mentioned many decades ago, the small farmer, especially when not owner of his land, has always been considered a pariah by the other social classes, and this contempt is slow to die.[14]

In general, Corleone suffers from problems common to many economically underdeveloped areas: low income; poor health and nutrition; high illiteracy and a low educational level (40.5 per cent of the town's population lacks an elementary education); inferior roads, hospitals, and other public services; and poor housing.

The Mafia *in Corleone: Historical Development.* As in the rest of western Sicily, the modern Corleonese *Mafia* had its roots in the *gabellotti* class, which administered the estates of Corleone's nobility. First serving, and finally dominating the *gabellotti,* the local *Mafia* supplied protection to absentee landlords from resentful peasants, while exploiting the peasants for their own profit.

In the early years of this century, the *Mafia* fought Corleone's peasant cooperative movement which, by attempting to deal directly with the landlords, threatened the *Mafia*'s role as middlemen. Eventually, most of the peasant leaders were killed and their followers intimidated. While Corleone's *Mafia* suffered under fascism it quickly reorganized after the war, and at least eight large estates in the town were in the hands of notorious *mafiosi-gabellotti* in the late 1940's. When a new wave of peasant agitation arose, it was to the *mafiosi-gabellotti* that the landlords once again turned for intervention. Several of the *gabellotti* were named (though never convicted) as participants in the 1948 kidnap-murder of a young leader of the Corleonese peasant union.

In the late nineteenth century, in addition to extorting money from landlords and from tenant farmers, the local *Mafia* had also collected "protection

---

[14] Alongi, 1890, p. i; see also Danilo Dolci, *Chi gioca solo,* Torino: Einaudi, 1966, and his *Conversazioni contadine,* Torrino: Einaudi, 1962.

money" from small independent landholders. Eventually, the *Mafia* came to control most other sources of profit—legal and illegal—in the Corleone region. One of the most important illegal activities was cattle rustling. According to local sources, two *Mafia* families in the area fought for forty years to gain control of an extensive forest used as late as the 1950's as a collection point for stolen animals. Eventually, their battle left a total of 49 dead and 54 wounded.

Although the postwar *Mafia* thus retained many of the old traits, substantial changes were occurring in its activities. With the Land Reforms, large estates were broken up, and the central government began to involve itself in local agriculture. Cereal crops, which are grown extensively in Corleone, are pooled through a government agency, so that the *Mafia* cannot involve itself in the marketing. Accordingly, the *Mafia* has had to shift its emphasis from extracting money from landlords and peasants to other areas: infiltrating government bureaucracies, political parties, and the creation of new businesses. A brief description of the careers of two important and well-known postwar *mafiosi* in Corleone illustrates the change. Doctor Michele Navarra, head of the Corleonese *Mafia* until his murder in 1958, was a "transitional" type of *mafioso*. On one hand, he had full responsibility for *Mafia* leadership. On the other hand, he occupied, through *Mafia* influence, a whole range of official, legitimate positions (medical officer, consultant for insurance companies, regional health inspector, hospital director, president of the Christian Democrats), which permitted him to control a profitable network of illicit favors, and to engage in political power brokerage. For example, as health director he issued certificates of blindness and extreme myopia to hundreds of local women so that *mafiosi* could accompany them to the polls and make sure they voted Christian Democratic. While dealing in these novel areas, Dr. Navarra still retained the aura of the *"old manfioso,"* feared and respected as an *uomo d'onore.*

Luciano Liggio, born in Corleone in 1925, is by contrast a *"new mafioso"*: a gangster, American style. His early career as a cattle rustler and *gabellotto* was in the traditional mold. However, conflict with another cattle rustler, under the protection of Dr. Navarra, forced Liggio to move to Palermo, where he became involved in other activities such as slaughtering and trucking stolen animals. In this way he collided with traditional *Mafia* interests.

The most important fight between Liggio and Navarra was over the construction of the dam of the Piano della Scala. Liggio favored the construction because he expected to get the contract for transporting the construction materials, and because it would enhance the value of his own land. The *"old Mafia"* was opposed to the construction, say the local people who are willing to discuss it, because irrigation would have upset the economic equilibrium, and, by helping small farmers, would have undermined the basis of *Mafia* power. The conflict finally resulted in an unsuccessful attempt to murder Liggio, who replied by successfully assassinating Dr. Navarra.

If Liggio is typical, the *"new mafioso"* can be outlined as follows: His novelty lies in the fact that he clashed with other *mafiosi* less for control over the local *Mafia* than over disagreement on policy; he shows a flexibility to engage in new activities where old sources of profits seem to be drying up, and he is less disposed to recognize divisions of influence within the *Mafia* based on "respect"; he is feared because he is a killer, but he himself is not "respected"—he is not an *uomo d'onore*.

Modes of Recruitment. While the realms of Corleone *Mafia* activities are changing, the mode of recruitment has not altered much. Usually, the *Mafia* recruits its new members from among young men of poor origins who have proven themselves to be "courageous," and possessed of a high sense of "honor," as revealed by their appropriate behavior in delinquent activities and in regard to the police. The prisons often provide a site for recruitment. There potential or confirmed delinquents come into contact with jailed *mafiosi*, render services to them, and prove their *omertà*. In jail as nowhere else, the hierarchy of the *Mafia* is exalted: the "man of respect" is honored; his word is law for other inmates, and he shows his power through special privileges the guards grant him.

Farmers, laborers, and shepherds have traditionally been recruited for the lowest rank-and-file positions. Shepherds have been especially desired not only because they knew the countryside well, but because their interests were in conflict with those of the farmers. Separated from the world by their poverty, ignorance, isolation, and fear of losing their pasture land, they have consistently refused to join in the local peasant movements and thus have been likely candidates for *Mafia* membership.

Kinship ties have traditionally provided the main channel for *Mafia* recruitment in Corleone. An elderly *mafioso* introduces to his "friends" a young relative who has shown himself to be a "man of stomach" (a man who can resist police questioning) and has already been useful to the *Mafia*. The candidate can be rejected by the leadership, but if he is accepted he will be a *mafioso* for life.

While the sons of *mafiosi* usually become *mafiosi*, high positions within the organization cannot be transmitted from father to son. The son has to prove himself, for the power a *Mafia* head can exercise is strictly related to his boldness and his ability to impose his will ruthlessly on others.

The Mafia in Corleone Today. In the last few years, *Mafia* activity in Corleone has slowed considerably. To some extent *Mafia* members have been eliminated by their own law of natural selection—mutual assassination—or have been scattered among thirty-odd prisons. Some who were unsuccessfully prosecuted have gone into hiding or left the region.

Changing economic conditions have also damaged the *Mafia*. The breakup of large estates has led to the collapse of the role of the *mafioso–gabellotto*. In addition, the heavy emigration of young men has deprived the *Mafia* of its main pool of potential recruits—impoverished youths.

As long as extensive cereal crops continue to be grown and pooled through the government agency, the parasitic and intermediary role which the *Mafia* plays in the marketing of other products will have no place in Corleone's agriculture. If, however, a new plan which forsees a shift from extensive to intensive culture is carried out, a return of *Mafia* control over the marketing and distribution of the produce could occur. The beneficiaries would not be the dying old *Mafia dei Feudi* (*Mafia* of the estates) but the aggressive *"new Mafia,"* which dominates the fruit and vegetable markets of Palermo, Villabate, and Monreale.

By decreasing the power of the *mafioso–gabellotto,* the Land Reforms have reinforced the town hall as the real center of clientism. Recent welfare and medical statistics from Corleone suggest that financial and medical assistance are being traded for votes, in maneuvers which have *Mafia* characteristics. When questioned about these maneuvers in the course of a 1969 Palermo newspaper interview, the mayor of Corleone replied:

> It seems an absurdity to say so here in Corleone, but according to me, the *Mafia* is an abstract thing . . . Throughout my political career, I have never met a *mafioso* . . . If there ever was a *Mafia* it would be difficult for it to return.[15]

The interview minimized the political role of the late Dr. Navarra. Two other doctors are now his successors as the heads of the Corleone *Mafia,* or so at least it was reported to us while we were there. Despite its decline, the Corleone *Mafia* still reaches out into the surrounding countryside to tie a vast number of people into a web of mutual obligations. How widely the *Mafia* is still spread in the region of Corleone is illustrated by the fact that while we were there, a major raid organized by the central (not local) *Carabinieri* headquarters to round up suspected *mafioso* nettled over 1,200 arrests and one anti-aircraft machine gun in forty-eight hours. That *mafia* is still very much a part of the local culture is also illustrated by the fact that, by the time we left, almost all 1,200 had been released for lack of evidence.

---

[15] Quoted in "Corleone sorvegliata speciale" by Mario Genco, in *L'Ora,* November 14, 1969, p. 12.

Mafia as a Form of Social Organization

Despite its origin and persistence as a *secret* society, we know enough about the *Mafia* as a form of social organization and about its place in the scheme of social groups to form some cultural and historical perspective within which to examine the Lupollos and other Italian-American crime "families." First, and foremost, the *Mafia* is not completely unique to Sicily although it has, admittedly had its most visible and dramatic development there. The *Camorra* and the Calabrian *Onorata Società,* while differing from Sicilian *Mafie* in some fundamental features, are obviously of the same genus. Like the *Mafia,* they draw their character as well as their structure from the southern Italian culture in which they thrive. It is the features of that culture —a strong family, a weak state, and a male role model which stresses individual honor—which have led to the development of these secret societies. We can assume that criminal secret societies such as the *Mafie* require a supportive ethnic base. If the code of silence is not a conspiracy of fear, admiration, or both with the local peoples, *Mafia*-type secret societies cannot function. Like Chairman Mao's archetypal guerrillas, *Mafie* are the fish who require a supportive sea of oppressed partisans around them in order to survive.

Mafia in the sense just described is more than a secret society. It is, as the Italians insist, a particular and peculiar state of mind. It also appears to be a basic form of organization with which to control or negotiate social conflict under some rather specific conditions. One of these conditions is a weak or absent state which does not produce an effective form of political socialization, or what the Italians call a *senso dello Stato*. When the state does become strong or authoritarian, as in fascism, the *Mafia* cannot operate and disappears, or at least goes underground. A second, closely related condition is a need for social mediation, a vacuum of political values, structures, and organizations. Here the *mafioso* can operate, essentially as a middleman. To the *mafioso* and his clients, this seems to be the natural order of things. In such a state, the *Mafia* offers protection and also a form of representation to the populace, which has no other means of negotiating with the power structure.

The base of *Mafia* power is personal relationship. The *mafioso* reduces every social relationship to a human level, a level in which he can feel and perform in a manner superior to other men because he has *omertà*—he is more of a man than others. Where the law is powerless, say the *mafioso,* the injured must have recourse to his own strength and that of his friends. Such relationships are not based on functional requisites, but on personal connections and relationships. This dependence on influence describes the exchange relationship of *mafia* which finds its persistence in the pattern of obligations and responsibilities established through favors and services.

Mafia as a form of social control also seems to provide some valuable lessons about the relationship of criminal or delinquent social systems to the society around them. The population's total obedience to the control of the *Mafia* is born out of the individual's overwhelming need for protection, a need that the southern Italian learns from his entire societal context—school, church, and above all family. As an attitude, *mafia* is socialized into the child by his family, and no other institution is strong enough to overcome it. In the Sicilian schools, the child is socialized to the same type of authoritarian role relationship established in the family. The conception of social hierarchy, typically *mafia,* is reproduced in large scale in the total society. The authoritarian relationship is not only established in the family and reinforced in school, but stressed in the relationship between the priest and his parishioner. Internalized by the child, it survives into adulthood without being counterbalanced by other behavior models. Since family, school, and church remain the only agents of socialization in Sicily, it constitutes the traditional and cultural base for *mafia.* Finally, the *Mafia* is a pattern of social relationships that is a viable social system. Once established, it persists through changing social, political, and economic conditions, simply performing different functions as the needs of the society differ with changing times. It can change from a political to a criminal organization and back again without too much internal disorder.

One question is as yet unanswered. Do changing functions imply a different organization, or does some core organization persist regardless of the function of the *Mafia?* Just as there are many *mafie* rather than a united *Mafia,* so they serve many functions. They are disruptive organizations involved in criminal activities and oppression, but they are integrative systems as well. The *Mafia* serves as a means of social control, a mechanism for the management of social conflict (although it generates some of the conflict itself), and a means of providing services to a public which would otherwise remain unserved.

As a kin-centered social system, the *Mafia* is Sicilian society in microcosm; it uses its cohesive and protective role to establish what the German sociologist George Simmel characterized as "the possibility of a second world alongside the obvious world."[16] That second world is what the *Mafia* has been in the south of Italy, particularly in western Sicily, which produced the Lupollos. Our question is whether Italian-American crime families like the Lupollos are such a second world in the United States. If they are, what does this say about their nature, their organization, and most importantly, their persistence?

---

[16] George Simmel, "The Sociology of Secrecy and of Secret Societies," *The American Journal of Sociology,* Vol. 11, No. 4, 1906 (translated by Albion Small), pp. 441–498.

3 / Immigration and Organized Crime

As we saw in Chapter 2, "the Sicilian *Mafia*" is actually a collection of quite independent *Mafie* and not an organization that (as some have claimed) could have made a decision to export the *Mafia* to the United States for criminal or any other purposes. It is also unlikely that any one of the *Mafie* made any such decision to export itself or any other. Italians (including Giuseppe Lupollo) did, however, bring the cultural attitude of *mafia* with them, and it has affected their relationship to organized crime in America. For a short period, 1925–1930, an organization of Italians existed which closely resembled the *Mafie* of Sicily. But before and after that period, Italian involvement in organized crime has been molded by a unique combination of Italian and American cultural values and social conditions. As acculturation proceeds, the relative weight of American as contrasted to Italian values will continue to increase.

In preparing this chapter, we have examined historical, anthropological, and sociological accounts of the Italian-American experience. We also interviewed Italian-Americans—some involved in organized crime, but most not—who lived through the period of migration and the formation of Little Italies in major urban areas in the United States.

The Immigration

From 1820 to 1930, an estimated 4.7 million Italians came to the United States. It was the longest and largest exodus from any European nation to the United States in modern times. The northern Italians came first, traveling on to California where they became farmers and fishermen and later bankers and businessmen. Only a very few of the early émigrés—musicians, artists, and a few political refugees like Garibaldi—stayed in the East. After 1870, however, the emigration from Italy rose sharply, and southern Italians began flocking to the United States to fill the need for cheap labor in the cities. Between 1900 and 1910, a total of 2.1 million Italians emigrated to the United States, over 80 per cent of them from the *Mezzogiorno*. Most had been day laborers or simple village artisans. Illiterate and parochial, few had ever ventured beyond the sound of their village church bells, and they viewed anyone not part of their kindred as inimical strangers. Unlike the earlier northern immigrants, who brought their families and intended to settle, the southern males often came alone and usually planned to stay just until they had saved enough money to buy farms or small businesses when they returned to their native villages. In fact, nearly half of those who came over after 1900 had already returned to Italy by 1910. In that year only 1.3 million foreign-born Italians remained in the United States.

Alone, cut off from the family system which had been the basis for personal security in Italy, unable to communicate except with *paesani* from their own area, the new immigrants clustered in ethnic enclaves in the large cities of the East. They sought out fellow villagers and kinsmen immediately on arrival. Some even arrived with labels tied around their necks indicating the name and address of the nearest kinsman, and, like freight, were shipped on by immigration authorities. Many remained in New York. There they replaced the Irish as construction laborers and found employment in light manufacturing. Others followed the building of railroads or found work in the iron-ore or coal-mining areas of the country. But they seldom went more than a few hundred miles from New York, the more easily to return to Italy once they had made their fortunes. This pattern continued throughout the years of mass migration (See Table 1). As late as 1930, about 75 per cent of the Italian-American population lived in the Little Italies of urban centers in six Middle Atlantic and northeastern states. And the tristate area of New York, New Jersey, and Pennsylvania had more Italian-American residents than all the rest of the country combined.

Table 1. Percentage Distribution of the Foreign-Born from Italy
1870–1930 *

Year	New England	Middle Atlantic	North Central	South Atlantic	South Central	Mountain	Pacific
1870	4.1	27.0	16.1	4.6	18.6	2.2	27.5
1880	7.8	44.0	12.4	3.1	9.9	5.3	17.6
1890	9.2	55.8	12.0	2.7	6.7	4.1	9.6
1900	12.7	60.1	11.4	2.2	5.4	3.0	5.4
1910	13.4	58.4	13.7	2.9	3.0	2.6	6.1
1920	14.8	57.5	14.7	2.5	2.2	1.7	6.5
1930	14.1	58.4	15.5	2.2	1.6	1.3	6.8

* Adapted from various volumes of the United States Census, 1900 to 1930.

Within the cities, the Italians settled in well-defined Little Italies, and within these colonies they tended to congregate with others from the same province and even from the same village. In New York's Mulberry Bend Italian colony, for example, where Giuseppe Lupollo first settled, Elizabeth

Street was Sicilian from one end to the other, while the Neapolitans inhabited most of Mulberry Street. On Elizabeth Street, neighbors from the Sicilian city of Sciacca huddled together in the same tenements, just as people from Palermo lived together in other blocks. The Italians succeeded in bringing their village culture with them, and that village culture—rather than any new Italian-American or even any emergent *pan*-Italian culture—set the standards for their behavior and beliefs. Here is an early description of life in an Italian colony on East Sixty-Ninth Street in New York, where about 200 families from the Sicilian village of Cinisi had settled:[1]

> The colony is held together by the force of custom. People do exactly as they did in Cinisi. If someone varies, he or she will be criticized. If many vary—then that will become the custom. It is by the group, collectively, that they progress. They do not wish the members of the colony to improve their economic conditions or to withdraw. If a woman is able to buy a fine dress, they say: "Look at that *villana* (serf): In the old country she used to carry baskets of tomatoes on her head and now she carries a hat on it." "Look at the daughter of so and so. In Cinisi she worked in the field and sun burnt her black. Here she dares to carry a parasol."
>
> So strong is this influence that people hesitate to wear anything except what was customary in Cinisi. Everywhere there is fear of being *"sparlata"*—talked badly of. A woman bought a pair of silk stockings and the neighbors talked so much about her that her husband ordered her to take them off. To dress poorly is criticized and to dress sportily is criticized. In this way one had to conform or be ostracized.
>
> • • •
>
> As a group they have certain very marked characteristics—reserve, suspicions, susceptibility to gossip, timidity, and the desire to *"fa la figura."* Intense family pride, however, is the outstanding characteristic, and as the family unit not only includes those related by blood, but those related by ritual bonds as well (the *commare* and *compare*), and as intermarriage in the village groups in a common practice, this family pride becomes really a clan pride. The extent to which family loyalty goes is almost beyond belief; no matter how disgraced or how disgraceful a member may be, he is never cast off, the unsuccessful are assisted, the selfish are indulged, the erratic patiently borne with. Old age is respected and babies are objects of adoration.
>
> • • •
>
> The colony has no newspapers, except one woman who is known as the *"Giornale di Sicilia"* or the *"Journal of Sicily."* She carries the news and spreads it as soon as said. She has now gone to Italy and the one who takes her place

---

[1] This material was collected by Gaspare Cusumano in the early 1900's as part of a Carnegie Corporation–supported study of Americanization. Parts of the manuscript have previously been published in Robert E. Park and Herbert A. Miller, *Old World Traits Transplanted,* New York: Harper and Brothers, 1921.

is a gossiper who is known as a *"too-too"*—referring to the "tooting" of a town-crier's horn. She is, moreover, malicious, and gives a version of a story calculated to produce ridicule. She not only talks about the breakers of customs, but about those who are financially low. To be financially low is looked down upon, and the *Giornale di Sicilia* warns people to look out for such and such a person, as he may ask for a loan. To be willing to lend means that one has accumulated money and thus the secret of the lender is out. So this is the reason they refuse to lend to one another and if one is down and out he would rather get money from a Jew than from a *paesano*. So deceptive are they as to their financial standing (partly through fear of blackmail) that it is customary to figure out a Cinisarian's fortune not by what he says, but how many sons and daughters are working.

Now and then some Cinisarian takes his chances in the business world. He writes to his relatives in Cinisi, has oil, wine, and figs, lemons, nuts, etc. sent to him, and then he goes from house to house. He does not enter in a business way, but goes to visit some family, talks about Cinisi, then informs them that he has received some products from the home town. And sure enough, the people will say, "You will let us get some eh?"

"Of course, tell your relatives. I can get all you want."

In this way the businessman makes his sales. He progresses until he gets a place opened and then come his worries. He must forever show that he is poor, that he is barely making a living, for fear of some attempt to extort money from him.

Not many men of Cinisi group are in business in New York, the reason being that one Cinisarian will not compete with another in the same line of business.

In the Cinisi colony there are no political parties. The group has not been interested in citizenship. Of 250, one or two were citizens before the war and now all those who returned from the war are also citizens. These young men sell their votes for favors. The average Cinisari, like all foreigners, has the opinion that a vote means $5. The Cinisari knows of corruption at home. In Cinisi there is very much of it. Money is raised to build a water system for Cinisi year after year, and it gets away without a water system coming in exchange.

The Cinisi group are more interested in Cinisarian politics than in American. They talk of the parties, of the artisans, of the gentlemen, of the *villani*, of the hunters, in Cinisi.

Most of the Cinisari in the Sixty-ninth Street group intend to return to Sicily. The town of Cinisi is forever in their minds: "I wonder if I can get back in time for the next crop?"—I hope I can get back in time for the *festa"*—"I hope I can reach Cinisi in time to get a full stomach of Indian figs," etc. They receive mail keeping them informed as to what is going on here. They write home of people here who have transgressed some custom: "So and so married an American girl. The American girls are libertines. The boy is very disobedient." "So-and-so who failed to succeed at college in Palermo, is here. He has married a stranger"—that is, an Italian of another town. In this way they blacken a man's name in Cinisi, so that a bad reputation awaits him on his return.

The reputation given them in Cinisi by report from here means much to them, because they expect to return. Whole families have the date fixed. Those who express their intention of remaining here are the young Americanized men.

The village culture, the primacy of ties to kinfolk, religion, and superstition—all of these the immigrant brought with him. Even his characteristic indifference to an absentee central government was simulated here, since his only contact with American governmental agencies was through the Irish cop on the corner and they consciously ignored each other. He was unable to read newspapers, seldom traveled outside the "village," and found his recreation among kinfolk and townfolk in the small social clubs which sprang up in every neighborhood. The only major change he had to make was in occupation. But even here, he could not change overnight from a semi-feudal agricultural serf to an urban manufacturing worker; the process had taken two centuries to complete in Europe. He fell back on a system that he brought with him; he worked not as an individual but as a part of a gang along with other *paesani,* and with a *padrone* as their collective agent. The *padrone* was usually a fellow villager or *paesano* who spoke enough English to make the necessary arrangements with employers for the sale of Italian labor. The *padrone* would send back to his village for male workers, negotiate their salaries, collect the money, and divide it among the workers, keeping a share for himself. In addition, he usually received some concession from the employer, such as the right to rent out living space or sell food to the workers. Thus a new feudalism developed in the *padroni* system, and few of the workers had any real contact with employers of the outside world. All these facets of southern Italian village culture came with the immigrants, and more than any other major ethnic group they clung to them in their enclaves. Our question, of course, is this: Did they also bring the *Mafia* with them, and is it also a part of what they have retained?

Crime and the Ghetto

It is deceptively simple to answer this question with a well-documented "no." The Sicilian *Mafia* could not and did not migrate as an organization to the United States. The various *Mafie* in Sicily are engraved on the daily life of the communities in which they live, and they are not for export. Despite the cultural affinity of the mainland Italians, no *Mafia* ever took root there; the *Mafie* even found the eastern end of Sicily inhospitable and so remained in the west. While there are examples of feuds and conflicts between various

Mafie in Sicily, no *cosca* ever attempted to annex or even invade the territory of another. Why should they then attempt to cross the ocean?

The characteristics of the Sicilian and south Italian migration to the United States also inhibited *Mafia*'s exportation. It was a proletarian emigration, and even so was considered a temporary move by most of the emigrants. At the turn of the century, all of the heads of the local *Mafie* in Sicily were men of some wealth, considerable power and prestige, and hard-earned middle-class status. There was no reason for them to leave the island until Mussolini and his Prefect Cesare Mori began arresting and killing suspected *mafiosi* in the latter 1920's and early 1930's. Some few individual minor *mafiosi* may well have come over earlier, but they did not represent any potential leadership; otherwise, they would have remained in Sicily. Like the vast majority of Sicilian immigrants, they came as individuals, and probably not to stay. The possibility that they were an advance party sent ahead to seek new territory and colonize is patently absurd. The local *Mafie* were rooted in sentiment and power in the local community; and there was no central organization or "grand council" that could make such a decision on a larger than local level.

Having set aside the contention that the *Mafia* set up branch offices in the New World, we find it comforting as well as plausible to fall back on our distinction between *Mafia* and *mafia* and say that what the migrants did bring with them was some primeval "sense" of *mafia*. Thus, while the organization itself did not move to the United States, it may be that, as Luigi Barzini muses:[2]

> In order to beat rival organizations, criminals of Sicilian descent reproduced the kind of illegal groups they had belonged to in the old country and employed the same rules to make them invincible. The convicted American gangster, Joseph Valachi, once explained the facts of life of the Sicilian village, probably as old as Mediterranean civilization, the principles guiding Homeric kings and heroes in their decision, to a Senate committee and an awe-struck twentieth century television audience. He patiently pointed out that an isolated man was a dead duck in the American underworld; that he had to belong to a "family," his own, or one which accepted him; that "families" were gathered in large groups, the groups in alliances, and the alliances in a loose federation called *Cosa Nostra,* governed by an unwritten code.

This diffusionist explanation, however, does not account fully for Italian-American involvement in organized crime. Certainly Sicilian-Americans did apply their genius for people and power with some success in illicit sectors of American life, as well as in business and politics. But the explanation fails in certain important ways.

The emergence of Italian-Americans in a dominant role in organized crime is a post-1930 phenomenon. The strict diffusionist approach must as-

---

[2] Luigi Barzini, *The Italians,* New York: Atheneum, 1964, p. 273.

sume that the concept of *mafia* lay dormant among the Italian-Americans for decades, and then suddenly emerged, in exactly the same form, as an archetypal model to organize their involvement in crime. Further, it must assume that the acculturative experience of Sicilian-Americans did not allow them to find better models in the American setting.[3] These assumptions do not bear up under analysis.

The diffusionist approach also ignores the issue of environment. E. J. Hobsbawm, the British social historian who has studied *Mafia* as a generic form of primitive social rebellion, sees it as "essentially a rural phenomenon" and cites the difficulties that barred its urbanization in Sicily.[4] How much more difficult for *Mafia* to make its way in an American urban setting. However potent the *Mafia* model was in southern Italian culture, it had to be Americanized to be successful here. Looking at the social history of the Italian-Americans from 1900 to 1930, one finds that some elements of southern Italian culture did have an important effect on the development of Italian-American criminal syndicates. It is just as clear, however, that social and economic developments in this country had an equally important role in play.

A number of social scientists have analyzed the relationships among ethnicity, organized crime, and politics in American life. Daniel Bell, for example, describes the transfer from one wave of European immigrants to another of a "queer ladder of social mobility" out of the slums which had organized crime as the first few rungs.[5] The Irish came first, and early Irish gangsters started the climb up the ladder. As they came to control the political machinery of the large cities, the Irish won wealth, power, and respectability through consequent control of construction, trucking, public utilities, and the waterfront. In organized crime, the Irish were succeeded by Jews, and the names of Arnold Rothstein, Lepke Buchalter, and Gurrah Shapiro dominated gambling and labor racketeering for a decade. The Jews quickly moved on up the ladder into the world of business, a more legitimate means of economic and social mobility. The Italians came last and did not get a leg up on the rungs of crime until the late Thirties.

In the early days of the Italian ghettos, the crimes reported in the press were, in fact, *Italian* crimes. They were the traditional crimes of the *Mafia* and *Camorra*—extortion through threats of death and bodily harm, vendettas or blood feuds (particularly between Neapolitans and Sicilians), and kidnapping of brides. But the criminal activity was not organized. At the same time, protection against these crimes was left almost entirely to the immigrants them-

---

[3] See Francis A. J. Ianni, "Time and Place as Variables in Acculturation Research," *American Anthropologist,* Vol. 60, No. 1, February 1958, pp. 39–45.

[4] E. J. Hobsbawm, *Primitive Rebels,* New York: W. W. Norton, 1965, p. 42.

[5] Daniel Bell, "Myth of the Cosa Nostra," *The New Leader,* Vol. 46, December 23, 1963, pp. 12–15.

selves; characteristically, the American attitude toward minority-group crime is indifference, so long as they keep it among themselves. And the Italians did. As Giuseppe Lupollo's son Joe puts it:

> Can you imagine my father going uptown to commit a robbery or a mugging? He would have had to take an interpreter with him to read the street signs and say "stick 'em up" for him. The only time he ever committed a crime outside Mulberry Street was when he went over to the Irish section to steal some milk so that my mother could heat it up and put in my kid brother's ear to stop an earache.

The most famous of these internal crimes were the activities generically known as Black Hand—threats, murders, maimings, and bombings as means of extorting money from the immigrants—because the notes demanding money were signed with that symbol of terror. These criminal operations were described in 1908 by the White Hand, an early Italian-American reformist group, which aimed to publicize the crimes and sought help from the police:

> Whole Italian families, in which a blackmailing letter or a threat in another form has been received from the Black Hand, live in continued anxiety and fear of the vague, unknown, but always terrible danger which hangs over them, and nobody knows whom it will fall upon, the father, one of the children, a relative, or all-together, in the destruction of the house or little store, demolished and set on fire by the explosion of a dynamite bomb. . . . Even business men of conspicuously strong character, and professional men of unusual ability, frankly admit that, after a threatening letter, a certain time has to pass before they were able to attend to their business with all the composure and energy required. . . .
>
> The letter in its classic form is short, written in an unassuming and sometimes friendly tone. It contains the request for money, with an indication of the place where it is to be delivered, and a threat, sometimes veiled by mysterious allusions, and sometimes expressed with a brutal lack of reserve.
>
> At the place designated the victim does not find anybody; but at the house he finds, a few days later, a second letter, in which the request is repeated, also the threat, in an aggravated form. And thus at brief intervals comes a third and fourth letter, each containing more violent threats than the preceding, expressed either in words or symbols, such as drawings of pierced hearts, of pistols, daggers, crosses, skulls and crossbones, bombs, etc. All these letters are prepared with a system of progression which shows in the author a mind by no means crude and untrained, but shows, rather, a consummate skill acquired by practice in this class of crime.
>
> In this manner the victim is intimidated to such a point that there is not left in his veins another drop of blood beyond that needed to nourish his fear, and to enable him, in such a depressed condition of mind, to lay hold on the anchor of salvation which is pointed out to him in one of the letters, that is, to apply to "friends." Some phrase in the letter hints vaguely at so-called friends; sug-

gests that whoever seeks will find; gives to understand, in short, that somebody might intervene between the victim and the mysterious and terrible god that has made the demand, and is threatening with all the thunderbolts in his possession, so that the matter might be adjusted in some way. In one letter in the possession of the White Hand, this "friend" who is to be the intermediary, and who in reality is the accomplice if not the author of the blackmail, is indicated with sufficient precision. He must be a Terminese from Termini, says the letter, meaning from the town of Termini, not from the country, and must live in the same street as the victim, which is a very short street.

So the unfortunate victim finally looks for the "friend" who can save him from the threatening peril, and has no difficulty whatever in finding him. For some time there has been continually at his side somebody who has shown himself more solicitous than ever before, if known for a considerable time; obliging and exceedingly friendly, if of recent acquaintance. This man sometimes guesses, sometimes induces the other to tell him the trouble which has destroyed his peace of mind, and curses the assassins who blackmail poor people and who ought to be hung or put in the penitentiary. He knows some mysterious people, banded together, who live and have a good time with money extorted from honest, industrious people. . . .

In the district itself it is considered very bad form to discuss these affairs. No one alludes to them voluntarily, or in plain terms speaks of a murder. A murdered man is spoken of as the "poor disgraced one," and the murders or persecutions as "trouble." Certain men are called *"mafiosi,"* but this generally means only that they are domineering, swaggering, and fearless, and no one would think of making a direct accusation. There are men who are said to be "unwilling to work for their bread," and certain names are never mentioned without a significant raising of eyebrows. The term Black Hand is never used except jokingly, nor does one hear the words vendetta, *omertà* or *feudo,* though every one is imbued with the sentiments for which they stand. In the whole colony there is no one so despised as an informer, nor is it thought desirable to show an interest in another's private affairs. There is a general belief that men who are murdered usually deserve their fate. Murdered men are not buried from the church unless a large sum is paid for a special mass.

The American press and police attribute all these "Italian killings" to the Black Hand and consider them inevitable. Every so often the newspapers print an interview with a police official in which a certain number of murders are prophesied to occur in this district, and the public are given to understand that the situation is hopeless. When a murder is committed its is either reported as a minor occurrence in a single paragraph, or absurdly elaborated in highly romantic style. A few years ago the chief of police, on being urged to have a careful study made of the situation, dismissed the matter by saying, "Oh, we've always had trouble up there; they never bother anyone but each other."[6]

---

[6] *La Mano Bianca,* p. 18. A report issued by the Italian White Hand Society, Chicago, 1908.

Some informants—not members of the Lupollo family—have told us that Giuseppe Lupollo not only lent money (at exorbitant rates of interest) to victims of the Black Hand, but often offered his services as a negotiator for the victim with the Black Hand group involved. Since, say these informants, Giuseppe was himself a Black Hand extortionist, he reaped double profits from the operation. When the extortion demands increased and the business-man could no longer pay the interest on Giuseppe's loans, Giuseppe would offer to negotiate a final settlement with the Black Hand in return for a partial interest in the business. Since this type of extortion demands that the business-man has ready access to cash, the function that Giuseppe is said to have per-formed was in fact an indispensable link in the whole Black Hand process.

The Black Hand activities were the work of individual extortionists or small gangs, and there is no evidence which suggests that there was any higher level of organization or any tie with the *Mafie* in Sicily or the *Camorra* in Naples.[7] Without the protective network of family and kindred, the immigrant was easy prey to anyone who appreciated his vulnerability, and individual entrepreneurs could operate freely in the police-less colonies. In the dozens of Black Hand letters examined for this study, we never once found an ex-plicit or implied threat that the *Mafia* or *Camorra* was in any way involved. This omission supports the position that the Black Hand was not a transplant of either of these secret organizations into the fertile soil of the early Little Italies. It also suggests that the cultural awe of these organizations was strong enough that no one dared use the terms lightly.

There is some evidence that individual *mafiosi* or *camorristi* may have emigrated from Italy to become Black Hand extortionists here. Enrico Alfano, a leader of the Naples *Camorra* who was known as "Erricone" ("Big Henry") was arrested in New York in 1907 by the same Sergeant Giuseppe Petrosino who was later killed in Palermo. Newspapers at that time suggested that Al-fano had come to New York to organize the Black Hand gangs, but there was no real evidence to support the claim. From all of the evidence, it seems clear that the Black Hands, which lasted about fifteen years (from the turn of the century to the First World War), were not an offshoot of the *Mafie* and, from the family histories of present reputed Italian-American crime families, nei-ther were they precursors of a modern *"Cosa Nostra."*

---

[7] See, for example, H. W. Zorbaugh, *The Gold Coast and the Slum: A Sociological Study of Chicago's Near North Side,* Chicago: University of Chicago Press, 1929: "Black Hand is not an organization. Its outrages are the work of lawless individuals or of criminal gangs," or Arthur Woods (New York City Deputy Commissioner of Police) writing in *McClure's Magazine* ("Problem of the Black Hand," Vol. 33, No. 40, May 1909, p. 40): "The Black Hand is not a cohesive, comprehensive society . . . Given a number of Italians with money and two or three ex-convicts, you have all the elements necessary for a first rate Black Hand campaign.

Mafia and *Camorra* did have another and somewhat more attractive legacy to offer, however—that of providing order where the larger society failed to do so. The self-contained immigrant colonies of early twentieth century America were in a real sense frontier settlements. As had been true on the frontiers of the westward expansion, the absence of established institutions and their sanctions provided an environment of "lawlessness" where conflict and violence always seethed just below the surface. The newspaper files of any large city will testify to the frequency with which violence erupted, particularly between rival gangs of Neapolitans and Sicilians, as in New Orleans in 1890.[8] While details varied, the pattern seems always to have been the same: a shoot-out occurs between a group of Sicilians and a group of Neapolitans. One or two on each side are left dead; everyone else is silent, including passers-by. These vendetta-like feuds grew out of the intergroup hostility of the Neapolitans and the Sicilians—by far the two largest groups among Italian immigrants—and do not seem to have been associated with any *Mafia–Camorra* war. Inter-familiar feuds also occurred occasionally, often in relation to the courting behavior of the children.

The frontier-colonies, lawless within their borders, also lacked any externally imposed pattern of legal recourse. The police were largely indifferent so long as the immigrants did not venture outside the colony, and so long as they voted the Tammany ticket. Faced with such an absentee government, the immigrants did just as they had done in Italy and just as a previous generation of frontiersmen had done in the West. Rough-and-ready internal policing developed, along with a set of "courts" which arbitrated disputes and meted out justice to wrongdoers. In Italy, the custom had been to go to a "man of respect"—a leader in the *Mafia* or *Camorra*—for redress of ills and protection from the vagaries of peasant life; in the American ghetto it was the same, and the informal courts held by real or reputed *mafiosi* continue in diminished power even today. As recently as 1967, the Mayor of New York City found it expedient to call on one faction in an Italian-American crime family to "cool off" intergroup hostility between gangs of Italian-American and Black youths in Brooklyn. And they did it. The power of this informal parallel system of internal policing is an intriguing but still unstudied feature of the history of social control in the ghetto. As one seventy-year-old Italian-American said of these informal courts in the early 1900's in the Lower East Side of New York, "If you did bad, they did bad to you, but if you did good they did good to you."

While the immigrants seldom wandered outside the ghetto, and thus maintained a cultural solidarity, their children had first-hand contact with American

---

[8] Dr. Pietro Russo of the Institute for American Studies of the University of Florence was most helpful in reviewing these articles.

society. This second generation, alienated from the past without really being adjusted to the cultural present, was in conflict.[9] Like the Irish and Jews before them, they formed streetcorner gangs as much to escape their overcrowded homes as to seek compatible peer-group relationships. One important function of these gangs was to protect their "turf" against marauding bands from outside the colonies. The Jews had formed such gangs to protect themselves from the Irish, and Italian youths came into conflict with both. As Giuseppe's son Charley says about his schooldays, "the Irish and Jewish kids used to beat the living shit out of us until we got smart enough to fight together in gangs like they did." The strength of the peer-group relationships established in these gangs and the importance of their role as a halfway house for socialization of the second generation has been well described and documented by Frederic M. Thrasher and, more pertinently, by William F. Whyte's later study of an Italian-American street gang in Boston.[10] These bonds continued into adulthood just as they did among the Irish and Jews, and represent an important element in the development of Italian-American criminal syndicates.

Prohibition and an American Mafia

Let us stop for a moment and consider where we have been and where we are going in this brief history of the formation of Italian-American crime "families." All of the social conditions and cultural imperatives which had led to the formation of *Mafie* in Sicily did, in fact, exist in the early ghettos. In their transplanted villages, the immigrants preserved their imported cultural models—their strong family system with filial respect for the mother and obedience to the father, and their antagonism to police and state. Harsh and impoverished living conditions, exploitation by employers and the *padroni,* and exclusion from the routes of social mobility were also present to produce social conflict. Yet the immigrants did not form a new *Mafia.* Despite all they brought with them and all they found discouragingly familiar here, three important elements of a *Mafia* were missing. The first missing element was time. It had taken the *Mafia* and the *Camorra* hundreds of years to grow in the friendly soil of southern Italy; twenty years were insufficient for a successful flowering in the United States. The second missing element was the established pattern of relationships—the social system of *mafia.* Despite the affinity of co-villagers in the ghetto, the migrants had come as individuals, and they

---

[9] Cf. Francis A. J. Ianni, "The Italo-American Teen-Ager," *The Annals of the American Academy of Political and Social Science,* Vol. 338, November 1961, pp. 70–78.

[10] Frederic M. Thrasher, *The Gang,* Chicago: University of Chicago Press, 1927, especially Chapter X; and William F. Whyte, *Secret Corner Society,* Chicago: University of Chicago Press, 1943.

had to establish new patterns of authority and new sources of power and profit. Without established networks of relationship and patterns of authority, *Mafia* cannot exist. Although the immigrants could not join together in a *Mafia*-model brotherhood, the Sicilian legacy of fear and police indifference to crime within the ghetto enabled them to operate as individual Black Handers.

The third missing element of a *Mafia* was the reinforcement by school and church of the Italian pattern of respect and obedience. The children of the immigrants were educated in American schools, and there the lesson was individualism, not family loyalty. Social workers' accounts of Italian-American family life in the ghettos are filled with astonishment at the strength of the family system, and with detailed accounts of how school and settlement house, to say nothing of streetcorner gangs, were breaking down this solidarity. *Mafia* as a form of social organization is impossible without the respect and obedience learned in the father–son and mother–son interaction models and reinforced in school and church.

After 1920, however, two developments changed all this. In Italy, Mussolini began his all-out attack on the Sicilian *Mafie*, and a number of Sicilian *mafiosi* came for haven to their kinsmen in the United States. In this country, National Prohibition provided a new source of illicit profits and thus a new and accelerated route to riches for both the immigrant and the second-generation Italian-American. Closure of legal liquor supplies opened illegal markets for beer and booze, and open warfare among rival gangs of bootleggers riddled the 1920's. What is not so well known, is that this new market supplied the first opportunity for immigrant *mafiosi* to work *together* for power and profit. Italians had traditionally produced their own wine, and converting home wineries to home stills was not difficult. Some of them quickly became large enough to make significant profits. Central organizations that collected the alcohol from hundreds of home stills, just as dairies collect fresh milk from independent farmers, became an important source for the producers of illegal whiskey.

While the immigrants produced illegal alcohol, and even organized collectives for it, their reluctance to leave their colonies and their lack of outside contacts hindered them from becoming engaged in the distribution process. Not so their sons, who, through membership in street gangs, were being socialized into the non-Italian world of the gangster. While the flamboyance of Al Capone has given an Italian characterization to the popular stereotype of the Prohibition gangster, the Italian-Americans by no means dominated the rival bootleg gangs. During the 1920's the Irish were being replaced by the Jews as the dominant ethnic group in organized crime; the Jews' ascendancy was not threatened by the Italians until the end of the decade. The names of O'Bannion, Moran, O'Donnell, Buchalter, Kastel, Lansky, Seigel, Weiss, and

Zwillman were far more important if less notorious than those of Aiello, Capone, and Torrio. At this time the Italian-Americans in bootlegging gangs more often performed lower-echelon enforcer roles than leadership roles. The role-model ideal for these newly mobile and aspiring underlings was the Jewish gangleader, and not the old-country–oriented *mafiosi* they contemptuously called "greenhorns," "greasers," "handlebars," or "Moustache Petes." Thus, the culture and social organization of American organized-crime gangs became an element in the development of Italian-American criminal syndicates.

While the second generation was enjoying access to the demi-world of organized-crime gangs, there were some important developments among the first generation in the ghettos. Bootlegging not only supplied a source of funds, but provided a functional basis for organization among those immigrants involved. Since the immigrants could not handle large-scale distribution themselves, the second-generation Italian-Americans who were gang members served as liaison between the immigrants and the distributors. Thus an informal alliance developed between immigrant and second-generation Italians, and between second-generation Italians and non-Italian gangsters, particularly those who were Jews.

The written history of Italian-American criminal syndicates between 1925 and 1930 is sparse and sometimes contradictory. This chapter's speculative reconstruction of this period is based upon such documentary evidence as seems non-contradictory, and upon data we discovered in field work. Our interpretation differs from the usual reconstructions in that it focuses on the transmission and transformation of culture, not on the development of criminal behavior through organizational continuity. Our primary interest is in the cultural features—both Italian and American—which seem to have served as organizational guides for developing Italian-American secret crime "families," rather than in the specific careers of individual Italian-American criminals.

As we have said, two of the missing socio-cultural ingredients necessary to form an Italian-American *Mafia* were added with the onset of Prohibition. Now the potential *mafiosi* could locate extra-colony sources of money and power. The second element that Prohibition supplied was the American gang —a new kinship-like network and hierarchical pattern of organization that could serve in place of the traditional (and critical) son–father obedience and son–mother respect socialization models which had been so weakened by the Americanization of the second generation. In the 1920's, the formation of new alliances and working relationships was made possible by the lucrative opportunity of Prohibition. The infusion of Sicilian *mafiosi* in the flight from fascism accelerated this movement. By the mid-1920's, all of the necessary ingredients for a new Italian-American *Mafia* were available, and it promptly began to take form.

The name most frequently associated with the Italian-American *Mafia* that emerged in the 1920's is the *Unione Siciliana*—often mispelled as Sici-lliano or Sciliane even in government documents. The origin of the name is unknown. An organization called the *Unione Siciliana* was established in Chicago in 1895 as a fraternal organization, with membership at first restricted to Sicilian-Americans, but eventually extended to any Italian-American. It has never been clear whether this organization was associated with the *Unione* of Prohibition, but since both seem to have centered in Chicago, some connection seems obvious. One of Giuseppe Lupollo's sons, who was involved in bootlegging activities in Brooklyn throughout Prohibition, told us:

> . . . at that time [1928] all the old Sicilian "moustaches" used to get together in the backrooms of the club—it was a *fratellanze* [brotherhood] and they used to call it the *Unione Siciliana*. They spent a lot of time talking about the old country, drinking wine and playing cards. But these were tough guys too, and they were alky cookers and pretty much ran things in the neighborhood. They had all of the businesses in [an Italian-American section of Brooklyn] locked up and they got a piece of everything that was sold. If some guy didn't pay up they leaned on him. Everybody paid attention to them and if some guy caused trouble in the neighborhood they called him into the club and straightened him out.

Various agencies and authorities present different histories and theories of the organization. Running through all of the often contradictory accounts, however, is a common thread of agreement that the *Unione* was Sicilian-American in origin and started among Sicilian Black Handers and bootleggers. The criminologist Donald R. Cressey, for example, in his *Theft of the Nation,* quotes attorney J. Richard Davis, who defected from an organized-crime combine in the 1930's to support his position that there was (and is) a nationwide alliance of organized criminals:

> The Dutchman [Schultz] was one of the last independent barons to hold out against a general centralization of control which had been going on ever since Charlie Lucky [Luciano] became leader of the *Unione Siciliana* in 1931. . . . The "greasers" in the *Unione* were killed off and the organization was no longer a loose, fraternal order of Sicilian Black Handers and alcohol cookers, but rather the framework for a system of alliances that were to govern the underworld. In Chicago, for instance, the *Unione* no longer fought the Capone mob, but pooled strength and worked with it. A man no longer had to be a Sicilian to be in the *Unione*. Into its highest councils came such men as Meyer Lansky and Bugs Siegel, members of a tremendously powerful mob, who were partners in the alcohol business with Lucky and Joe Adonis of Brooklyn. . . . It still number[ed] among its members many old time Sicilians who [were] not gangsters.[11]

---

[11] Donald R. Cressey, *Theft of the Nation,* New York: Harper and Row 1969, pp. 55–56.

Our own view is that the *Unione Siciliana* was a loose confederation of local groups of Sicilian-Amercians involved in selling extortion and protection in the Little Italies and in bootlegging activities, particularly in organizing the cottage industry of home distilling in the ghettos. We maintain that by the late 1920's this organization had all the cultural and organizational features of a new *Mafia* in the United States. Like the *Mafia* in Sicily, it served the Little Italies as a means of social control, a mechanism for the management of social conflict (and again like the Sicilian *Mafia,* a generator of some of the conflict itself) and as a means of providing services to a public which would otherwise remain unserved. But it was dependent on the preservation of those south Italian values which led to its formation in the first place and, while Italian-Americans have clung to their familialism and to their values longer than most immigrants, time and acculturation inevitably win out.

By the end of the 1920's, the stage had been set for an inevitable clash between the *fratellanza* or *Mafia* model of the *Unione Siciliana* and the achieving, second-generation Italian-American mobsters who were now moving into leadership roles in the gangs. Once again social change in the general society intervened to speed organizational change in crime. The Great Depression and the prospect of inevitable repeal of Prohibition forecast the end of the era when there had been enough illicit profit for everybody. With the end of Prohibition it would be necessary to find new sources of wealth. Some areas, such as gambling and labor racketeering, were attractive to both generations. Others, such as prostitution and drugs, were reprehensible to the aging "Moustache Petes," who saw such activity as unworthy of a man of respect. Other conflicts of interest and influence were also involved as various groups struggled in the inevitable quest for power.

The Castellammarese War and Its Aftermath

In 1930, Giuseppe Masseria, a Neapolitan prominent in the gang world of New York, ordered the extermination of a number of Sicilian "old moustaches" whose associations were with the *fratellanza* groups. There has been continuing speculation as to why he did this. Some say it was because of conflict over future areas of exploitation; others believe that he was simply hungry for greater power. Whatever his reasons, the move touched off a war in New York which eventually spread throughout the country. With Masseria were such non-Sicilian Italian-Americans as Vito Genovese, the late Joe Adonis, and Frank Costello, whose alliances with non-Italian (principally Jewish) mobsters had been forged in the world of the gangs. Opposed to Masseria were the old-time Sicilian-Americans who had risen to prominence in the *Unione.* Many of them, like Joe Bonnano and Stefano Magaddino, had come from or around the small town of Castellammare del Golfo on the western coast of Sicily. The Castellammarese and other Sicilians, such as Joe Profaci and Gaetano Gagliano, gathered behind Salvatore Maranzano and fought back.

As the war raged throughout 1930 and 1931, the "old moustaches," particularly the Castellammarese, were the most frequent victims; in one forty-eight-hour period, close to forty of the Sicilian leaders were killed. Despite his victories in these battles, Masseria was soon losing the war to Maranzano and sued for peace. Maranzano refused to offer terms. Thereupon Masseria retreated to a heavily armed fortress in New York, determined to hole up and hold out. His followers, however, did not go with him. Five of his lieutenants —Genovese, Luciano, Livorsi, Straci, and Terranova—surrendered to Maranzano, and on April 20, 1931, the Castellammarese War came to an end, as three of them murdered Masseria in a Coney Island restaurant while they were having dinner together. Maranzano's victory did not last long; he was assassinated by his own lieutenants on September 11, 1931.

Whatever else it was or did, the Castellammarese War brought the short melancholy life of the Italian-American *Mafie* to an end. The old "Moustache Petes," the custodians of the *mafia* tradition, were either killed off or passed into obscurity. The younger immigrants and the second and succeeding generations saw in the urban American gangster, not the Italian *mafioso,* a model filled with the excitement and promise that their parents' nostalgic associations with the social banditry of the *Mafia* and *Camorra* could no longer provide. They formed gangs of their own in the new mode of the urban criminal syndicate, not the old rural brotherhood. The new syndicates did not follow provincial lines, and working relationships with non-Italians, particularly Jews, were established.

An Organized Underworld?

After 1930, the Italian-Americans succeeded the Jews as the major ethnic group in the ranks of organized crime. At about the same time, they also began to gain some legitimate power in major cities, particularly in the middle-Atlantic and northeastern states where a vast majority of southern Italian immigrants had settled. Now, the new judges, lawyers, prosecutors, councilmen, and even police had grown up in the Little Italies, along with the new leaders in organized crime. They had lived together as children and strong bonds had been established; the associations remained, through friendship and marriage. Alliances of power, friendships, and kin relationships all merged, and today it is difficult if not impossible to sort out those associations which are corrupt or corrupting from those which merely express the strength of kinship relations among southern Italians and their descendants. Whether innocent or corrupt associations result, there is no question that the family still forms

Figure 1. A Developmental History of Italian-American Crime Families

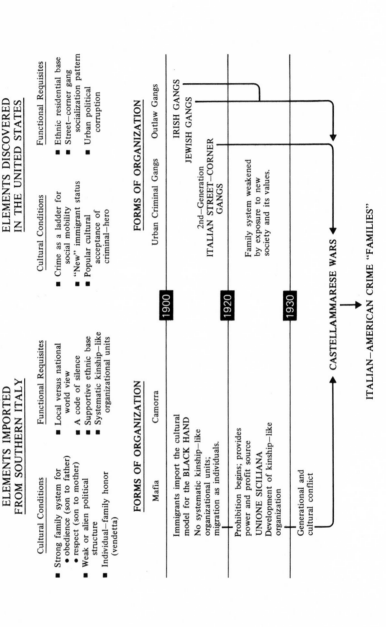

the basic network which ties the Italian-American community together, and that kinship is the pivot of that community. The *Mafia*-model *Unione* was a peculiarly southern Italian institution which could not and did not survive long in the New World. The acculturation process works in crime as elsewhere, and the values which activated and informed the old *Mafia* model were, by 1930, no longer prized. But while the organizational form of the *Mafia* disappeared, it could have left a heritage of kinship which still binds crime families and characterizes the involvement of Italian-Americans in organized crime. Whether some new organization was formed or whether the survivors of the Castellammarese Wars regrouped into new alliances is not a question which we can answer with any validity at present. As we report field observations in later chapters, we shall comment on this question in the context of what we have learned about the Lupollo family. For now, some general remarks must suffice.

The relationship between society and the development of the *Mafia* in Sicily holds true for organized crime in this country as well. There is no organized crime "underworld." Rather, organized crime is an integral part of our cities. It is the result of an individualistic, predatory philosophy of success, the malaise of laissez-faire economic and political practice. Organized crime is that part of the business system operative in the illicit segment of American life. The degree and tenure of minority-group involvement in this business enterprise is basically a function of the social and cultural integration of the group into American society. At their first entrance into this society, immigrants and their children grasp at the immediate means of acquiring what the New World has to offer. As they are acculturated, their crimes become more American and in time merge into the area of marginal legitimate business practice. Where one stops and the other begins is not always easy to see.

4 / The Lupollo Family

Describing the Lupollo family is difficult for several reasons. In the first place it is necessary, of course, to change names and to adjust dates and places to preserve the anonymity of the family. Yet it is very important that the basic structure of the family be preserved, since what is most intriguing for our concerns is the functional relationship between the family as a business syndicate and the family as a kinship unit. Actually, as the kinship chart of Figure 1 indicates, the family contains four separate lineages—the Lupollos, the Salemis, the Tuccis, and the Alcamos. But perhaps most perplexing to those who are not completely familiar with the southern Italian concept of family, is the fact that the association of these four lineages as a kinship group and their alliance as a business organization are one and inseparable. Functional roles in the business enterprises—whether legal or illegal—are nearly always a function of kinship and usually parallel generational position. The family business itself is an associated and integrated series of more than twenty legal business enterprises and a number of illegal ones which is clearly identifiable as a unit and which functions as such. Many members of the Lupollo family—whether Salemis, Tuccis, Alcamos, or Lupollos—have other, "outside" business activities or professions which are completely separate, but they have little or no effect on their functional roles within the Lupollo family business.

The Beginnings of the Family

The patriarch and founder of the family empire, Giuseppe Lupollo, was born of peasant parents in the district of Corleone in western Sicily in the early 1870's. Little is known of Giuseppe's life in Sicily. He left school at the age of ten to work with his father. Then, according to some family members, he worked as a gamekeeper for the *gabellotti* on the estate of the local baron until he was eighteen, when he left to farm a small plot of land owned jointly by his father and an uncle. Others claim he continued working for the *gabellotti* even after he began to farm. According to the latter version the *gabellotti* was head of one of the *cosche* of the *Mafia* in that region and Giuseppe worked with him in *Mafia* activities. No one in the family maintains that Giuseppe was a member of the *Mafia* in Corleone, but as one of his grandchildren told

Figure 1. The Lupoll

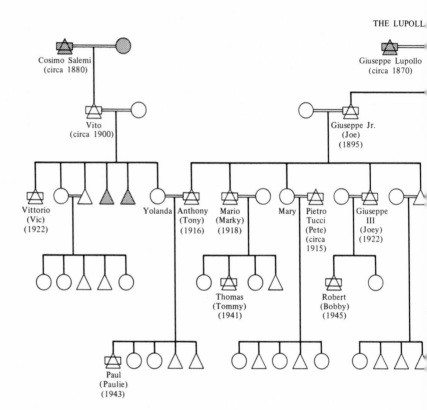

Family Kinship Chart

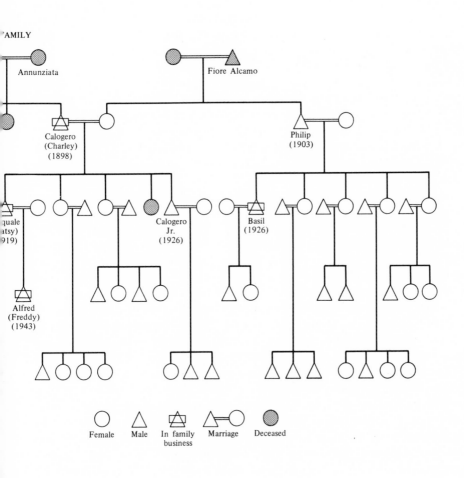

Female Male In family business Marriage Deceased

Annunziata

Fiore Alcamo

Calogero (Charley) (1898)

Philip (1903)

quale atsy) 919)

Calogero Jr. (1926)

Basil (1926)

Alfred (Freddy) (1943)

us, "In Sicily everybody worked with the *Mafia* or for it, and the old man was too smart to be on the other side." When Giuseppe was nineteen he married the niece of the *gabellotti* and for a time lived with her family. Knowledge of his wife is sparse. Her name was Annunziata, and she walked into the town every market day to sell produce from the garden she tended. She bore three children; a daughter, Adelina, who died at the age of two, and two sons, Giuseppe Junior, born in 1895, and Calogero, born three years later.

Giuseppe's reasons for leaving Sicily are subject to family dispute. Some claim he left to make money, return to Sicily, and establish himself on a larger landholding. A more romantic version pictures him escaping the wrath of a rent collector whose daughter had caught Giuseppe's eye. In any case, he arrived in the United States in 1902 with his wife, two sons, and four hundred dollars. The money may have come from scrimping and saving, or it may have come from his involvement with the *Mafia;* no one is certain. It was, however, a considerable sum; compared to other Sicilians, many of whom arrived penniless, he was a man of sizable fortune.

Giuseppe was settled among *paesani* from Corleone in the Mulberry Bend Section of New York's Lower East Side, he used his money to establish two businesses: he imported olive oil and candies, and he ran an "Italian bank." He sold the imported foods door to door in the Sicilian areas of the Lower East Side and soon expanded to other Sicilian neighborhoods.

The "bank," which Giuseppe operated from his home, loaned money to neighbors and *paesani*. It was not chartered, and he charged whatever interest rates he chose. Immigrants had no real property or other assets, and could not get loans or credit from normal banking institutions or any other source. Giuseppe and other "Italian bankers" provided the one sure source for loans. People outside the family claim his bank was actually the beginning of what later became a loan-shark operation. Everyone agrees that his rates were high, but members of the family claim that they were reasonable considering the circumstances. If the interest was high, so were the risks, for Giuseppe was investing in a group that was poor and could only afford to pay back in small amounts. In addition, since the police were indifferent to Italian-colony affairs he had no legal recourse for default. No one talks directly about what occurred when someone defaulted, but there are suggestions that Giuseppe was tied in with one of the Sicilian Black Hand gangs, and those unfortunate immigrants who were unwilling to repay him would themselves be repaid with physical violence and in some cases even death.

The "bank" was instrumental in starting Giuseppe on his rise to power and profit in the community. Italian-Americans entering business were forced to approach storefront banks for capital. In time, Giuseppe wrote off parts of the loans in exchange for an interest in the business. Having obtained partial control, he would then advance money for expansion and, in return, enlarge his interest in the business. Soon Giuseppe established himself as partial or complete owner of an ice-delivery service; an Italian bakery and confectionery store; a retail grocery store which specialized in Italian cheeses, olive oil, and condiments; and a small combination bar and card parlor on Grand Street in the Lower East Side. Around 1910, Giuseppe Lupollo began the family gambling interest setting up a branch of the "Italian lottery," which was the precursor of the policy or numbers racket. Through the First World War he concentrated his efforts on consolidation of these diverse interests within the Italian community, expanding beyond its borders only to purchase real estate in an Italian section of Brooklyn.

By 1915 Giuseppe Lupollo was an established and feared "man of respect" in the Italian-American community. He had achieved considerable financial success, and while his "loan-shark" and gambling activities were well known and, at least according to outside informants, he was involved in Black Hand activities, his status in the community was that of a banker and businessman. Active in local community affairs, he helped *paesani* to bring friends and relatives from Sicily, seemed willing to assist his less fortunate countrymen, and was a pillar of his church. On the feast day of St. Antonio, the patron saint of Corleone, he was usually selected as the marshal of the parade and always played a conspicuous part in the *festa*.

One *paesano* who came to New York through Giuseppe's generosity was Cosimo Salemi. Salemi was from Mezzoiuzzo, a village in the same district as Corleone, and was a distant cousin of Giuseppe's wife. Soon after he arrived Giuseppe employed him in the Italian lottery. We do not know Salemi's role in the business, but in about 1917 the lottery was raided as the result of a fracas between two customers, and Salemi was arrested. This was the first of the few times that any member of the family has suffered the scandal of arrest. Giuseppe was never implicated, but he learned through this incident that his power and status were safe only so long as police and politicians chose to ignore what was happening in Little Italy. He also learned that only an organization built on family loyalty could give him the personal security necessary for continued success.

Giuseppe Lupollo's two sons—Giuseppe Junior (Joe) and Calogero (Charley)—grew up and attended school in the Lower East Side. Despite their father's status in the community and his rapid accumulation of wealth, both remember this period as one of extreme hardship. Charley, for example, has vivid memories of the tenement in which he grew up:

> Joe and I talk a lot about the old neighborhood sometimes and it's funny the things you remember. A lot of characters that we knew in the neighborhood, like old Filomena who used to see visions of Saint Calogero and we used to make all kinds of noises outside her room to bring on visions and how my

mother, God bless her, used to raise holy hell with me because she said that Saint Calogero was my saint and that it was *infamita* for me to make fun of someone who had visions of him. . . .

More than anything else I remember the smells in the neighborhood. You can't believe how many people lived together in those houses. There were six or seven tenements on Elizabeth Street where we lived and in those buildings, which were maybe five or six stories high, there must have been fifteen or sixteen hundred people living. And everybody took in boarders, too. A lot of the guys who came over from Sicily were not married or had left their families in Italy. They were only there at night since they were out working all day, and at night there must have been another seven or eight hundred guys sleeping in the building. We had it pretty good because there were only four of us—my mother and father, Joe and me—in three rooms, but in some of the other apartments you had seven or eight adults and maybe ten kids living in an apartment the same size.

Some of the smells were good. I can remember, for example, that early in the morning, say five o'clock, you could smell peppers and eggs frying when the women got lunches ready for their sons and husbands. But more than anything else I remember the smell of human bodies and of garbage. There was no such thing as garbage collection in those days and everybody just threw it out in the street or put it out in the hallways. Christ, how it stank!

From the beginning, in his family as well as in his business, Giuseppe Lupollo wanted status and legitimacy or at least their trappings. He refused to accept the old Sicilian proverb "Don't make your children better than yourself," and insisted that one son get a good education. Accordingly Charley completed high school at the age of eighteen. He himself knew that in the United States education was not only possible but essential for "getting ahead in the world." He still comments that his father had the vision to see that all the things he had gained could not be preserved unless somebody in the family had enough education that "the Jews and the politicians couldn't put anything over on him." Charley wanted to be a lawyer, but "at that time Italian kids just didn't go to college." After graduation from high school, he worked for his father in the ice-delivery business, and got involved in politics. He was chosen by his father and suited by his own predilections to be the respectable and legitimate family member.

Joe (Giuseppe Junior) left school at fifteen to work for his father. He started as a "helper" in a bakery and later began working with Cosimo Salemi in the family's Italian lottery and served as an enforcer in the family loan operation. Because his lesser education prevented involvement in politics and legitimate business, and because of his early involvement in his father's affairs, Joe gradually became responsible for the less legitimate family enterprises. In 1915 Joe married Serafina Saietta, cousin of Ignazio Saietta, who played an important role in the early attempts to organize the various and disparate

Black Hand gangs in New York City. This was the family's first important connection in the city-wide organization of the nascent Italian syndicate. Four years after young Joe's marriage, however, Ignazio Saietta was arrested and sentenced to thirty years.

In late 1916, Charley married Giuseppa Alcamo, the daughter of a stonemason who had emigrated in the early 1900's from Sciacca on the western coast of Sicily. Giuseppa, like Charley, had graduated from high school, and this, combined with the fact that she did not come from the Corleone district, created tensions in the family. The young couple moved in with his parents, and Giuseppa still remembers that sometimes Charley's mother would pointedly set the table for just three people—herself, her husband, and Charley. However, gradually if grudgingly, the old woman accepted her new daughter-in-law, largely because of Charley's conscious effort to keep peace in the family.

The 1920's

By 1920, old Giuseppe had three grandchildren—Anthony (Tony) and Mario (Marky) by Joe, and Pasquale (Patsy) by Charley. Both his legitimate and illegal enterprises were prospering in the beginning of the postwar boom. Late in 1920, partly as a result of the social and residential mobility which characterized many Italian families at that time, but also because Giuseppe decided it would be good for business, the family moved to an Italian section of Brooklyn.

In Brooklyn, old Giuseppe continued to run both the family and the family business with an iron hand. And the business, which now involved a number of diverse activities ranging from the Italian lottery and loan-sharking to the ice-delivery business, remained one business. Each separate part reported directly to old Giuseppe and each part contributed to the others. For example, by 1921 the ice-delivery business, which had branched out to include coal, was replacing its horse-drawn wagons with trucks. When the trucks were not needed, they did not stand idle; they were used to make deliveries from one grocery store to another or from the bakery to the grocery stores.

The cohesiveness of the business was rooted in Giuseppe's firm resolve to keep all the activities within his own family and, moreover, to employ relatives—of whom there were many—at every level of every enterprise. In the bakery, for example, every employee was either a family relative or a *paesano* from the Corleone district. As each enterprise grew, Giuseppe would select promising relatives or in-laws for leadership positions. The Lupollo business was becoming a major operation in the Italian-American community, but it was sufficiently cohesive to be manageable as a family oligarchy.

At some time in the 1920's the family entered the garbage-and-refuse hauling and disposal business. The family ascribes old Giuseppe's decision to enter into this area largely to his shrewd sense of potentially profitable business areas, but also to the corporate nature of the family business enterprises. By 1922 the family was heavily involved in the production of illegal alcohol. The residues from the home stills had to be carted away by someone, so the family began using the ice-and-coal company's trucks. However, as the operation grew the use of ice-and-coal trucks became conspicuous, and the family purchased a separate truck to haul residue. This truck also began hauling garbage from the other family enterprises. Soon more trucks were added, and the family was in the garbage business.

Within the Italian colonies in Brooklyn and the Lower East Side, everyone knew of the Lupollo family's legal and illegal business involvements. The Lupollos were safe in their community, and flourished because they did not venture outside it. Their contact outside the ghetto was still only occasional and even then was for business rather than social purposes. Joe Lupollo's son Tony once described the kind of isolation the ghetto afforded:

> What's so hard to explain to anybody who never went through it is how Little Italy and living there is a life all in itself. You ate, slept, played, fought, and moved only in Little Italy. When you were outside you felt you were outside and you felt a difference when you went back inside the borders. But even more important is what it did to your thinking. We kids knew that there were other kinds of people; we saw Irish kids, Jewish kids, and even a few colored people in school. But even my father, who was only seven years old when he came to this country, lived and acted as if there was nobody else except the people in Little Italy. When I was growing up there were four kinds of people: Italians, colored people, Jews, and *Americans*. Anybody who wasn't one of us or colored or Jewish we always talked about as an American. Sure, sometimes we would say that he was Irish or even that he was German, but we lumped them all together as Americans.
>
> In 1932 or '33 my grandfather's bakery added a line of sliced sandwich-style bread like you see in stores today. I never heard anybody in the family or for that matter anybody in Little Italy ever call it anything but "American bread." I remember that my mother used to make sandwiches for us to take to school for our lunch and we used to always argue with her to make the sandwiches on American bread because that seemed to show that you were more American than Italian. She didn't do it for a long time but when she finally did I still remember the trouble we used to have trying to eat pepper-and-egg sandwiches made out of that thin crustless bread. The olive oil made the bread soggy and it would always fall apart.

After 1925 the Lupollo family moved into the distribution as well as production of alcohol and alcoholic products. According to a popular story, old Giuseppe was approached by a "Jewish beer baron" wanting to lease his trucks for the distribution of beer and other alcoholic beverages smuggled in from

Canada. Giuseppe gave no immediate answer; instead, he sent for Cosimo Salemi and asked if he could find outlets for whiskey and brandy. Salemi assured him that he could, and Giuseppe made arrangements to "import" liquor himself. He used his own trucks for delivery, and used his grocery, bakery, and importing enterprises to cover the bootlegging business.

Old Giuseppe was still firm in his decision to develop legitimate and illegitimate businesses separately, and to have different relatives involved in each. Charley stayed in charge of the legitimate businesses and used his influence in politics to protect the lottery which Joe gradually took over, making the gambling a relatively low-risk illegal activity. When the time came to move into bootlegging, Giuseppe chose neither Charley nor Joe to head the operation, but instead placed Vito Salemi, Cosimo's son, in charge. Vito was the only member of the family group other than his father who had been arrested, and he had the necessary contacts in the community to set up the network. But no one in the colonies thought of the bootlegging as Vito Salemi's operation or the ice-and-coal business as Charley's, or the lottery as Joe's. Each was in every sense a family business. And Giuseppe as head of the family was the head of each separate enterprise. Moreover, the income from all the family enterprises flowed into one central account—Giuseppe's.

Both the legal and illicit business activities of the Lupollos prospered during the 1920's. Some difficulties were, however, generated by the power struggle among the emerging Italian-American syndicates. Ignazio Saietta's imprisonment in 1919 had frozen the attempt to organize the Black Hand gangs. In the 1920's, however, partly as a result of the power-and-profit market provided by Prohibition and partly because of the growing movement of second-generation Italian-Americans into organized crime, a new power struggle emerged. Three general geographical power areas, which came to be called "chairs," began to develop in New York City: one in East Harlem, one in Greenwich Village, and one in Brooklyn. The Lupollos held a good position in East Harlem because Ciro Terranova, the major power there, was related by marriage to the Lupollos. But the Lupollo operations were in Brooklyn and lower Manhattan, and the family was therefore deeply involved in the struggle for those "chairs." The Downtown and Brooklyn chairs were fought over by the Joseph Masseria–Frankie Yale faction and the Salvatore Mauro–Umberto Valenti group. Giuseppe had the power to tip the balance, but his emerging empire could be wiped out if he chose incorrectly. Charley Lupollo once described to us how old Giuseppe made such decisions:

> Pop used to talk to Joe and me on how important it was for the business to be protected and to make sure that we had friends who we could trust. If he told us once, he told us a thousand times that you couldn't trust the judges and the politicians to do anything for you because they didn't understand the way things worked in the Italian district. Judges did everything by the book

or even worse, they did what they were told by the politicians who were out to get all they could from hardworking souls. The only protection was to take care of yourself and to make sure you had friends you could count on when the time came. Pop always said that he trusted Italians more than Americans, Sicilians more than Italians, his *paisani* more than other Sicilians but most of all he trusted his family. And family to Pop means not just those of us within the family but everybody who was related to us. Even there, however, he made it clear that blood was more important than marriage and the closer you were related to somebody the more important to have their trust. A lot of people say bad things about my father because he worked with people like Joey Doto [Joe Adonis] and Ciro Terranova but what they don't say is that these were relatives and that my father trusted them when he couldn't trust anybody else.

Along with the Dotos (Joe Adonis and his father), old Giuseppe threw in with the Yale and Masseria faction. Whether distrust of non-family members or his own inherent shrewdness motivated Giuseppe is unknown, but his choice was good: Masseria emerged as the major power in Manhattan and Yale took over in Brooklyn. Shortly after this, however, in about 1926, Giuseppe decided to concentrate in Brooklyn and began to close some operations in lower Manhattan. His legitimate business enterprises were continued both in Mulberry Bend and in other Italian sections of Manhattan, but he gradually moved the Italian lottery and the storefront bank to Brooklyn.

The 1930's and 1940's

With the onset of the 1930's and the end of Prohibition, the Lupollo business complex underwent another change. A very profitable sector had been closed off, but Giuseppe had already begun the Italian lottery and was developing it into the new numbers or policy game. He had now moved out of the ghetto for some operations, so that the protection afforded by the ghetto was insufficient, and Giuseppe had to deal with the political power structure. At this point Philip Alcamo, the younger brother of Charley Lupollo's wife, entered the family business. "Uncle Phil," as he is always called, had completed law school and was active in Democratic politics. Charley had also been increasing his political contacts, but after 1932, it was Uncle Phil who forged the links with the political structure which have since served to protect the family interests. With bootlegging profits and new gains from gambling, Giuseppe expanded into new, legitimate areas of business.

Even while they were moving toward respectability in the 1930's, the Lupollos struggled to maintain their position among the growing number of Italian-American crime families. The Castellammarese War which racked the gang world in the 1930's had indirect but important consequences for the family. This war between the insurgent second-generation Italian-American and the immigrant "Moustache Petes" caused no internal conflict within the Lupollo family; old Giuseppe was obviously one of the "Moustache Petes," but his sons and other family members were completely loyal to him. If the young insurgents took over, they would probably not deal with old Giuseppe, identified with the "moustaches," and his empire might be carved up. His earlier decision to place Joe in operational control of the illicit portions of his business empire now paid off. Joe represented the family in negotiations during this difficult period, and the numbers and loan-shark operations remained secure for the family.

The Castellammarese Wars and the earlier struggle over the Brooklyn and Manhattan "chairs" impressed on Giuseppe the insecurity of illegitimate enterprise. After 1932, he moved with even greater dispatch and resolve to strengthen the legitimate enterprises of the family while reducing the illicit activities.

Around 1940, when he was approaching seventy years of age, Giuseppe relinquished control of the family enterprises and made his son Joe the active head of the family. Since then both the illegitimate and legitimate enterprises have reported to Joe. Old Giuseppe died in 1950.

Despite its rising wealth throughout the 1920's and 1930's, the Lupollo family continued to live conservatively. Their houses in Brooklyn appeared no more luxurious than any others in the neighborhood. Old Giuseppe acted and dressed the role of a successful Italian-American businessman, and was very well known and powerful in the Italian community, but he did not permit himself or either of his sons to take on the lavish life style they could have acquired. Though Giuseppe still had no social contacts outside of the Italian colony, within it he traveled freely among Italian-American politicians, newspaper owners, businessmen, and the emerging group of Italian professionals. But while his covert role in illicit business activities was well known within the Italian colony, no member of his immediate family had ever been arrested, and his name was virtually unknown to the outside world.

Joe and Charley Lupollo continued to provide grandchildren and heirs for old Giuseppe. Joe's daughter, Marianina (usually called Mary), was born in 1921, another son, Giuseppe Lupollo III (Joey), in 1922, and his last child, Salvatore, in 1926. During the 1920's, Charley had four children. His three daughters—Clara, Helen, and Annunziata—were followed by a son, Calogero Junior (Charles).

The Family Today

Today Joe looks back on his selection as head of the family business as an inseparable and almost inevitable result of his father's determination to

consolidate the family's gains by moving it more and more into the mainstream of American society:

> Pop really loved Charley and me the same and he didn't even think of us
> as two different people but as the sons of the family. He always told us that
> business and politics are full of people who would just as soon see you dead
> if it meant that they would make an extra nickle. He used to say in Sicilian
> that life is so difficult that God gave everybody a family to make sure that he
> had somebody who would always help him. I remember that I was always
> surprised about how much he knew about American business and politics. He
> never read the newspapers except the Italian ones and when we used to listen
> to Walter Winchell or some other newscaster he would always say that the
> newscaster's mouth was wired to somebody else's brain and that you should
> only believe whatever you can see.

When Joe took control of the family business he began consolidating
diverse enterprises and assigning functional responsibility to family members.
He continued his father's practice of assigning relatives and *paesani* to all
supervisory positions. By the beginning of the Second World War, the grocery,
bakery, and importing businesses had been consolidated into one major bakery chain and one nationally known food-products firm. This part of the family
business is managed by Pete Tucci, who married Joe's daughter, Mary, in
1942. Pete is not a Sicilian but comes from the mainland province of Calabria.
Charley once remarked that in the old days Giuseppe would never have permitted his granddaughter to marry a Calabrian, and if she had, he would have
ostracised her from the family. A *Calabrese* having a role in the family business would not have been allowed in old Giuseppe's day. Nevertheless, Pete
Tucci is in it now, and has expanded the food-products firm by adding farms
and packing plants in New Jersey and California and a frozen-food line.

Joe's elder sons, Tony and Marky, manage the family's substantial real
estate holdings in Brooklyn. In addition, Tony has his own clothes-manufacturing concern which produces a line of men's clothing sold in many large
department stores. Joe's third son, Joey, works directly with his father and
serves as an official with two family companies. Joey is also a stockbroker and
has considerable real estate holdings of his own in upstate New York. The
youngest son, Sal, graduated from a Catholic college in the East after the
Second World War and went to medical school. He is now married and prac-
ticing medicine in New Jersey. He still visits his father and mother and his
brothers and sisters and usually appears at large family gatherings. He has no
business contact with the family.

After Joe became head of the family business, the original ice-and-coal
delivery company was transformed into a fuel-delivery enterprise and expanded to include a limousine-leasing business in Brooklyn and a trucking
firm. Charley heads this enterprise and also the garbage-hauling business,

which has expanded to the Bronx. Actually, however, Charley's main role in the family is in politics and public relations. He shares this role with Phil Alcamo—not without a certain amount of competition between the two—and the two together represent the political interests of the entire family. Charley's connections are primarily in local, city, and state politics. He is on friendly and familiar terms with numerous politicians, judges, union leaders, and city and police officials.

Charley's son Patsy now manages the trucking and limousine-rental interests of the family, and is also said to have independent real estate holdings in Las Vegas and Reno, Nevada. Of Charley's other four children, none seems to have any contact with the family business. Clara, a registered nurse, is married to a physician and lives on Long Island. Helen married a pharmacist. She is a schoolteacher and lives in the Bronx. Annunziata entered a teaching order of nuns; she died in the 1940's. Charles went to college in Florida and took a law degree at the University of Virginia. He is now in the real estate business in Arizona, and as far as we can determine has no contact with the family business, although he does return to New York occasionally and visits the family.

Phil Alcamo's principal political connections center in Washington. He travels to the capital frequently and meets with and entertains Congressmen and government officials, particularly those in regulatory agencies. In addition to his involvement in the family business, Phil also has his own public-relations firm and a travel agency. He and his wife, a nurse of English-Irish descent, have four daughters and a son. One daughter, who has recently remarried after a divorce, is living in Tenafly, New Jersey; one is married to a naval officer and lives in San Diego, California; one is the wife of a liquor distributor in the Bahamas; and one is married to the owner of a chain of hairdressing shops in the Philadelphia area. Phil's son, Basil, is a certified public accountant. He works with his father in the travel agency, handles the accounting for most of the family businesses, and also has his own independent accounting firm.

Since Cosimo Salemi's death in 1938, his son Vito has managed the gambling interests of the family. He is also active in the loan-shark operation. Vito had five children. Marty was shot and killed in a Bronx bar in the mid-1930's. Philip was killed in the Pacific during the Second World War. Dominica (Domenique) married a German-Irish clothing manufacturer. They live in Florida, where they own two motels and an apartment building. Vito's daughter Yolanda is married to Tony Lupollo (Joe's son). Vito's surviving son, Vittorio (Vic), has been working with his father in the loan-shark business since he graduated from high school.

Vito Salemi and Vic, who is a bachelor, live together in Brooklyn, but the rest of the family has moved elsewhere. In 1947 Joe Lupollo moved to

Forest Hills, Long Island, and all three of his sons live in the same area. Pete Tucci lives in the Astoria section of Queens and also has a large summer place in Ventnor, New Jersey. Charley and his son Patsy both live in Lynbrook, Long Island, and Charley also has a summer place in the Pocono mountains. Phil Alcamo maintains a large apartment in Manhattan and has an estate in Old Westbury, Long Island, near his son Basil's establishment.

The family members who have moved out of Brooklyn have become a part of the various communities in which they live. Joey, for example, is a member of the yacht and racquet clubs in his community as well as the local country club. He has his own plane, a large power cruiser, and a fleet of cars. His home is considered a "showplace" in the community. He entertains his neighbors frequently and lavishly and is a sought-after guest as well. Like most of the third-generation Lupollos, Joey is still an active member of the church and gives frequently to both his local parish and the Archdiocese. He gives generously to community campaigns and to other special philanthropic appeals.

In 1970, forty-two fourth-generation members of the Lupollo-Salemi-Alcamo-Tucci family could be identified. Their movement towards legitimation seems almost complete. Only four of the twenty-seven males we traced are involved in the family business. Even when their fathers are active in the family business, most of the children are in legitimate enterprises. Tony and Yolanda Lupollo have five children. Their two daughters married "outside"— one to the son of a judge—and the youngest son attends a liberal arts college in upstate New York. Another son is a member of the English department in a liberal arts college. Only one son, Paulie, works with his father in the family business. Marky Lupollo has two daughters; one is a teacher married to a dentist, and the other is completing a master's degree in psychology. His son Frank is a lawyer. Only one son, Tommy, works with his father in the real estate sector of the family business. Pete Tucci and his wife, Mary, have five children; one son is a physician, one son is a lawyer, and the three daughters are all married "outside." None of Pete's children is in the family business. Joey Lupollo has two children. His daughter is in college; his son Bobby is a stockbroker and is also involved in the family business. Patsy Lupollo's only son, Alfred, is also involved in the family business. Basil Alcamo has two children. His daughter attends a private school in upstate New York, and his son is currently attending a Catholic college outside of Philadelphia.

While the family business has increasingly concentrated on legitimate sectors of the economy, the illegal activities of the family continue. The gambling activities—which formerly included bookmaking as well as the policy or numbers game—are still in operation in Brooklyn but are gradually being phased out. Loan sharking, however, continues to be a major activity and is increasing rather than disappearing. The family has a major interest in this area and there appears to be no intention to move out.

Life Styles in the Lupollo Family

The Lupollo family exhibits the range of similarities and differences typical of families everywhere. Each member is a distinct individual, yet each fits into a role category. The most obvious scheme of classification is by generations. Each of the three surviving generations of the Lupollo family has a characteristic style which marks its members off from the other generations. We were never able, of course, to observe the behavior of old Giuseppe or of Cosimo Salemi, but from family recollections and accounts of individuals outside the family who knew them, they seem to have shared more with each other than either did with their children or grandchildren.

Giuseppe was a man of considerable talent and charm, self-educated, and a shrewd judge of people and situations. A security patrol officer who grew up in the neighborhood with Giuseppe's children knew him as an important and influential neighbor and describes him as "always aware of what was happening around him and always in control of what was happening in the neighborhood." Others described him as intelligent and absolutely determined to have his way. One story tells of Giuseppe, making his rounds selling condiments, being set upon by a gang of Irish toughs. The gang of six or eight men abused Giuseppe and demanded his money and his merchandise. He refused and was severely beaten, but managed to protect both his money and his goods. No one knows whether Giuseppe, in true Sicilian style, later avenged himself. Charley says that such set-to's probably happened more than once, because in the early days of the Italian ghetto anyone who wandered outside was fair game for "American" toughs who preyed upon immigrants.

At first Giuseppe's style of life was not noticeably different from that of other immigrants. If any characteristic set him apart it was, say former neighbors, his ability to find a profit in anything he turned his hand to. He was generous with neighbors and *paesani* who needed help; he could always be counted on for a job for an indigent relative or passage money from Italy for the relative of a friend. Indeed, when the immigrant arrived Giuseppe usually had some sort of job waiting. Probably Giuseppe's friendly and supportive behavior was related to his constant need to find people he could trust to work in the growing business. Relatives were always more dependable than others; and, failing kinship, cultural affinity and the network of friendship were almost as secure.

As Giuseppe prospered in business his tastes seemed not to have changed a great deal. When he moved to Brooklyn, his row house was no different from the others in the lower-middle class neighborhood. While his children and grandchildren were using their growing wealth to move to suburban areas, Giuseppe remained in Brooklyn until he died. From all accounts he was a patriarch, at once kindly and domineering. Within the family all important decisions were reserved for him, and where he did delegate authority, it was still subject to his approval. Outside of the family he was feared and respected. It was characteristic in the early Italian-American ghettos to see power as positive, regardless of the fashion in which it was attained. He was conservative in political and social attitudes and in every respect a "Moustache Pete," associating with the old *paesani* from the Corleone region. He devoted himself to his family; Joe and Charley speak of him today as a kindly if stern father who always had their best interests at heart.

We know little about Cosimo Salemi. What we do know comes from his great-grandson Paulie, who, because he is a link between the Salemi and Lupollo lineages, often presents the Salemis as "not so bad as they're always made out to be." Cosimo seems to have worked for Giuseppe from the day Giuseppe financed his migration from Sicily to the United States. Moreover, Cosimo remained entirely within the illegal operations of the family, and that tradition has continued in the Salemi lineage to the present. From other, random sources, Cosimo seems to have been boisterous but friendly and to have instilled fear rather than respect into those who worked with him or knew him. Like Giuseppe, his relationships were with *paesani* and always within the ghetto. He never moved from the row house in Brooklyn in which he lived from the 1920's on.

Isolation and insulation within the ghetto were characteristic of both Giuseppe and Cosimo. They were unwilling (and unable) to move freely in the world outside the Italian colony. Their business and social activities and experiences were contained within it throughout their lives. Their very isolation within that enclave allowed them to prosper. Whether difference in ability or sheer situational factors made Giuseppe the leader and Cosimo the underling is a question, but this relationship has persisted between the Salemis and the Lupollos ever since.

Today the second generation—Joe and Charley Lupollo, Cosimo's son Vito, and Phil Alcamo—make up the senior leadership cadre of the family. Phil, who was in his mid-sixties in 1970, is somewhat younger than the others; they are all in their early seventies. These four senior leaders in the family business vary in their degree of acculturation but all are distinctively Italian-American in life style. Vito Salemi is the least acculturated; he speaks English only grudgingly and dresses in the conservative dark suit and black tie of the successful immigrant businessman. He continues to live and function in his old neighborhood in Brooklyn and is uncomfortable outside it. Even in the summer, when he spends a month in Atlantic City, he lives in an area where neighbors and cronies from Brooklyn also have homes. The few friends and contacts he maintains outside the family circle are all Italian-American and are known in the community as either involved in or related to organized-crime activities.

Of the four senior family members, Vito most nearly fits the stereotype of the Italian-American mobster. He oversees the illegal sectors of the family business and numbers among his relatives and friends several well-known and much-feared Italian-American hoodlums. Yet there is another side of Vito, which emerges at family gatherings such as weddings and baptisms. Within the family social circle he is noted for his generosity, particularly with young children. He delights them almost as much with his fracturing of the English language as he does with his gifts. Repeating his malapropisms is a favorite pastime in the social life of the family.

Joe Lupollo, who has headed the family both as a business enterprise and as a social organization since the 1940's, is also much more Italian than American, but less Italian than Vito. When he moved to Forest Hills in 1947, it was mostly at the insistence of his children who wanted him "to start enjoying some of his money." His associations and interests, however, have remained in Brooklyn. He travels in from Forest Hills daily to oversee his business empire, and on Sundays he still comes in to his old parish church for early mass, returning to Forest Hills to hold open house for all of his children and grandchildren in the afternoon. Despite his considerable wealth and even more considerable power, he never seems comfortable in Forest Hills. In Brooklyn he still sees childhood friends from time to time, and attends the weddings of his many godchildren. His large and spacious Forest Hills home is more an extension of his life in Brooklyn and a meeting place for his children than a part of the surrounding community.

Unlike Vito Salemi, Joe does not view the world outside the Italian-American community as alien and inhospitable. He belongs to a number of clubs and organizations which, while heavily Italian-American in membership, are not exclusively ethnic in purpose or makeup. His sons are also members of some of the same organizations, including one which is an athletic club. While his children use it as a social and athletic center, Joe goes there only occasionally to meet his sons, to have dinner, or to meet non-Italian-Americans on matters of business. Joe is also active in Italian-American and Catholic fraternal and civic organizations and is known as a generous donor to various Catholic charities.

Joe travels only to visit relatives or do business. He usually spends some time each summer with one of his children, all of whom maintain summer places outside the city, and occasionally he visits relatives in Pennsylvania and upstate New York. Joe has not been outside the United States since his father brought him here. He has no memories of Sicily, but still speaks of the ghetto life in lower Manhattan with a mixture of nostalgia and irony. Often such remarks are made in response to some complaint by one of the younger Lupollos and are intended in part to remind them of their distance from the family's humble beginnings and the cost of that journey in stoicism and vitality.

Joe's younger brother, Charley, shares this attachment to the Italian-

American community, but he is better educated, thinks in less traditional patterns, and moves freely in the larger American community. Like Joe, he conducts most of his business activity in Brooklyn, but his home in Lynbrook is the center of his social life; he mingles with his neighbors and, particularly in recent years, he has begun to take an active part in community life. He often chides Joe for being so old-fashioned and has tried on several occasions to interest him in social and sports activities but with little success. Charley is an avid fan of all sports, particularly boxing and professional football, and attends as many events as he can. To a lesser extent Charley also follows baseball and basketball, but only because football is seasonal and boxing, in his words, "is now a bunch of clowns and actors who put on a better show outside the ring than inside." Charley has friends and contacts in the sports world and, through his son Patsy, has recently been mingling with show-business personalities and the vast array of hangers-on who people the periphery of that world. While Joe is active in Italian-American and Catholic organizations, Charley finds his associations in the political world of New York City. He has never been a candidate for office himself, but he is active in politics at the local level and seems to know any number of politicians, in and out of office, on a first-name basis.

While Joe Lupollo fits in function if not in title the classical description of the "boss" in an organized crime family, Charley seems to be a roving ambassador between the family and the business and political system outside the Italian-American community. It is Charley who travels frequently, handles relationships with the police and political establishment, and represents the family in the non-Italian world. It is Charley, rather than Joe, who goes to testimonial dinners for retiring judges and city commissioners and advises the younger members of the family on the wisdom of new business enterprises. But inevitably Charley defers to his older brother whenever business or family matters are being discussed. He very seldom challenges Joe's business or family decisions. To an extent this behavior relates to Joe's reputation for suddenly erupting into violence when he is angry, but it also indicates Charlie's recognition of Joe's authority as head of the family.

Phil Alcamo is the most acculturated of the four senior members of the family, and so the least tied to the Italian-American community. A lawyer, he is as much at home in the world of politics as he is in the Lupollo family's other world. And it is in the political milieu that Phil finds the greatest challenge and enjoyment. He frequently entertains businessmen, politicians, and stage and sports personalities in his Manhattan apartment. City councilmen, commissioners, judges and Congressmen attend parties and dinners there. On these occasions, Phil discusses art as well as politics but still manages to prosecute his own and the family's case on such matters as pending legislation and problems with federal regulatory bodies.

Much more than other senior family members, Phil enjoys the cultural advantages of New York; he frequently attends the opera and the legitimate theater and has gained some reputation as a collector and connisseur of art. His apartment is not very different from that of other wealthy business or professional men in the city, except for the many autographed photographs of well-known political and entertainment personalities. Phil's life style draws both envy and criticism from other family members. The Lupollos love to tell of old Giuseppe's wife Annunziata visiting Phil's apartment. Her comment on the lavish collection of paintings was *"manga nu Santa"* ("not even one saint's picture").

Within the family, Phil adjusts his role and style to fit. When he is with Joe Lupollo he becomes more Italian. With Charley he is far more American, and with the younger members of the family he is the model of the Italian-American businessman who has made it socially and financially in American society. While Charley is sought out for advice on business matters, it is Uncle Phil who is the arbiter of taste and counselor in politics.

The children of these four senior members form the largest generational grouping within the fifteen members of the Lupollo family who form the leadership cadre of the family business. Of the seven members of the third generation in the family business, those in the Lupollo lineage—Charley's son Patsy and Joe's sons Tony, Marky, and Joey—are a cohesive subgroup which shares a similar life style. All live on Long Island near their respective fathers, and all have integrated their families into their local communities. Yet while they live on Long Island and their families are established there, they still spend most of their time in the city. For Tony and Marky "the city" is Brooklyn, where they carry on their business activities and still retain their major social contacts. Patsy Lupollo also works in Brooklyn; his social interests center about night clubs and East Side parties in Manhattan. Joey spends most of his business day in the Wall Street area looking after the family's investment interests, and divides his social activities between business friends in Manhattan and his family on Long Island.

Each of the four third-generation Lupollos is a different personality— Tony is a dour and suspicious loner, Marky an outgoing and friendly businessman, Patsy the family playboy, and Joey the heir apparent to his father's power—but the closeness of the Lupollo lineage and the compelling milieu of the family business mandate certain similarities in life style. Whatever their legal and illegal business activities, they are always kept out of the communities in which they live. In many ways they are no different from any number of other prosperous businessmen who live on Long Island and commute to offices in the city. In fact, one of the striking differences between this generation of Lupollos and their fathers and sons is how closely they resemble their predominantly Jewish neighbors on the Island, even to the frequent use of

Yiddish words and phrases in business conversation. To some extent this is probably the result of their adaptation to the communities in which they live, but much of it seems to be emulation of the ethnic group which most immediately preceded them into the security of upper-middle-class American society.

Pete Tucci, who married Joe Lupollo's daughter Mary, is also in this middle age-grade in the family. Pete is in the uncomfortable position of simply acting for his father-in-law in the food-products company, and he has no "outside" business interest of his own. He has neither power nor prestige in the family circle. His home in Astoria is fairly modest by the standards of his family contemporaries, and he maintains the life style of a successful Italian-American businessman whose work and family occupy his whole life. He is considered conservative and traditional by other members of the family and, while he always attends family social functions, he usually does not take an active part. His wife, on the other hand, is outgoing and is said to dominate him completely, an unusual arrangement in this highly patrifocal group. Inevitably, some observers attribute this to Pete's entry into the family business through his wife's lineage; significantly, neither of Pete's sons has any connection in the family business.

Vic Salemi is a bachelor living with his father Vito and working with him in the gambling and loan-shark sectors of the business. Unlike his father, he seldom appears at family social gatherings. Paulie Lupollo, who is his nephew, describes him as somewhat dissatisfied with the subordinate role the Salemis have had to play vis-à-vis the Lupollos and says that he is anxious to move into some of the legitimate businesses. Vic may be dissatisfied with the Salemi lineage's assignment to the illegal sectors, or he may simply be interested in expanding his own business activities; we do not know. But the apparent difference between Vito's acceptance of his role in the family business and Vic's growing rejection of it has implications for the future relationships among the various lineages.

Phil Alcamo's son Basil has moved further than any other member of the family executive group into non-family social and business life. Like his father, he is better educated than his age mates in the executive group, and his training as an accountant gives him a role as a specialist which affords him some degree of autonomy within various family business activities. Of all the third-generation members of the Lupollo family, Basil most actively rejects Italian-American ancestry as an identifying feature of his life. His estate in Old Westbury is nestled among those of prominent socialites, and he enjoys the role of the part-time country squire. His daughter rides and shows her own horses, and his son has some reputation as an up-and-coming young yachtsman. Characteristically, however, Basil does not associate himself with Joey Lupollo, is less "American," less outgoing, and, less social.

Few fourth-generation Lupollos have followed their fathers into the family business. Most of the sons have entered professions, and most of the women have married professional or businessmen, usually but not always Italian-Americans. Some have left the New York area, but all keep in contact with their immediate families. The four men in this generation who have active roles in the family business are all Lupollos—Tony's son Paulie, Marky's son Tommy, Joey's son Bobby, and Patsy's son Freddy. All four are college graduates who, with the exception of Bobby, attended Catholic colleges in the Middle Atlantic region. They maintain continuing business and social contact with their fathers and with one another, but their associations are weaker than those of previous generations and they are less involved with the Italian-American community. Freddy, for example, spends a good deal of time golfing and playing tennis with non-Italian friends and neighbors. Why these four remained in the family business while their brothers left to enter professions is not known. Nor is it possible to assess the significance of the fact that one son of each of the third-generation Lupollos stayed in the family business while no member of the Tucci or Alcamo lineage did (there are no male Salemis in this generation). It is difficult to say whether the members of the fourth generation who left the family business did so to escape it, or whether the continuing social mobility of Italian-Americans simply made it possible for them to aspire to professional roles which were denied their parents. However, contact with those fourth-generation members who did remain in the family business revealed their feeling that by the next generation the Lupollos will have completed their transition from the Italian-American community into American society, and, if allowed to, will complete the process of legitimation which old Giuseppe started in the 1920's.

The Value Structure in the Lupollo Family

Each of the four generations of the Lupollo family has moved closer to the mainstream of American social life. In this transformation, each of the generations has developed its own life style as south Italian values have given way to a more American way of life. But some vestigial Italian values still characterize the family as a social system which transcends generations. While they are less obvious and compelling in the fourth generation than they were for Giuseppe and his children, they are still important guides to family behavior, and to an understanding of the way the family operates and survives.

The most obvious and, in our experience, the strongest of these values is the importance of kinship and family as the bases of both social and business organization. In one sense this value is even stronger here than it was in the south of Italy. In the rural south of the old country, positive attitudes toward familialism and kinship strongly sanctioned the extended family as the ideal. The vagaries and harshness of peasant life, however, ruled against extended family patterns in residence or work; the land and the economy made it impossible to support so large a group. Yet, as we have seen earlier, the extended family continued as an ideal, always dreamed of, if seldom achieved. In this country, however, the Lupollo family has managed to achieve that ideal. Success in business has allowed them to encompass the entire extended family of related lineages in one social–business unit. In fact, their familialism becomes self-reinforcing, since family unity adds to business success.

Closely related to the value of familialism is the patrifocal character of the lineages and of the family itself. The Lupollo family is a man's world; women have no place in it except as wives and mothers and as linkage points to ally the lineages. Almost without exception, the women in the family are uninvolved in and seemingly unaware of the nature of the business empire which their husbands serve. Wives may be socially and interpersonally aggressive and even domineering in home life, as in the case of Mary Lupollo Tucci, but they have no role in business activities. The strength of this male bonding is such that sons spend considerable time with their fathers not only in business but in social activities. Members of the same generation also seem to show some preferential association with one another, particularly with those of the same lineage.

Male dominance and bonding is also associated with the third primary value in the Lupollo family—honor. Among the Lupollos as in the south of Italy, the individual's allegiance to *onore e famiglia* recognizes the cultural fact that individual and family honor are one and inseparable. Although this value is not as dramatically obvious among the Lupollos as it is in Sicily, it is nonetheless operative. Even fourth-generation males identify with the family as a unit and count any insult or slight to it as a personal affront. Similarly, since each lineage is identified as part of the family any loss of face or dishonor of one lineage or one member is a blot on the honor of the entire family.

These three primary values—familialism, male dominance and bonding, and honor—are noticeably stronger in the Lupollo family than in other Italian-American families we have observed. That is, the Lupollo family appears to be more traditional and conservative of these south Italian values than most Italian-American family groups. Their conservatism in values both develops from and explains the cohesiveness of the family unit. It may also explain other value orientations which seem family-wide. Politically, they are ultraconservative and express a strong support for "Americanism." They are "hawks" on the question of United States involvement in Vietnam, scornfully oppose student activism of any type, and generally regard most schemes for social welfare as leftist and dysfunctional to society. Their social values are consonant with their politics; Black and Puerto Rican militance is assumed to be Communist-inspired or an attempt to get something for nothing, and such movements as Women's Liberation are subject to ridicule. The strongest social disapproval, however, is reserved for Jews. Anti-Semitism is so strong within the family that one must assume that competition is at the heart of it. Members of the family attribute most political corruption as well as most business problems to Jews. For example, in 1969, former Water Commissioner James Marcus, a friend and supporter of Mayor John Lindsay, was indicted along with reputed underworld figure Anthony Corallo and contractor Arnold Fried for conspiracy and bribery in the issuing of construction contracts in New York. One second-generation family member observed:

> They'd give Corallo the chair if they could but those two Jews [Marcus and Fried] will come out smelling like roses. They'll get Carmine De Sapio too, but the Jews who say they bribed him will get off. Haven't you noticed that it's always Jews like [Bernard] Goldfine, who offer the bribes? It's the way they do business and whenever you get to the bottom of one of these bribery cases it's always a Jew who starts it. Then it gets blamed on the Italians, or some poor bastard who worked all of his life to get ahead is left holding the bag because the Jew lawyers know that if they can find some guy with an Italian name he is a sure setup for the newspapers.

Other family members agreed.

The Lupollo family continues in Catholicism, but here there are more obvious generational differences. Generally, the younger members of the family are more religious—at least in the American sense—than their parents. The senior members show the Italian male's traditional reluctance to attend church, letting their wives go alone. The younger members of the various lineages, most of whom attended parochial schools, are more Irish-American in their religious habits.

There are other values which are shared by members of the extended Lupollo family, and which they in turn share with other Italian-Americans and with other Americans as well. But generally, those we have just described are the ones which dominate the social system of the family. We observe in coming chapters how these values originating in the south of Italy have structured the family, directed the distribution of power, authority, and prestige, and shaped the rules which govern the behavior of the Lupollos.

5 / Business and Social Organization in the Lupollo Family

Many charges are made against Italian-American criminal families, but few are as disturbing as the allegation that they are infiltrating and "taking over" large areas of legal business enterprise. Though the public appears to tolerate organized crime's control of such "harmless" areas of illicit profit as gambling, many people are troubled by reports connecting underworld figures with the ownership of legitimate businesses such as food-processing plants, construction and trucking firms, importing offices, restaurants, bars, and race tracks.

One reason for public and governmental concern, of course, is the idea that the syndicates will use the profits from their legitimate businesses to expand their illegal activities still further. Another, more disturbing cause for concern is the fear that criminals, by operating their legal businesses with illegal methods, will make it impossible for legitimate businessmen to compete. In addition, virtually all federal law-enforcement officials believe that Italian-American syndicates are allied in a nationwide criminal conspiracy, and this belief makes the movement into legitimate business seem even more sinister. Obviously criminal organizations pose more of a threat to legitimate business when they act in concert than when they act alone. Moreover, the mere allegation of conspiracy suggests that criminal syndicates have a subversive purpose in mind in entering legitimate business fields.

Though it is easy to draw up the legitimate business portfolios of many known underworld figures, it is more difficult to uncover the reasons why such portfolios are assembled. The answer espoused by most criminologists is that the rich criminal organizations need new areas in which to reinvest illicit profits. As these criminologists point out, buying, starting, or muscling into legitimate businesses also permits underworld figures to evade income-tax prosecution, and provides a respectable "front" behind which to continue their dirty work. A different if not entirely incompatible explanation imputes a less rational motive to the criminal who moves into legitimate business: the desire that he and his family play a legitimate, respectable role in the American community.

While the motivation for organized crime's movement into legitimate business has been much discussed, little is known about the legitimate business activities of a typical criminal syndicate, or about the relationship between such a syndicate's legal and illegal business activities. Our study of the Lupollo family gave us the opportunity to examine these questions closely. Two findings about the Lupollo family business should be underlined from the outset. Current popular opinion has it that the movement of Italian-American criminal syndicates into legitimate business is a recent development. The history of the Lupollo family, however, contradicts this view. Rather than being a recent step, the Lupollo family involvement with legitimate business began when the family began, almost seventy years ago, and its movement toward legitimation—toward the acquisition or creation of legal enterprises—seems to have been a steady trend for forty years, and the main motive in the growth of the family empire.

In this chapter we present data from the field on the organization of the family's business empire. We describe the structure of both their legitimate and their illegitimate enterprises, and relate what we know of the linkages between them. In this chapter we are also concerned with the ways in which the family's business enterprises relate to patterns which have traditionally structured family behavior, and the ways in which social and cultural change have affected the family as a business organization. And finally, we consider the rules which determine how family members are assigned to positions in the management of the family business.

Almost all of the information on the organization of the family business that we present in this chapter was gathered through field research, participant observation, and interviewing. All summary and descriptive field data included were either directly observed or substantiated by at least one subsequent interviewer (except where we specify that this is not the case).

The data on the structure of the legitimate family enterprises were gathered from family members or persons involved in business operations with the family. Wherever possible, we also checked these data with standard business listing services and references. Providing the same kind of control for data on illegal activities was, of course, more difficult, since there are no record forms for factual checking. However, all of the data presented on the family gambling and loan-sharking activities were checked for internal consistency and constantly compared with what is known about such operations in organized crime in general.

There are, of course, many things we were unable to discover. Just how the legal and illegal enterprises are integrated we were only able to surmise on the basis of what we saw and heard, and what family members were willing to tell us. For example, while we were able to determine that funds from loan-sharking activities find their way into some of the legitimate enterprises because we know that family member X is involved in both, we do not know the exact nature of the gambling and loan-sharking operations—precisely how much money is involved, how much of it must be used to buy protection, how closely the two operations are interwoven. Our data are particularly thin regarding the relationship between the Lupollo family and other families involved in organized crime. We have no evidence that would indicate that the family is part of any national or international syndicate. Neither, of course, do we have any conclusive evidence that they are not.

Organizational Structure of the Lupollo Family Business

Legitimate Enterprises. The consolidation of the Lupollo family's legitimate businesses into eleven interconnected enterprises began when Joe Lupollo became head of the family. He and Charley Lupollo and their brother-in-law, Phil Alcamo, began to pare off some of the family's less profitable enterprises and to shore up and combine some of the more profitable ones. One of the most important new companies to emerge was the Brooklyn Eagle Realty Company, a real estate and management corporation created around 1940.[1] The family had earlier begun to dispose of much of its real estate on the Lower East Side of Manhattan and to concentrate on holdings in the Brooklyn and Long Island areas. Brooklyn Eagle Realty brought these holdings together. Joe Lupollo's sons Tony and Marky are co-owners of record of the company; Tony's son Paulie and Marky's son Tommy are also officers in the company. However, Joe still retains direct functional control of the real-estate company. Both Tony and Marky must clear all business negotiations and decisions with Joe, and it is generally known in the Italian-American community that Tony and Marky "run the business for their father." The company has a main office in Brooklyn and two branch offices on Long Island; its holdings are three to five million dollars in the Brooklyn–Queens–Long Island area. In addition, the Brooklyn Eagle Realty Company also manages properties in other parts of the country for members of the family.

A second important corporation which developed out of the consolidation is Contessa Foods, Inc., a combine which includes two subsidiary companies, the Reale Baking Company and CFI Foods, Inc., a food-processing company: Contessa, which is a nationally known producer of Italian food products, is now a public corporation although Joe and Charley are the largest stockholders. Pete Tucci, Joe's son-in-law, is vice-president of Contessa, and Basil Alcamo (Phil's son and Charley's nephew) does the accounting for the company. Pete Tucci is also president of CFI Foods, Inc., a wholly owned

---

[1] The names of the various companies have been changed to protect the anonymity of the family. In some cases we have also changed a product or service supplied for the same reason.

subsidiary that operates farms, packing plants, and wholesale outlets in New Jersey and California. Reale Baking Co. produces and distributes Italian bread, bread products, and pastries in the Middle Atlantic and lower New England regions. Charley Lupollo heads this company; Joe's son Joey is a company officer. The family interest in both companies is well known, and some of Reale's products are distributed nationally through Contessa. In the late 1940's, the family also started a catering service in Brooklyn and Long Island which serves Bar Mitzvahs, weddings, and other social functions in Brooklyn and Long Island. Joey's son Bobby is presently manager of Brookwood Catering Company as well as co-owner, along with his cousin Freddy (Patsy's son) of R & A Pizza, a small chain of pizza parlors on the northern shore of Long Island. Financial backing for both the catering company and the pizza-parlor chain came from Joe and Charley Lupollo, who are "silent partners" in both enterprises.

After the Second World War, the family's ice-and-coal delivery and garbage-disposal enterprises were expanded into four related companies. The Lupollo-Livale Trucking Company, a hauling-and-drayage concern, does business in the states of New York, New Jersey, and Pennsylvania, and in 1968 expanded into Connecticut, Rhode Island, and Massachusetts. Bruno Livale, who is listed as co-owner (with Charley Lupollo) of Lupollo-Livale, is Joe Lupollo's wife's brother-in-law and has been retired since 1962. Charley Lupollo is also the owner of the Corona Fuel Company, which is managed by his grandson Freddy (Patsy's son). Patsy himself operates the Royale Limousine Service, which leases automobiles and maintains a small taxi fleet on Long Island. Charley's nephew Joey is president of Stema Disposal Corp., a garbage and refuse-hauling company which operates in Brooklyn and recently expanded to the Bronx.

Phil Alcamo is president and manager of P. A. Previews, a public-relations firm which handles accounts for both Contessa Foods and Reale Baking. P. A. Previews has other accounts as well, however, and recently expanded to convention development and management services in addition to public relations. Phil's son, Basil, is the accountant for this firm.

These eleven companies form the legitimate sector of the Lupollo family business. Their combined assets are in excess of $30 million dollars. We are certain that these eleven companies do form a cohesive business syndicate and that the Lupollo family controls their operations. With the exception of P. A. Previews, which is owned by Phil Alcamo, all are directly owned or financially controlled by Joe or Charlie Lupollo. P. A. Previews itself is at least partly financed through Contessa Foods, and we include it in the family business structure because, as we shall show later, it functions in the exchange system which has been established among the various companies.

A number of other businesses, operated independently by members of the

Lupollo family or their relatives, may be classified as family-related on the basis of their publicly declared control by members of the central family or their relatives, although we have no evidence that the proceeds flow into the central family coffers. We were able to identify ten business enterprises in which members of the Lupollo family have some interest, but there are probably many more. Joe Lupollo is the principal stockholder and actual owner of Vital Shoe Company, which is operated by one of his cousins; he is also owner of the Absford Linen Service, operated by an in-law of the Salemis'. He also has a partial interest in Island Plumbing and Heating Company, operated by a cousin, and Giovanni Beauty Shoppes, a chain of women's hairdressing parlors, operated by his son Patsy's nephew by marriage. Joe's son Tony is president of Danny Boy Clothes, the largest of the family-related businesses, a men's clothes-manufacturing concern with plants and distribution outlets in the New York–New Jersey–Pennsylvania area. Phil Alcamo has an interest in three of the companies we classify as family-related. Phil's son Basil and Joe's son Joey are co-owners of a stock investor service called New Investor's Service Company. The company maintains offices in New York City and is a "hedging fund" operation. Basil and Joey have accumulated something over $600,000 from members of the family which they use to purchase blocks of stock. There is no public sale, and only the partners are involved in the purchase. Joey, who is the president of the company, handles most of the transactions. Joey's son Bobby also has "a piece" of this operation. Phil's sister, Rosa Parone, is the owner of record of Melrose Cigarette Company, a cigarette-vending-machine company which operates in the Bronx and in Miami, Florida. Rose's son, James Parone, is the manager of P. A. Travel, a travel agency established by Phil in 1964. Basil also has an interest in P. A. Travel.

Two other businesses seem more distantly related to the family enterprise structure: Arva Realty, an Arizona real estate company operated by Charley's son Charles Lupollo Jr., and B & R Paving Construction Company, owned by Peter Livale, the son of the Bruno Livale who is Charley's partner in the Lupollo-Livale Trucking Company.

A structural model of the legitimate portion of the Lupollo family business empire is shown in Figure 1.

Illegal Operations. The legitimate business structure of the family is complemented by a similar structure of illegal enterprises. From the time that old Giuseppe Lupollo established his first bar and card parlor on Grand Street, gambling has been an important part of the Lupollo family business. The concentration on this area was not accidental. While gambling is, of course, an illegal activity, it is characterized by both low visibility and high tolerance from society. Few are really concerned about the prevalence of gambling, in-

Figure 1. The Lupollo Family Business

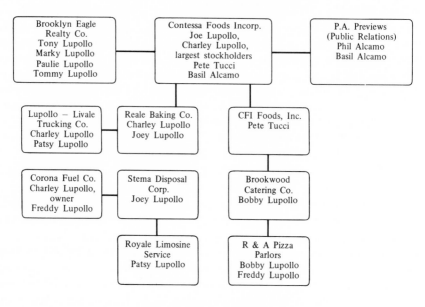

FAMILY RELATED BUSINESSES

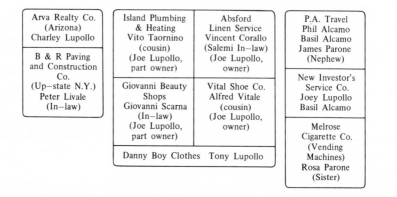

cluding the authorities. In the New York area, where the Lupollo family operates, the police tend to look upon gambling as a minor social vice which, whether carried on in the stock market or in the horse parlor, doesn't hurt anyone. People gamble by their own choice, and the gambler is merely providing a service for a population which demands to be served. Exposure of gambling syndicates, no matter how large, very seldom produces any widespread indignation, and the penalties usually assigned by courts for gambling violations reflect this lenient attitude.

Recalling the days when old Giuseppe ran the gambling enterprise, Phil Alcamo says:

Old Giuseppe always used to say that it was people's weaknesses and not his own strength that allowed him to make money . . . He used to say that what he did [in running a gambling syndicate] was to help people do what they wanted to do and that he never forced anyone to gamble who didn't want to. The cops never gave him very much trouble, because they felt that nobody would bring much "heat" on them if there was gambling in their area. If there was a highjacking or a mugging or if somebody was killed, then a lot of attention was called to the area and somebody above them would put "heat" on to get things straightened out. Gambling went on all the time and the only time there was trouble was when some independent bookie or numbers writer refused to pay off and drove people into a beef.

Giuseppe opened up the Grand Street bar and card parlor soon after he came to the United States. Immigrant laborers would come to the card parlor to play *ziganetta,* an Italian card game which involved betting in much the same manner as the game of poker. Sometime during the First World War, Giuseppe began operating an Italian lottery out of the same bar and card parlor. Cosimo Salemi, the founder of the Salemi lineage, was associated with him from the outset. While the precise nature of the relationship is uncertain, Lupollo did supply the funds and ran the "bank" portion of the enterprise, while Salemi ran the actual operation itself.

The Italian lottery was the forerunner of the policy or numbers game which is today the most prevalent illegal lottery in large cities. In this form of lottery, the player must successfully guess which three-digit number (for example, 5–8–4) will result from some previously agreed-upon tabulation, such as the final digits of the United States Treasury cash balance, or the total amounts bet in the horse races at a given track on a given day. The New York Exchange is also a popular source for the daily number. The odds are, of course, 1,000 to 1 in favor of the "house." If the gambler does guess the proper three-digit number, he is paid off at odds which run only as high as 600 to 1.

Within the Lupollo family today, Vito Salemi directs the gambling enterprise. He operates out of a storefront "bank" in Brooklyn which is known in the family as "the regional office," "the bank," or "the main office." The actual gambling operations take place through a number of distinct and separate "district offices" in Brooklyn, Queens, and Long Island. Each of the districts is called a "wheel" and has a franchised "manager" with territorial and functional control over organized gambling in that particular district. Of the eight district wheels we were able to identify as part of the Lupollo family bank, five are controlled by managers who are related to the Lupollo or Salemi lineages by blood or marriage. Two of the Brooklyn district wheels are managed by Puerto Ricans who have purchased franchise rights from the Lupollo family, and one Long Island wheel is directly controlled by Vito Salemi.

Each of the district wheels is fully guaranteed and protected by the family, and for this service each pays a stipulated percentage of the gross back to the bank. As far as we were able to determine, each district wheel funds its own local operations, and the bank only supplies emergency funds on a loan basis if there is a "run," or if there are too many winners at the same time in one wheel. Each wheel is completely autonomous from the others, and there is no functional relationship between them. None of the wheel managers comingles his receipts with those of any other manager.

Each district manager establishes and operates his own organization. The bets are picked up on the street, in "numbers drops" located in small business establishments, or even within large industrial concerns, by "runners." The money and the bet slips are picked up from the runners by "collectors." The collector turns the funds and slips over to a "controller" who operates out of one of the branch banks of the district wheel. The money and number slips from each of the branch banks are turned over to the "district controller" who operates the lottery in that district. The district controller is not the same person as the manager. The manager is the entrepreneur who owns and finances the district wheel; the district controller is his employee, and actually operates the enterprises. Payoffs on winning numbers follow the reverse of the route for cash income. Figure 2 charts the organization of the Lupollo numbers enterprise.

Although the numbers game is managed by Vito Salemi, the Lupollo family retains functional control. Joe Lupollo is the overall "banker" and he underwrites the entire activity. Phil Alcamo also has a financial interest in the numbers game. His work is that of layoff banker, or financial backer for the bank. If the bank or one of the district wheels cannot handle all the bets that have come in on a given day, Phil will accept some of the bets at a different set of odds from those at which the manager would have to pay off his clients. If the wheel or a branch bank is hit hard, the bet with the layoff banker cushions the blow somewhat. Phil says that he does this for "sport" and that he really is not directly involved in the operation. On the other hand, Paulie Lupollo told us that Phil "picks up a bundle" through his layoff role, that it is strictly business for Phil, and that he is very cautious about accepting layoff bets. Phil, along with Charley Lupollo, is responsible for maintaining the necessary political and police contacts and protection. This involves a regular "payroll" in which payoffs are fixed at a given rate depending on the status of the receiver.

A Comparative Note. As we mentioned in Chapter 1, we are able to conduct field work with the De Maio family, which operates the gambling en-

Figure 2. Organization of the Lupollo Numbers Enterprise

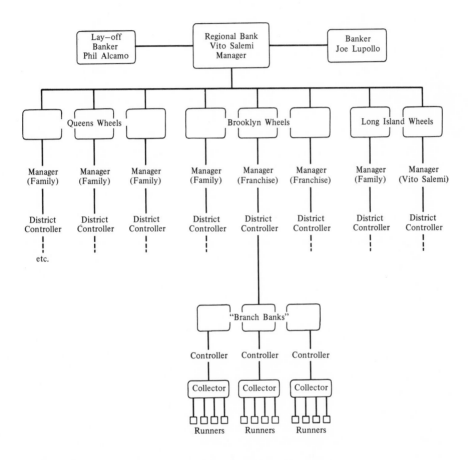

terprises in East Harlem. The family is headed by Joey De Maio. His son-in-law Dominick Maisano operates a district wheel in partnership with his brother Paul Maisano. The operation shows some interesting differences from the Lupollos. For one, the East Harlem wheel operated by the Maisano brothers does not use branch banks in the same sense that the Lupollo operation does. The functional roles of controllers, collectors, and runners are present here also, but the men appear to work directly out of the East Harlem wheel rather than a branch bank. Branch relationships are maintained instead by "neighborhood controllers" who operate out of the wheel, but have responsibility for a particular neighborhood. The neighborhood collectors report to a head collector.

A second difference is that the telephone is used more frequently in East Harlem as the means of communication between runner and collectors, and between collectors and the controllers. This difference is probably due to the fact that in East Harlem one can play the numbers three or four times a day rather than once, and therefore communication has to occur more rapidly. There are also "night numbers" when the nighttime trotting races are run. Finally, the Maisano brothers operate the East Harlem wheel as managers, but serve the role of collectors as well.

Paul Maisano feels the future of his wheel is not very bright. There are now a growing number of "independent" lottery operations in East Harlem, particularly the *bolita* lottery that Puerto Ricans and Cubans patronize. In addition, there is increasing pressure from Blacks in the area who want to take over the numbers operation that is still controlled by the De Maio family. Paul Maisano's reaction is interesting:

> What the hell. Those guys want to make a little too. Everybody wants his turn at making it, we had ours and I guess it's their turn now. But if you watch the way they run the operation, it's not going to be the same. A lot of times they refuse to pay off. That leads to trouble and trouble always brings heat. In the twenty years I'm here in East Harlem, we never refused to pay off even when we were sure we were being taken. Now nobody knows what the hell is going to happen.

We shall return to the De Maio family in Chapter 8.

Loan Sharking. The loan-sharking operations of the Lupollo family have grown considerably from old Giuseppe's Italian bank. No loan seems to have been too small for Giuseppe's consideration in the early days; one informant reports that he always borrowed $2.00 from Giuseppe on Wednesdays and repaid $2.50 on Saturdays. Some loans were as low as fifty cents in the days before 1920. His rates of interest were usurious according to some who lived in the community, but his family does not hold the same view.

Whatever the case with old Giuseppe's bank, today loan-sharking or "shylocking" is a major part of the Lupollo family's illegal empire. Like gambling, it sustains little risk vis-à-vis the police and courts, and is viewed with tolerance by society. Except for the widespread belief that loan sharks kill or maim defaulters, few really condemn the individual who lends money, even at exorbitant rates; rather, they suspect the improvident who must borrow. The loan-sharking activities of the family seem to be prospering and growing. In this they differ from the gambling operations. The latter are under strong pressure from Blacks, Puerto Ricans, and Cubans whose mobility in organized crime is gradually forcing the Lupollo family either to accommodate through franchises or to move out. There is not much pressure from insurgent Blacks and Puerto Ricans in the loan-shark business, however. In fact, while both the gambling and loan-shark operations are centralized under the direction of the Salemis, the loan-shark operation in Brooklyn, at least, lends money to the very Black and Puerto Rican gamblers who are pressuring for a piece of the Lupollo gambling empire.

One client of the loan-sharking operation describes it as follows:

> What we have here again is a separate bank set up with a large sum of money. The main operational force in the shylocking or loan-sharking activity is the bank which loans out the money. For lack of a better word I will call them sharks or money-lenders. These are the guys who go out and actually make contact to keep the money moving. Another important part of this total operation is the enforcement section. What usually happens is most of the sharks are given a large bankroll. They move around the community looking for people who are in one kind of jam or another and who need money in a hurry. You find most loan sharks hanging around crap games, gambling parlors, the private clubs that usually house the poker games and other games. The loan sharks hang around these different places and they make it known that they have money to loan at high interest rates. What usually happens is that a person who wants to borrow money has to give his marker, and his marker states that when he borrows the money he will pay it back in a certain amount of time. If he doesn't pay the money back that he stated on his marker, he has one or two alternatives. He has to write another marker which ups the interest rate and it also determines an amount of time for the money to be paid. If it is not paid by that time he has to write another marker which ups the interest rate and it also determines an amount of time for the money to be paid. If it is not paid by that time he has to write another marker. Most loan sharks only accept one or two markers. If the money isn't paid by that time, the whole operation is then handed over to the enforcement part of the organization and they begin to take action. This action usually starts out by a few strong verbal threats, moves into physical violence that sometimes might even be followed in the more drastic cases by loss of the borrower's life.
>
> The most important part of any loan-sharking operation is the ability to keep your money moving. Some loan-sharking banks have as many as fifteen or twenty money lenders out covering various sections of the city. In the Manhattan area you have loan sharks who follow all of the floating crap games that are also operated by the family. The people who play in these games play for large sums of money and when somebody is busted a loan shark is right there to loan him money or to take up his marker right away. So you've got one group of sharks who definitely follow all of the crap games and all of the poker games, and they make money readily available to any of the big losers. They are ready to pick up a marker from him right away because they feel that the men who gamble in these games will be able to pay off their loans in a short period of time.
>
> One of the biggest loan-shark operations is the one that is located along

the docks. On nearly every pier, the Lupollo group, controls a whole loan-shark-ing operation. And anybody working on the pier who is getting paid on a weekly basis is able to borrow money with the realization that his marker is going to be picked up in a week.

In recent years the family have become a little more sophisticated in their loan-sharking activities. . . . They have amassed enough capital now to loan money to different businesses who for one reason or another might need money in a hurry. Some of these businesses might want to expand, others of them might be having financial difficulties of one kind or another, and they need money in a hurry. What happens here is that the men who are in business pick up a marker or give their marker and if they can't pay off their loans in a period of time, the members of the family or whatever else you want to call them, then instead of using force or anything like that they want to use the money that they have loaned these different business men as a way of buying into different businesses.

So what we have now is: a whole operation has been set up where the loan sharks or the shylocking business has decided that they want to move into legitimate business. And one of the ways that they do it is that instead of . . . I shouldn't say instead of. I think that a lot of businesses who want money in a hurry and who don't want to go through all of the hangups of trying to borrow it from banks now know that the loan sharks or certain organiza-tions like the loan sharks that are controlled by the *Mafia,* the family will loan them money on a short-term basis realizing that once they have borrowed this money and if they can't pay it back, they then have to accept members of the *Mafia* or these other organizations as partners.

The organizational structure of the Lupollo "family" loan-sharking oper-ations roughly parallels that of the numbers game. While the Salemis manage the operation, its control centers between Joe and Charley Lupollo. Both Joe and Charley have heavy investments in loans, and both have territorial control over sections of Brooklyn and Long Island. In gambling the territorial control is complete, and no "independent" can operate very long without some diffi-culty from either the police or the Lupollos, or both. In loan-sharking, how-ever, there seems to be both a territorial and a functional division of control. In Brooklyn, for example, Joe has control over the lending of money on the docks and "on the street." Charley, on the other hand, has the heaviest in-vestment with businessmen and large accounts, dealing with corporations. Phil Alcamo works quite closely with Charley but also has money on the street with Joe. Not only is there a distinction in terms of the potential debt-ors; the operation of the areas is also somewhat different. In the waterfront and street operations, Joe works through a number of "bankers" who are similar to the controllers in the numbers operation. Joe supplies money to the bankers at a 2 per cent per week rate of interest, payable every week. The banker then makes loans directly to the borrower, or in some cases operates through a street man, who, like the runner in the numbers operation, is the person actually in closest contact with small borrowers. The banker charges the street man 3 per cent, and the borrower must usually pay 5 per cent per week. However, none of these rates of interest is fixed. During the stock market decline in 1969–70, when investors were faced with the dilemma of having to obtain money during a tight-money period, the rates to borrowers were as high as 8 per cent per week.

The portion of the loan-shark business controlled by Charley Lupollo operates somewhat differently. Unlike Joe's empire, which is based on the territoriality of the docks and the streets, Charley's operation is not limited to a specific territory although he operates in Brooklyn most frequently. This portion of the family's illegal enterprises has a connection with the legal businesses. Just as all of the family gambling centers tend to have a resident loan shark for gamblers who need money, so the Brooklyn Eagle Realty Company salesmen are able to arrange loans with little difficulty. We have never noticed the same arrangement in New Investor's Service, but both Charley and Phil Alcamo are known to be able to arrange loans for business associates.

Although the future for the loan-shark operation in general is a bright one, the waterfront and street operations are not as sure of continued success as Charley and Phil's dealings with businesses. Once at a family gathering celebrating a baptism, Patsy Lupollo (who is involved in Brooklyn loan-sharking) commented on the current state of lending on the waterfront:

> I wouldn't put out any money even at 15 per cent now because operating costs are so high. Half the guys who borrow are on dope and no matter what you do, they aren't going to pay you back because they end up on Rikers Island or getting shot by the cops. I told Joey that I like his stock market thing much better because even if it ain't sure, you don't have all those creeps and bums to work with.

Relationships Among Legal and Illegal Business Enterprises. Tracing the relationships among the illegal activities of the Lupollo family and their legitimate business enterprises is a difficult and uncertain task. In the first place, all data on these relationships come from observation, inferences drawn from patterns of business, social, and personal interaction among family members, and some sketchy interview data obtained from non-family members. A second difficulty in describing the relationship between the Lupollos' illegal activities and legitimate enterprises is that the relationship has changed over time. Over the last forty years, there has been a gradual movement toward legitimation—an increasing acquisition of legitimate businesses, and an increasing separation of legitimate and illegitimate activities. But the character of the movement to legitimation has not been the same at all times. Young Paulie Lupollo has different reasons today for wanting to separate the family's legal and illegal businesses than his great-grandfather did forty years ago. In fact, the structure of relations between the family's legitimate and illegitimate enterprises has been transformed at least twice since old Giuseppe Lupollo founded the family in the early 1900's.

When Giuseppe first came to the United States, he operated both the legal and illegal activities as part of one organization, and he himself controlled and operated both of them. The foods he imported from Sicily he sold door to door himself, and the small Italian bank which formed the basis for his reputed loan-shark activities later operated out of the same dwelling—his—as the importing business. Later, when he added the card parlor and bar, he operated all of his business activities out of this "office." In these early years of the family business structure, the distinction between the legitimate and illegitimate portions of the organization was minimal, since Giuseppe ran all of the activities as the visible and sole owner. Profits from illegal activities were placed directly into legitimate activities, such as the purchase of real estate or business enterprises such as baking and grocery stores. Defaults on loans allowed an increasing control in numerous small businesses. Illegal and legal business activities, no matter how small, were centered in Giuseppe himself, who linked the two areas together.

Some of the information gathered from family members and some data from non-family members indicate quite forcefully that the linkages grew out of the nature of ghetto life itself during that period. As we saw in Chapter 3, Black Hand extortion was widespread and greatly feared. The immigrant businessman could not or would not turn to the police and so, in order to pay the extortion money, he had to borrow money from Giuseppe's Italian bank. As we reported in Chapter 2, non-family members have told us that Giuseppe not only lent the money so that the businessman could pay the extortion, but often offered his services as a negotiator, and was himself a Black Hand extortionist. When the extortion demands grew and the interest on his loans became unbearable, he would offer to negotiate a final settlement in return for a partial interest in the business. Since this type of extortion demands that the businessman present cash, Giuseppe's reputed function of loan-sharking was in fact indispensable to the Black Hand process. At the same time, however, his legitimate business enterprises provided him with a respectable role which he enjoyed and promoted. He was a man of some wealth in a community where poverty was the rule; he was a banker and a businessman among laborers and simple artisans. Gradually as his wealth and power increased, his social status within the Italian ghetto community also grew.

The first transformation of the Lupollo family business began after 1920. As Giuseppe's business enterprises grew and prospered, it became necessary to delegate some responsibility to others. In this phase, Giuseppe began to diffuse control, always following two organizational guidelines. The first was to build business on kinship. During his lifetime, no position of importance was ever assigned to anyone who was not a relative. Moreover, the higher the position in the organization, the closer the relationship. The second organizational imperative was to divide the family into those who would operate the legitimate businesses and those who would perform in the illegal world.

Giuseppe took a pragmatic approach in deciding what family member should go where. When the illegal gambling and banking activities became large enough, he employed a distant cousin of his wife, Cosimo Salemi, to work for him in the gambling enterprises, but he kept the bank himself. Eventually, Cosimo's son Vito took over from his father and the kinship relationship was solidified when Vito's daughter Yolanda married Giuseppe's grandson Tony, and the two lineages were joined. At about the same time, Vic took over the bank, which now operated on the street as loan-sharking. Since that time, the Salemis have remained the lineage most closely associated with the illegal activities of the family although, as we pointed out earlier, they now have some involvement in a few of the legitimate business enterprises as well.

Giuseppe's older son, Joe, began his illicit career working with the Salemis in the Italian lottery. Later, however, when the legitimate businesses became large enough, Joe was moved out of the illegal area and gradually came to control the various legal business enterprises, eventually being designated by his father as the head of the family business organization. Joe thus has had experience in both the legal and illegal ends of the business. On the other hand, Charley, Giuseppe's second son, always seemed by inclination and training destined to move into the respectable areas of business. From the outset, Charley operated openly only in the area of legitimate businesses. Whether or not old Giuseppe designed it deliberately, the division, with Joe controlling the illegal areas and Charley appearing to be the legitimate member of the family, continues to this day.

While illegal and legal activities were thus on the way to becoming two distinct operations, there was no clear separation between them. During Prohibition, as we said in Chapter 3, the trucks that Charley used for ice delivery not only delivered groceries for the importing company but were used in the bootlegging operation as well. Also, while Giuseppe divided the two areas of responsibility between his sons, he still maintained firm control over both kinds of activity, and they were integrated through his leadership.

During this period, Giuseppe began welding together an efficient business empire—dropping some of the faltering enterprises, concentrating on the more profitable, and adding some new activities as well. The consolidation had social as well as economic benefit to the family. Giuseppe's role as head of a growing business empire afforded him the highest social status within the Italian-American community. And his increasing wealth and power accelerated his upward mobility outside the ghetto community he controlled. He enjoyed the comforts and privileges that he could afford in the outside world—expensive automobiles, beach-front vacation homes—but he was never really at ease outside the ghetto. Giuseppe's son Joe never feels comfortable in the outside world, but this is not so of Charley, nor of Giuseppe's grandchildren.

As the succeeding generations moved more freely into American society, the importance of avoiding the appearance of criminal activity became greater. Yet so long as old Giuseppe stayed in control, the case with which money, equipment, and power moved back and forth between illegal and legal activities made a completely respectable posture impossible.

After the Second World War, the Lupollo family moved out of the ghetto into the mainstream of American business and social life. The various legitimate companies were gradually taking shape as distinct corporations. Illegal activities continued also, but now that the family's legitimate enterprises operated outside the protective walls of the ghetto in the relatively open world of American business, it was important that the legitimate businesses be insulated from the unlawful activities.

This was the aim of phase two of the legitimation process, in which two major changes took place. In Giuseppe's day, services had been rendered by one company to another, and some illegal activities were serviced by legal enterprises. Cash was also transferred from activity to activity regardless of distinctions in legality. Now, however, monies and services were transferred from person to person, rather than from company to company. Cash and services flowed only through individuals. For example, as layoff banker Phil Alcamo receives money from the numbers game which may have an important effect on his legitimate business activities. Nevertheless, there is no direct transfer of funds from the numbers game to P. A. Previews or to P. A. Travel.

Legal and illegal activities seem to be further insulated from each other by the use of two companies as centers for the transfer of funds. The money from gambling goes to Joe Lupollo, who as banker controls this area, or to Phil Alcamo, the layoff banker. Charley Lupollo may or may not be involved at this point. All three—Joe, Charley, and Phil—invest heavily in Brooklyn Eagle Realty, and in investments managed by the New Investors Service Company. After the money from gambling is "cleansed" by reinvestment in legal activities, the profit is then reinvested in loan-sharking. (See Figure 3.)

While Vito Salemi technically heads the loan-sharking operation, all of the members of the family invest money in it although Vito is the only family

Figure 3. Conversion of Income from Illegal Activities into Legitimate Income and Reinvestment in Illegal Activities

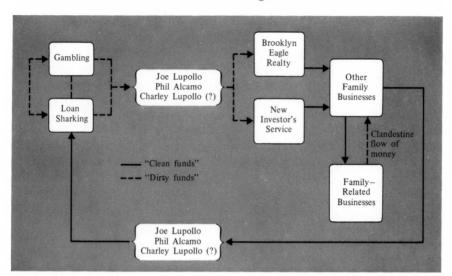

member who actually engages in the process of "shylocking." On one occasion, a documentary filmmaker mentioned to Charley and Phil the financial difficulties he was having as a result of the prolonged stockmarket decline. Charley suggested that he get in touch with a "business associate" by the name of John Spinoza, "whose company sometimes finances films" on a short-term basis. Later that evening, while the three of us were having dinner, Phil mentioned Spinoza as one of the real estate salesmen for Brooklyn Eagle Realty. I asked whether Brooklyn Eagle was in the loan business as well as real estate, and Charley explained that Spinoza and some of the other salesmen at the company liked to put their money into short-term loans, and that filmmakers were among their favorite clients. Phil said that "a lot of guys" preferred lending money to putting it in the stock market, and that the risks involved were no greater. He went on to add that many of the borrowers are steady customers and "like gamblers" spend part of their lives raising money; another part of their lives is devoted to betting it or spending it, and a third part is spent worrying about how to get the first two parts together. Charlie mentioned a well-known New York City builder and a famous male stage star who are "so strung out" in loans that they have difficulty meeting the interest payments. The tone of their comments indicated that this kind of behavior represented weakness on the part of the borrower, and that the role of the lender was simply to supply money for people who were unable to manage their affairs wisely.

The Staffing of the Lupollo Family Business

Over the last forty years then, the Lupollo business organization has undergone considerable change. Not only have legal and illegal activities been separated from one another, but there has also been a tendency toward decentralization of the ever more numerous legitimate businesses.

But while the family business empire has grown both in the interests it encompasses and in the functions its executives must fulfill, it has not followed the usual organizational practice of adding a new department to serve each new function. Rather, the empire has reached into itself for a member-relative to fill each functional role.

In effect, it is people rather than organizational functions that define the organization, and it is through people that the family operates. An executive rarely defines or shapes his role within a corporation. The reverse is true of the Lupollos. As we shall see in the next chapter, the tasks and skills of family members often take form as they organize and conduct the various enterprises. In a corporation, no man is indispensable because someone else can always be hired with roughly the same area of expertise. In the Lupollo family, certain members are indispensable, because the success of the business depends very much on their personal qualities and contacts. For example, without Charley's and Phil's contacts in the "legitimate" world of business and politics, the family enterprises probably could not function.

Another reason why certain family members are irreplaceable is that the kinship-based organization of the family restricts the field from which the family's executives can be selected. The fifteen men who run the empire are all closely related by blood or marriage. Joe is the undisputed head of the group, and Charley and Phil form a "directorate" working with him. The other members of the group perform lesser but still important organizational roles, many of them related to special areas of competence. Basil Alcamo, for example, is known in the family as a mathematical wizard, and whenever profit percentages or business projections are involved he is always sought out.

The usual distinction between line and staff roles does not hold in the Lupollo family organization. All executives in the family whether Lupollos, Tuccis, Salemis, or Alcamos contribute directly to profits by producing the "product." None is exclusively a staff executive in the usual sense of the term. Various members do have facilitating roles, performing some services and providing specialized information, but each also has direct responsibility for some functional segment of the business.

In addition to the central family—the executives—there are three other levels in the Lupollo family organization. Below the central group there is a second-level group of near and distant relatives who function as supervisory personnel. While this part of the familial system is not as extensive as it was while Giuseppe was alive, it is still significant. Relatives are actively recruited and moved up the hierarchy by all the members of the central family. A cousin who completes college is placed in one of the businesses for a period of time and is watched by the family member responsible for that business. If the cousin does well, he moves up rapidly; if not, he is at least assured of his current position for as long as he wishes. In this way, ties between members of the four lineages remain strong, and no alienation of relatives occurs. We observed both recruitment and advancement, but saw no case of a relative leaving the organization.

The third level of organization is not one we have seen in any typical business organization. The closest analogy is with the political world and even there the analogue is not perfect. Just as in most civil-service structures there are numbers of employees who hold mid- and lower-level positions through the intercession of a politician, so the Lupollo family organization includes numbers of lower-level employees who are there because of the influence of some member of the central family group. Neither "patronage" nor "family retainer" describes the situation completely; rather, the workers of this class seem to have some personal connection with some family member and so are part of the organization. Phil Alcamo, for example, has as his office manager the husband of his former secretary's sister. When he pointed out this relationship to me one day, I asked why he had hired the man. His reply was that his former secretary had been a faithful and honest employee for many years and that he could trust her with anything. When she left to join her husband, who had taken a job in South America, she asked Phil if he would hire her brother-in-law, who was then looking for a job. Phil, always looking for "dependable, hard-working, and loyal employees," hired him and eventually promoted him to office manager. This same pattern of close association with family groups of employees occurs elsewhere in the organization, and there are numbers of families—Italian-American and otherwise—who have such relationships with the family.

So far, we have described three organizational levels which are characteristic of both the legal and illegal sectors of the family business. The fourth (and final) level is found only in legitimate areas. It consists of the thousands of employees of the legitimate business enterprises who are no more aware of the illegal operations of the family than any other private citizen would be.

Organizational Rules in the Lupollo Family Business. From our study of the Lupollo family business, it is possible to extract a set of rules that governs the organizational structure of the business empire and assigns individuals within it.

- The family operates as a social unit with social organization and business functions merged.
- All leadership positions, down to "middle-management" level, are assigned on the basis of kinship.
- The higher the position in the organization, the closer the kinship relationship.
- Leadership positions are assigned to a central group of family members, all of whom have close consanguineal of affinal relationships.
- Members of this leadership group are assigned to either legal or illegal enterprises, but not to both.
- Transfer of monies from illegal to legal and back into illegal activities takes place through individuals, and is part of the close kin-organization of the family.

The successful blend of illegal and legal enterprises which constitutes the Lupollo family business empire has been seventy years in the making. Over that period, its constantly increasing prosperity has enabled the heads of the family's various lineages to provide their relatives—from children and grandchildren to distant cousins—with jobs and financial security, and even with a lavish life style. In this sense it can be said that the kinship-based clan organization of the Lupollo family business has enabled family members to preserve and even embellish a kind of extended family system which the counterpressures of American life could have otherwise easily destroyed.

6 / Authority, Power, and Respect: Roles and Recruitment in the Lupollo Family

Like other investigators of organized crime, we were interested in uncovering the structure of the Italian-American crime family we were studying. But unlike many previous investigators we did not start out with any model of criminal-syndicate structure in mind. Instead of trying to define organization roles in the family by borrowing from other systems, we determined roles by seeing how people acted toward one another.

Our main interest in studying the family's structure was not, moreover, to label functions or to arrange them in a hierarchy. That there was a hierarchy within the family was plain to see: what we wanted to understand was how and why that hierarchy was established, and what rules dictated behavior and relationships within it. Since we were obviously looking for something rather different than previous investigators, we cannot claim that our work supersedes theirs. But we do feel that our observations give a truer—if more complicated—picture of how an organized-crime family operates than that provided by many of our predecessors in the field.

Ever since the hearings of the Kefauver Committee in 1951, and increasingly since the 1963 appearance of Joseph Valachi before the McClellan Committee, federal law-enforcement agencies and their consultants have been trying to delineate the organizational structure of the Italian-American criminal syndicates. Their approach emphasizes a "formal organization" model of analysis which views the criminal organization as a social unit deliberately designed, like a business or government bureaucracy, to achieve specific goals. Noting that "organized crime is big business" and that the syndicates form a sort of "invisible government," students of organized crime have looked to the structure of our large legitimate corporations or to government for models on which to base an analysis of the criminal syndicates, and they have produced elaborate organizational charts of the structure of the model organized crime family. Donald Cressey draws a direct parallel between corporate and business bureaucracies and the structure of organized crime groups, endowing the latter not only with a similar hierarchy of job titles and functions, but also with the same rationality and impersonality.

Cosa Nostra . . . is indeed an organization with both formal and informal aspects. Where there are specialized but integrated positions for a board of directors, presidents, vice-presidents, staff specialists, work managers, foremen and workers, there is an economic organization. When there are specialized but integrated positions for legislators, judges, and administrators of criminal justice, there is a political organization. Like the large legitimate corporations it resembles, Cosa Nostra has both kinds of positions, making it both a business organization and a government.[1]

Cressey adds, that like any large corporation, the *Cosa Nostra* family "continues to function regardless of personnel changes" because it is "rationally designed with an integrated set of positions geared to maximize profits."

Cressey's use of the bureaucratic analogy depends on a structuralist view which sees "organization" as defined by positions, a hierarchy of jobs to be filled and carried out, and as a blueprint which can be used to construct and reconstruct organizations everywhere. Our research, however, has shown us that "organization" in the Italian-American criminal syndicates cannot be described in this way without major distortion. Secret criminal organizations like the Italian-American or Sicilian *Mafia* families are not formal organizations like governments or business corporations. They are not rationally structured into statuses and functions in order to "maximize profits" and carry out tasks efficiently. Rather, they are traditional social systems, organized by action and by cultural values which have nothing to do with modern bureaucratic virtues. Like all social systems, they have no structure apart from their functioning; nor, as we noted in Chapter 5, do they have structure independent of their current "personnel." And when the cultural values which underlie the social system weaken, the families also weaken and die.

In one respect, Cressey's analysis is a new departure in the study of criminal syndicates: four of the job classifications he describes are drawn from the study of actual behaviors involved in organized crime. The first of these functional roles "the corrupter," grows out of the need for criminal organization to secure immunity from legal process by bribing or intimidating public officials. A second role grows out of the need to enforce decisions where there is no recourse to due legal process. Cressey sees the role of "the enforcer" not so much as that of executioner, as that of the warden who makes all the necessary arrangements and then has some other functionary perform the actual execution. A third role develops out of the need to maintain some degree of anonymity for the leadership. This requires the use of "buffers," who intervene between the "boss" and the rank-and-file of organized crime. The buffer is both a courier and an observer; he reports rule violations and other data to the boss, and carries back his decisions and commands to others.

---

[1] Donald R. Cressey, *Theft of the Nation,* New York: Harper and Row, 1969, p. 110.

Finally, Cressey holds that the large amounts of money realized from illicit operations and the growing involvement in legal business ventures have created a role called "the money mover." Money movers are individuals skilled in finance who invest and reinvest syndicate funds and generally handle financial matters for families in organized crime.

While Cressey's model does pay attention to behaviors performed in organized crime, the model of syndicate organization known to most newspaper readers is less attuned to behavior. Here the emphasis is less on functional roles and more on the pyramid of authority, which is described in the quasi-military vocabulary used in the Sicilian *Mafia*. At the head of the organization is the "boss" (which translates to the Sicilian *capo*) who carries out his executive functions aided by an "underboss" (or *sottocapo*). The latter is the chief administrator in the unit, acting for the boss. While the "underboss" is a line position, there is an equivalent-status staff position called *consigliere*. He is often a retired or semi-retired member of the family whose wisdom and tact are respected, and who acts as the boss's alter ego. At the level of middle management, authority is vested in the *caporegime* (also called "captains," "lieutenants," or *capodecine*). They command platoons or companies of "soldiers" (*soldati*), the lower-level family members who operate illicit enterprises on a commission basis or own their own illicit businesses under family protection.

This widely accepted "organizational structure" of *Cosa Nostra* is similar to the structure found in most corporate enterprises and in government and military bureaucracies. In fact, we think that such a degree of similarity does not exist. Unlike most bureaucracies—the Bell System and national labor unions, for example—popular descriptions of the *Cosa Nostra* provide no equivalent of the corporate headquarters or "national office." This circumstance is intriguing, because it raises questions about whether or not such a national office does exist. Those who charge that there is a national conspiracy of Italian-Americans involved in organized crime must of course posit the existence of a national commission which oversees regional and local activities. But if in fact such a commission does exist, the *Cosa Nostra* would seem to be the one organization which has managed to prosper without relegating increased authority and power to the central organization.

But if a national committee does exist, why should a New York family accept its decisions, since it has no power other than the power of its individual members? Various reports suggest that the commission is able to rule because it commands fear on the part of *Cosa Nostra* membership, and because no boss is strong enough to take over complete control. Thus the commission is able to rule because the individual member families have agreed to subject themselves to its discipline in return for security against internecine warfare.

Another explanation is that cooperative enterprises require the exchange of services, and that the commission acts as a broker in facilitating these relationships. But it is difficult to imagine that the one small family in San Francisco would have much traffic with any of the large families, or that there would be much need of arbitration between them.

If *Cosa Nostra* has a national commission, typical organizational design would require that it have some headquarters staff and some organizational locus for review and appraisal of policy. For a national commission to operate as legislature, judiciary, and executive in the way *Cosa Nostra*'s rulers are said to do would require an elaborate corporate structure, but there is no indication that any such unit exists. Thus, if there is a commission, its real function seems to fall outside the sphere of the consciously constructed and rationally operated organization. It seems to be an integral part of a social network, rather than an organization unit. The corporate analogy may arise from honest attempts to explain syndicate organization in terms that are familiar to the public. However, it may have another, more suspect motivation, arising from the theory that organized crime is engaged in a "national conspiracy." The President's Commission on Law Enforcement and Administration of Justice holds that there is in existence

> . . . a society that seeks to operate outside the control of the American people and their government. It involves thousands of criminals working within structures as complex as those of any large corporation, subject to laws more rigidly enforced than those of legitimate governments. Its actions are not impulsive but rather the results of intricate conspiracies, carried out over many years and aimed at gaining control over whole fields of activity in order to amass huge profits.[2]

The "national conspiracy" theory demands the existence of a national organization with a set of goals aimed at corrupting and subverting the American way of life. Like the alleged Communist conspiracy which preceded it, and the Black power and youth rebellions which are succeeding it in public interest, the "*Mafia* conspiracy" requires a national *Mafia* organization.

The distortions introduced by the attempt to compare the structure of *Cosa Nostra* to an American bureaucratic organization are further compounded by the attempt to describe organizational positions in terms of equivalents in Sicilian *Mafie*. Roles and role behavior are very much conditioned by the environment in which they operate. Sometimes the physical or cultural environment may compel a society, a group, or an individual to see that certain role behaviors are performed; sometimes it may preclude such behaviors

---

[2] The President's Commission on Law Enforcement and Administration of Justice, *The Challenge of Crime in a Free Society,* Washington, D.C.: Government Printing Office, 1967, p. 187.

entirely. The socio-cultural system in Sicily both forces some behaviors and precludes others in the role of *capo;* it is reasonable to suppose that Italian-American society operates from a different set of constraints, so that an Italian-American family head's role could not compare exactly with that of the *capo.* The position terms *capo, sottocapo,* and *consigliere* are derived from the hierarchical structure of Sicilian *Mafia* families. But in Sicilian *Mafie,* as in other southern Italian secret societies, these positions resemble kinship statuses far more than organizational ones. The *capo,* for example, is often called *zu,* or "uncle." The position is often hereditary and it is an analogue of the *capo famiglia* who is the leader of the extended family in the south of Italy. Even more important is the nature of the relationship among the statuses in criminal secret societies. The position of *capo* is not comparable to that of company president or even government official, for the Sicilian *capo* is far less subject to organizational controls than even the most autocratic corporate leader or dictatorial head of state. The closest comparison would be with the leader of a military or paramilitary guerrilla band. Describing the various positions in Italian-American syndicates as "like" those in bureaucracies gives the impression that they are, in fact, formal organizations. But they are not.

The Structure of Authority in the Lupollo Family

Within an organized-crime family, authority—that is, legitimate power —does exist. There is a sense of legitimacy that permits the family to organize power into a hierarchical pattern, so that some members hold authority roles and others do not. Those who hold authority are able to commit the family's resources to the pursuit of goals and to command members to action in that pursuit. Those who have little or no authority act with all the deference to the authority figure that one would expect to find in any hierarchically structured social system.

The most obvious rule regulating the authority structure is that roles within it are distributed on the basis of generational affiliation within the various lineages. In every case, the older the generation, the greater the authority. The second rule is that the various lineages—the Lupollos, the Alcamos, the Salemis, and the Tuccis—enjoy differential status within the family so that generally, although not universally, a Lupollo has more authority than a Salemi of the same generation. There are exceptions to this rule, described later, but they are special cases resulting from the operation of the third rule of ranking: within the family, some members achieve authority on the basis of specialization or expertise. For example lawyers and accountants, whose skills become more valuable as the family business expands, can gain legitimated power on this basis.

Joe Lupollo is the undisputed head of the family both as a business empire and as a social organization. Members of the family acknowledge his leadership, and their behavior toward him is always deferential. Whenever there is an important business decision to be made he makes it, not only in all family business enterprises, but (probably) in all family-related firms as well. One hears such comments as "Patsy wants to go into building suburban shopping centers but his father nixed the deal," or "Charley represents his brother Joe's interest on the docks," and most frequently, "check with Joe." Throughout the Italian-American community in New York, Joe is recognized as the "head" of the Lupollo family. This means more than being the patriarch of his family. It means also that he is the accepted leader of the business family as well. Thus, someone wanting to make an important business deal with one of the family companies begins by contacting the family member who is nominally in charge of the business, but he knows that if the decision is big enough, eventually Joe will have to make it. One member of the family once commented on this state of affairs to me. During the intermission of a concert which I attended with Phil Alcamo and his son Basil, we met a manufacturer of cardboard boxes who asked Phil to "see what he could do" to get him some business with Contessa Foods. While he was talking to Phil, Basil commented to me:

> He wouldn't dare go see Joe because he thinks that he'll eat him up and ask him for some kind of kickback on the contract so he tries to get to him through my father. The same thing happens with me. People come to me and say "Hey, talk to your Uncle Joe for me, will you" and they give you a look that says they won't forget you if you do.

Joe also commands authority within the social structure of the Lupollo and associated lineages. When a baptism or wedding occurs, in any of the lineages, or even in the family of some distant relative or employee, Joe is expected to send the most expensive gift, and he seldom disappoints. When several members of the family agree to dine out together, whether for business or for social reasons, it is always Joe who chooses the restaurant (always one of his three favorites), and then picks up the check. And on the few occasions when the Lupollo family is approached as a group—for religious gatherings or for benefits in the Italian-American community, for example—it is always through Joe.

Although Joe is the head of the family, there seems to be no organizational title which goes with the position, or at least I never heard one. He is called "Joe" by his brother Charley, Phil Alcamo, and Vito Salemi; other members of the family use the appropriate kinship term. When members of the family speak to each other about him, they either refer to "Joe" or attach the kinship term which relates the speaker to him—"Uncle Joe" or "my father, Joe." I have heard him called "boss" by some of the younger members of the family. When Mario Puzo's book *The Godfather* came out, Bobby Lupollo began referring to his grandfather (who also happens to be his godfather) as "the Godfather." But this did not last long and no one else picked up the term.

Charley Lupollo and Phil Alcamo also hold important roles in the authority structure. Charley is the family surrogate for Joe and, in his absence, the decision-making role is his both in business and in family social life. Everything said of Joe is true of Charley when Joe is not present; in no case, however, does Charley enjoy this deference when Joe is present. Since Joe dislikes traveling, Charley usually handles any very important business dealings out of town.

When Joe and Charley are together at family gatherings or meetings, Charley defers to Joe and usually does not advance new ideas or even suggestions unless Joe asks for them. The family meetings witnessed for this study were not formally called; they were *ad hoc* situations in which some items of business came up during social gatherings. Whether this deferential behavior holds true in formal meetings (assuming there are formal meetings) has not been determined.

In addition to his surrogate role, Charley has another informal role in the family. He is far from garrulous, and when he does speak he is usually peremptory. He is also ultraconservative, views most new ventures with suspicion, and seldom asks for advice. His anger, when he shows it, is violent and abusive. Nevertheless, the younger members of the family usually find Charley more approachable than Joe when they want a decision or favor. Charley has close relationships with many of the junior members of the family, and is a good listener. He presents new ideas to Joe, advances petitions, relays unfavorable business data, and generally intercedes for other family members. He does this with considerable sensitivity and no little skill. He seems to have catalogued all of the requests and data and knows Joe's moods so well that he can fit the right request or drop the appropriate bad news to Joe at precisely the right time. The other side of this role has Charley carrying decisions back from Joe to other family members. Interestingly, Charley seems to perform this same role even for Joe's sons Tony and Marky—but not for Joey—at least where business affairs are concerned.

These two roles, Joe as boss and Charley in a role which seems to combine elements of the *sottocapo* and *consiglieri* described by experts as hierarchical roles in *Cosa Nostra,* and a little of the buffer role described by Cressey, are the only offices we observed (although we found a number of other roles). Some other members of the family do command more authority than the rest, but it appears to us that these differentials develop not from office, but rather through operation of the three ranking rules we described earlier. Tony Lupollo, for example, appears to wield more authority within the family than does Vito Salemi or Pete Tucci, but this is probably because he is a Lupollo.

Another role in the family is that of "heir apparent." It is held by Joey Lupollo, who seems to have been selected to take over control of the family from his father. This is generally accepted within the family and is obvious in some of the behavior relationships we saw. For example, Joey does not use his Uncle Charley as a go-between with his father, but approaches him directly. When Charley is unable to represent Joe at business meetings or to travel out of town, Joey goes instead. Most important, however, is the fact that Joey spends a great deal of time with his father, more than any other member except Charley.

The family displays a number of "specialist" roles—that is, roles developing as a result of the particular expertise of the individual. For example, Charley shares with Phil Alcamo the role of political contact for the family. As described in an earlier chapter, Charley is connected in city and state politics, while Phil has contacts in Washington, particularly with regulatory agencies. There is insufficient evidence to determine whether or not this role fits Cressey's definition of the corrupter. I have met judges, commissioners, members of federal regulatory bodies, and congressmen socially when I have been with Phil Alcamo. More frequently, however, Phil's contacts seem to be with administrative assistants or other aides of congressmen and federal officials. At these meetings Phil openly discusses the needs of the family where government is concerned and often asks for advice or favors. He also suggests favorable business investments or land-purchase opportunities and will "put someone in touch with someone who can do something for them."

Basil Alcamo and Joey Lupollo are considered the two best business minds in the family, and their advice is often sought on investments and business problems. Basil, who is a certified public accountant, is considered the technician, and Joey the possessor of good "business sense." When someone in the family needs help in organizing a new business or solving a problem with taxes, he goes to Basil; someone with a hot new business idea will probably test it out with Joey. Joey's specialty is the American Stock Exchange, and his recommendations on what to buy and when to sell were almost always accurate during the two years of study. Phil Alcamo is also considered to have good business sense, and generally is the arbiter and interpreter of national and international events and their probable effects on the world of the Lupollos.

The numerous other specialist roles in the family are more social than business specialties. Nevertheless, since the family is so much an integrated social and business unit, these roles also have some effect on the family as a business unit. For example, Bobby Lupollo is considered the sharpest dresser in the family (although the older members consider his dress somewhat extreme). He sets the style for the younger family members; but his views also carry considerable weight in the family-related Danny Boy clothing line.

Some specialist roles also grow out of the illegal activities of the family, but we have few data on them. On one occasion, when a Sicilian-American businessman complained to Phil Alcamo that he was having trouble with truckers who were stealing merchandise from his shipments, Phil suggested that he switch his business to Lupollo-Livale Trucking "where they know how to keep drivers and warehousemen from stealing." When the businessman pointed out that he had a long-term contract with the trucking firm he was presently dealing with, Phil said that it could be taken care of "by some friends in Brooklyn." Later I asked Phil if he meant the Salemis and he answered "among others." I surmised that Phil was implying the existence of enforcers within the family, but the evidence of such roles is weak.

The authority structure in the family is diagrammed in Figure 1. What this diagram shows is the operation of the three rules of ranking which we extracted from our observations and from interview data. What it cannot show, however, is that this pattern is not fixed. It is slowly changing, because the traditional placement of power in the authority roles is being challenged by new power sources developing in the family.

The Changing Bases of Power in the Lupollo Family

We have defined authority as legitimated power, but we have said nothing about "power." It is commonly defined as an individual's ability to compel or influence another to do his bidding. This definition implies that power is an attribute of the individual—it is his capacity to exert influence. But power does not reside in an individual, any more than authority rests in a position. Power is a property of a social relationship; it is an individual's capacity to influence someone or some group. The term "network" captures this sense of relationship far better than a term like "power structure," and so we shall use the former in our analysis of the flow of power in the Lupollo family.

The authority structure we have described represents the distribution of legitimated traditional power within the Lupollo family; it specifies which individuals maintain control over important matters. There is a generational distribution of power, with the Lupollo lineage having the greatest power within generations. Joe Lupollo, as the head of the family (the oldest of the Lupollo lineage has the most power, and his younger brother Charley must be considered the second most powerful family member. After that, however, there is no such certainty. Phil Alcamo has power, but it is specific to his role as political liaison, so that his power is situational rather than general. Joey Lupollo has power as the heir apparent, but in crime families as in royal families succession is an uncertain thing. Whether Phil or Joey has more power

**Figure 1. The Structure of Authority in the
Lupollo Family**

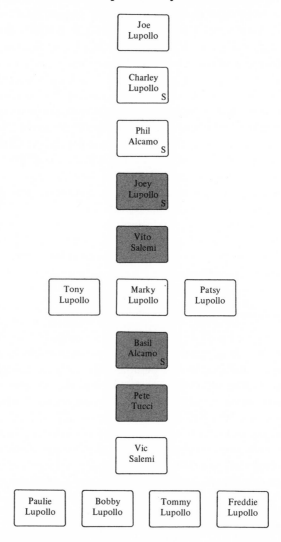

Note: The Rules of Ranking

1. The earlier the generation, the higher the rank. The authority of all family members conforms to this rule except for the four men shown in shaded areas. Joey Lupollo and Basil Alcamo rank higher, and Vito Salemi and Pete Tucci rank lower than would be expected on the basis of their respective generations.
2. Within generations, the Lupollo lineage takes precedence over the others.
3. Specialists (S) are ranked higher than generalists.

can only be answered if the questions "more power over whom" and "under what conditions" are first answered. Joey is a Lupollo and so one of the ranking rules places him ahead of Phil, who is not a Lupollo; but Phil is older than Joey, and so a second ranking rule is operative as well. Actually, relative power within the family cannot be assessed for individuals, but rather must be attributed to alliances and networks among individuals.

Management of power within the Lupollo family is remarkably disciplined. Joe Lupollo is "the boss" and receives all the deference due him in that authority role. Other members of the family fall in line with varying degrees of power, in a classical hierarchy of authority. Over the two years of our study, however, it became increasingly apparent that in the Lupollo family, as in any social system, the pattern by which power is distributed is not constant, for competing networks of power alliances cause the pattern to shift.

Three main power networks can be outlined; they are shown in Figure 2. The first and most obvious of these centers around Joe. As traditional head of the family, he is by far the most influential in deciding such power-based matters as the allocation of resources, the selection of goals, and the ordering of social and business life; his younger brother Charley is second most powerful. The exercise of Joe's power is based on the fear other family members feel for him in his role as traditional authority—a fear expressed in the form of a reluctance to initiate any new idea or social action, or to challenge the existing locus of decision-making. Family members express this as an unwillingness to "step out of line."

But if Joe is a control figure with complete authority within the family, the basis of his power seems to be shifting. He is boss precisely because he is the traditional head of the family, and this kinship-based role necessarily carries with it a conservative approach to control over the family empire. Joe's personality seems to have fitted him well for this role, and his experiences certainly did little to alter that fit. When old Giuseppe designated Joe as his successor, the two worked closely together during the transition period in which Joe learned from his father both the tasks and the role of family head. It was undoubtedly from his close association with his father that Joe gained his sense of family-oriented, kinship-based responsibility for holding the business-social unit together. Like his father, he operates entirely within the Italian-American community, where his contacts and associations are restricted to a relatively small group of family members, *paesani,* and other Italian-Americans involved in legitimate and illegitimate businesses.

While Joe maintains control over the family's businesses on the basis of his traditional authority, his brother Charley and Phil Alcamo operate outside the Italian-American community. Charley, better educated than Joe, is interested and involved in city politics and the business world where he seeks friends and contacts. He is joined in this quest by Phil Alcamo, and the two

Figure 2. Power Alliances in the Lupollo Family

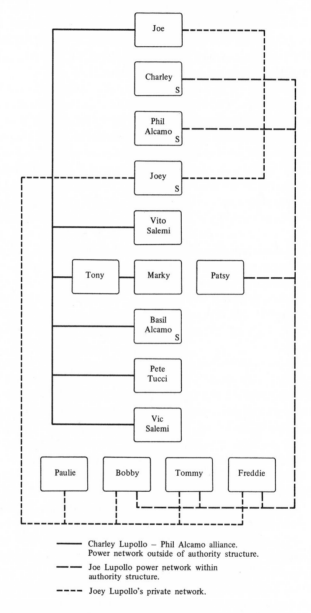

—————— Charley Lupollo – Phil Alcamo alliance.
Power network outside of authority structure.

– – – – Joe Lupollo power network within
authority structure.

- - - - Joey Lupollo's private network.

Note: Rules for Power Alliances

1. Kinship remains the most important basis for power alliances and forms the
   basis for legitimating power into authority.

literally compete for new alliances within the "American" business and political establishments. Neither Charley nor Phil is by any means "liberal" or "progressive" in politics or social attitudes, but each is far less conservative and dogmatic than Joe. All three look at New York City politics as a corrupt marketplace, but while Joe would say this is the result of the natural venality of man, Charley and Phil would say that the fault lies in the "system" and would see reform as possible if not desirable. Joe is more "Italian" than "American," not only in his affiliations but also in his outlook on life; the reverse is true of Charley and Phil.

These differences in world view and affiliation—Joe the conservative, kinship-oriented operator in the Italian-American community and the underworld, while Charley and Phil are oriented to the business and political establishments—are producing power tensions in the Lupollo family. As the family moves increasingly into the legitimate business establishment, Charley's and Phil's footholds there become more and more critical. Without these contacts, even the illegal activities would have difficulty; in fact, they probably could not survive. Thus, Charley and Phil have come to serve as power connections for the family, and in this role they inevitably challenge the supremacy of Joe's authority.

Faced with this challenge—which is implicit but seldom acted out—Joe has turned back into his own world of power, rather than seeking political and business connections of his own. The two sources of his legitimated power within the family are the Salemis and Pete Tucci. Vito and Vic Salemi have no important authority positions in the family, but they are masters of some of the power. In part, this grows out of their operational control of the illegal activities of the family. In part, it is because they report directly to Joe and wield power through that direct association. As well as his own associations in the underworld of Italian-American criminal syndicates, Joe has connections through the Salemis, and the potential power of these connections will be an important asset to Joe as he struggles in future to maintain his control. Pete Tucci, like Joe and Vito, is more conservative than Charley and Phil, and is oriented to the Italian-American community. Like Joe, he values the kinship bonds of the family and sees the social unity of the group as critical

---

2. In addition to blood and marriage ties, power alliances are formed through ritual kinship in the tradition of *compareggio* which allies generations and lineages together as well as individuals.

3. While consanguine, affinal, and ritual kinship are important bonds for the formation of power alliances, a system of reciprocal obligations within the family also operates to link individuals to each other and into power alliances.

4. Finally, where none of the above rules of alliance for power are compelling, mutuality of interests, friendships and self interest also provide motivations for new alliances.

to its survival. With these allies, Joe fortifies himself as the head of a conservative, constrained, and traditional family organization.

Joe was seventy-five years old in 1970 and the undercurrents of the power struggle going on in the Lupollo family must soon become someone else's problem. Here, the power networks come into play and provide some important insights into the future of the family. In the third generation of the family —the children of Joe and Charley Lupollo, Vito Salemi, and Phil Alcamo— more members affiliate with Joey than with Charley and Phil. Tony and Marky Lupollo exhibit complete filial deference to their father and, moreover, really seem to believe that Joe can and should use his traditional authority to hold the family together. Vic Salemi is also allied with Joe, and seems distrustful of Phil Alcamo and even more so of Basil Alcamo. Basil, on the other hand, is publicly deferential towards Joe, but privately he is often critical of Joe's "old-fashioned" ideas and stubbornness. He is openly hostile to the Salemis and contemptuous of Pete Tucci. The Salemis he sees as little more than hired hoodlums, while he considers Tucci, who operates part of the legitimate business empire as Joe's creature, an old-world sycophant playing peasant to Joe's *gallante uomo*. Patsy Lupollo is his father's man and allies himself with Charley and Phil. The key figure in the second generation, and indeed the key actor in the latent power struggle, is Joey Lupollo.

All of Joey's inclinations and values would logically lead to an affiliation with his uncles Charley and Phil. Like them he is connected in the American establishment, and sees the future of the family as dependent on nurturing and expanding these contacts. His tastes and style, like theirs, have climbed beyond the baroque attitudes and ostentatious life style of his brothers Tony and Marky. Yet in every observable act and social relationship, Joey allies himself with his father. Whether this behavior is genuine or calculated we cannot say, but the dissonance between Joey's attitudes and behavior are sometimes obvious. Once, on one of the few occasions when I was present during conflict within the family, Phil and Charley were trying to convince Joe that Mario Procaccino, the "regular" candidate for Mayor in New York City, could not possibly win either because people didn't take him seriously or were convinced he was a reactionary. Joe felt that Lindsay's term as Mayor had been so disastrous that the voters would turn him out, and that Procaccino, because he was the candidate of the Democratic machine, would win. This was more than idle political debate, because the whole scheme of influence and payoff of police and city officials could hang in the balance of the election. Generally, the assumption is that many police officials and civil servants will survive changes in administration, and will still be around—the "old reliables"—no matter who wins. In addition to myself, Joe, Charley, Phil, Joey, and Basil Alcamo were present. Basil was certain that Lindsay would win and argued insistently with both Joe and his father. Joey joined in the debate but said very little to indicate his own convictions. Finally, with no little show of exasperation, Basil turned to Joey and said "What *do* you think, Joey? Does Procaccino have a chance to win?" Joey spoke at some length and, to me at least, his argument seemed to support Basil's belief in the probable victory of Lindsay. Yet when he reached the summation, he expressed complete support for his father's belief that the Democrats would carry Procaccino to victory. Basil was visibly annoyed and later, when he was driving me home, told me that just two days before Joey had agreed in a private conversation with him that Lindsay would win.

There are, of course, obvious reasons why Joey would side with his father in the developing struggle for power in the family. As the heir apparent, he is slated to take over his father's traditional role as head of the family, and the challenges from Basil, Charley, and Phil are challenges to the legitimate authority of that role. In addition, his kinship ties with his father are strong ones and family loyalty may be important to him. And finally, he may simply be waiting for his father to step down before showing where his true allegiances lie. Whether his ambivalence is the result of a conflict between filial loyalty and his own ambitions for the family or is a means of waiting out the power conflicts to see what will happen, he remains a key to the future direction the family will take. In the improbable event that this latent struggle becomes an open one before Joe dies or retires, I would venture the opinion that Joey will end up on the winning side.

In the fourth generation, all of the family members save one tend to line up with Charley and Phil, rather than with Joe and Vito Salemi. Bobby, Freddy, and Tommy Lupollo all understand access to the establishments of the larger society to be far more potent than the traditional control of some piece or pieces of territory. All well-educated and quite comfortable in American society, they see little future in the old world of organized crime. The one exception is Paulie Lupollo, whose mother, Yolanda Salemi, ties him to that lineage as well as to the Lupollos. Paulie allies himself with his uncle Vic Salemi and, through him, with Joe.

All four of the fourth-generation members of the family are also allied with Joey Lupollo. Even Paulie Lupollo, whose matrilineal association with the Salemis leads him to resent the status differential between them and the Lupollos, sees Joe as the emerging power center in the family. These alliances come about in part as a result of the greater congruence of life styles and taste between Joey and the younger family members. It is to him that they relate most easily. For example, Joey is an antique car buff and sometimes exhibits his collection of exotic cars at national shows. The younger Lupollos find this pursuit more appealing to their own tastes than Joe's attachment to the Italian-American community or Phil and Charley's single-minded pursuit of business and politics. It also says to them that Joey has made it in the social world.

Another aspect of their alliance with Joey is that Joey has consciously sought their allegiance in a way which his father and uncles have not. All of the leading members of the family—Joe, Charley, Phil, and Joey—know that a network of supporters is crucial to anyone interested in gaining or maintaining power. Joey, however, has been the most successful in building such a network with the fourth generation because his direct access to his father enables him to extend special help or favors to the younger members. And so he has established a reciprocity relationship with them: his assistance is repaid by their loyalty.

Whether Joe was a confederate with his son in developing this new channel of communication, which bypasses Charley and so strengthens both Joe and Joey, we do not know. There is, however, no question that he tacitly approves of it. It could not work without his knowledge, since the favors must come from or at least be approved by him. Whether Charley and Phil are unaware of this, which seems improbable, or whether they also have an understanding with Joey, we do not know; but here again, the only visible opposition comes from Basil Alcamo:

> Joey is like a cute politician, he promises Freddy one thing and Tommy something else and keeps them both happy. Sometime, he's going to promise more than he can deliver or he's going to promise the same thing to different people, and then watch out.

These networks of power alliances are visible within the family, but at present they do not create enough static in the normal system of power flow to generate tension or dysfunction. They do, however, indicate the changing expectations and attitudes of family members. The traditional network of power is legitimated in the authority structure, and generational and lineage considerations are important in the allocation of power. But since the family's relationship with the old Italian-American and newer societal environments is shifting toward the latter, new power alliances are forming both within the family, and between family members and the external world. These new alliances are based not on kinship, but on association and on the reciprocity of service and return service. Increasingly the family is forging such ties with the power establishments of the larger society, and so those members of the family who relate to that society are enjoying new possibilities of power within the family. Of all members of the Lupollo family, Joey has the greatest potential for power, since he not only inherits his father's traditional, kinship-based authority but also has full access to the functional, performance-based power which grows out of contacts in the business and political world.

Thus, two basic patterns of social relationship—kinship, and reciprocity and associational ties—organize the structuring of power-alliance networks in the Lupollo family. The interplay between these two patterns is reflected in yet another network of alliances—godparent–godchild relationships. In an earlier chapter we cited the importance of *compareggio,* or the ritual, fictive kinship of godparenthood, in southern Italian culture in general and in secret societies such as the *Mafia* in particular. In the south of Italy, and traditionally within Italian-American culture, *compareggio* establishes three power linkages or alliances. The first links generations, since the godfather is usually of the same generation as the godchild's father, and so reinforces the kinship structure and generational authority. The second ties the child to his ceremonial sponsor or godfather and sets up a potent if putative relationship with reciprocal rights and duties which are similar to father–son relationships. Since these responsibilities are not taken lightly and since the godfather is literally responsible for raising the child in the event of the father's death or incapacity, one always selects a man of power and prestige as godfather for a son. Finally, the network of *compareggio* forms alliances between the two families involved, and the familiar term *compare* is extended to all members of both families signifying a relationship second only to blood. Within Italian-American culture, the practice of *compareggio* is more and more conforming to the American Catholic pattern, which stresses spiritual rather than kinship bonds in the relationship, but it is still potent in the Lupollo family.

Figure 3, which diagrams the godparent–godchild relationships we know about in the Lupollo family, provides several important insights into the power-alliance systems within the family. First, despite the growing practice in American Catholicism to have contemporaries as godparents, godparenthood in the family is always in the preceding generation for each case that we know of. Not only does this tie the generations together in ritual kinship, it also brings the various lineages together in one pattern, since there are now godparent–godchild relationships among all of them. The distribution of godparenthood also reflects the relative power of the lineages; Lupollos are more frequently godparents than any other lineage. While this circumstance could be attributed to the fact that there are more Lupollos than any other lineage in the family, more careful analysis indicates the power-alliance implications of preferential godparenthood. Old Giuseppe was also godfather to numerous other children of relatives, *paesani,* and other coethnics who sought his protection and favor. In the next generation, Joe as head of the family seems to have been sought after as godfather more frequently than his younger brother Charley. However, the last generation in our study seems to recognize that Charley and Phil, and to an even greater extent Joey, represent the future direction of power; and so they are chosen as the most promising sponsors for a child. This seems to be true of all save Paulie Lupollo, who once again shows his matrilineal ties to the Salemis by having his Uncle Vic as godfather for his only son.

Figure 3. Godparent-Godchild

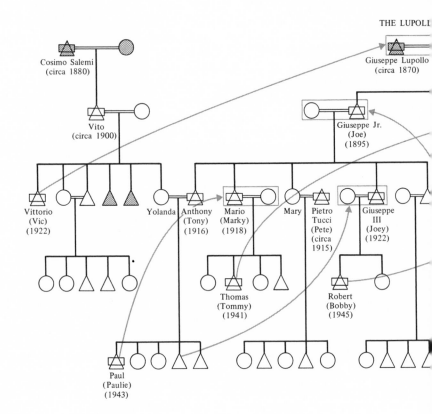

THE LUPOLI

Cosimo Salemi
(circa 1880)

Giuseppe Lupollo
(circa 1870)

Vito
(circa 1900)

Giuseppe Jr.
(Joe)
(1895)

Vittorio
(Vic)
(1922)

Yolanda Anthony
(Tony)
(1916)

Mario
(Marky)
(1918)

Mary Pietro
Tucci
(Pete)
(circa
1915)

Giuseppe
III
(Joey)
(1922)

Thomas
(Tommy)
(1941)

Robert
(Bobby)
(1945)

Paul
(Paulie)
(1943)

Relationships in the Lupollo Family

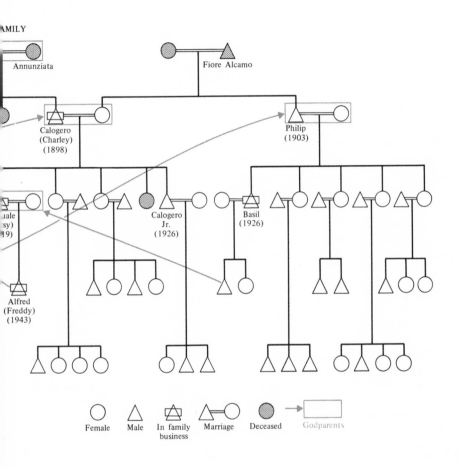

FAMILY

Annunziata

Fiore Alcamo

Calogero
(Charley)
(1898)

Philip
(1903)

uale
sy)
19)

Calogero
Jr.
(1926)

Basil
(1926)

Alfred
(Freddy)
(1943)

○ Female   △ Male   ⬂ In family business   △—○ Marriage   ● Deceased   → ▭ Godparents

Prestige Ranking in the Lupollo Family

In studying the Lupollo family, we were looking for patterns of social relationship which would establish who was related to whom, how, and under what conditions. In particular, we were interested in discovering a network of relationships which would define some members as more powerful than others, some who command, and some who follow. For example, we asked whether there was someone in the family who, under all circumstances, was always "the boss." If there was, what were the techniques of control, the sanctions, and the communications network he used to exercise his authority within the family, and how did he relate to others inside and out of the family?

We soon discovered that we were dealing not with one but with several behavioral structures which tie the Lupollo family members together. The first of these is the legitimated system of role-prescribed relationships which establishes power in a hierarchy of authority. In this system, the authority of the individual is largely inherent in the role itself; the individual is powerful because of the status he occupies. But within the Lupollo family, as elsewhere, authority and power are not always the same. We came upon this field-generated confirmation of an accepted theoretical position one evening when Basil Alcamo complained of his problems with the family's authority structure.

> . . . There are times when I don't know whether to give advice or just sit back and see what happens. Joe [Lupollo] is a great guy but he doesn't know for sure what's going on in the business world. If I tell him that he should get rid of something he waits and waits until he feels in his guts that it's time. If I tell him to buy something he does it, but not until he sits on it awhile. He's like his father and doesn't want anybody to think that he isn't his own man. He's the boss and wants everybody to know it. Charley [Lupollo] and my father [Phil Alcamo] have the same problem with him. They're connected downtown and know pretty well what's going on. He listens to them more than he does to me because he knows he can't move without their help, but he is so fucking stubborn that even with them he makes a big deal out of it.

What Basil was describing was the situation within a group in which the authority structure and the power relationships are not perfectly meshed. This discovery that authority and power did not go hand in hand among the Lupollos led us to search for another way of describing stratification within the family. Moreover, neither power nor authority explained certain forms of control behavior we observed, such as the operation of "deference." Eventually, our observations led us to a third ranking dimension, that of "prestige." Prestige, in the sense that we are using it, is the hierarchical ordering of the esteem in which a person is held by others in the social system which they share.

Studies of prestige are usually carried out by participant-observation—

the field worker immersing himself in the social system he is studying and observing the social distinctions—or by the use of some prestige-rating technique by which the members of the system rate each other. Regardless of the technique used, two problems confound such studies. One is that the natives of the system usually lack a set of specific terms to describe prestige, and so while there may be culturally useful ways to scale "it," there is no way of being certain that you are actually measuring "it," in the first place. A second problem is that most people don't really carry a prestige rating of others around with them; rather, they have internalized a set of culturally determined rules or criteria for ranking people. Within the Lupollo family, however, and within Italian and Italian-American culture generally, there is an accepted term which does combine all of the dimensions of prestige in one ranking device—"respect" (*rispetto*).[3] In the Lupollo family, respect is a constant characteristic of an individual, although it is enhanced by age. Old Giuseppe, for example, was *rispetto* because of his power and authority, but as he grew older his age earned even more *rispetto*. Cosimo Salemi, who was feared because of his personal power, did not have high respect, because he always had to defer to Giuseppe; as he grew older, however, his age also earned him increased *rispetto*.

In Italian-American society, *rispetto* is traditionally mediated as it is in Italy—through age, kinship (generational membership), authority, and power.[4]

Today, however, under the pressure of acculturation, the relative weight of these factors in ranking an individual is changing in Italian-American society. While age and kinship are still important factors, authority and particularly power are increasingly important and probably outweigh age and kinship. A successful young physician or politician earns as much *rispetto* among his fellow Italian-Americans, if not more, than an older nonprofessional. It is not just success in his role but the relative "importance" of the role which wins respect.

In the Lupollo family, respect is expressed in many different ways. It is the basis for protocol in both business and social interaction, and it determines who will make decisions for the group, no matter how important or how insignificant the matter to be decided. It even establishes the relative social power of the wives. At a family social gathering, positions at the table, order of the service, and even who serves and who is waited upon, are signs of the respect afforded each man. In business matters, the right to initiate ideas and make suggestions is a function of how much respect an individual commands. In

---

[3] For a perceptive discussion of the nature of *rispetto* and how it is used to stratify a central Italian village, see Sydel F. Silverman "An Ethnographic Approach to Social Stratification: Prestige in a Central Italian Community," *American Anthropologist*, Vol. 68, No. 4, August 1966, pp. 899–922.

[4] Cf. Sydel F. Silverman, *Ibid.*, pp. 906–907.

Figure 4. Respect Ratings by Lupollo Family Members

Rated \ Rater	Joe	Charley	Phil	Vito	Joey	Tony	Marky	Patsy	Pete	Vic	Basil	Bobby	Freddy	Paulie	Tommy
Joe		▲	▲	▲	▲	▲	▲	O	▲	▲	▽	▲	▲	O	▲
Charley	▲		▲	O	▲	▲	▲	O	▲	▲	▲	▽	▲	O	▲
Phil	▲	▲		▽	▲	▽	▽	O	O	▽	▲	▲	▲	O	▲
Vito	▲	▽	▽		▲	▲	▲	▽	O	▲	▲	▽	▽	▽	▽
Joey	▲	▲	▲	O		▲	▽	O	▲	▽	▲	▲	▲	O	▲
Tony	O	▽	▽	▲	▲		▲	O	O	▽	▽	▽	▽	O	▲
Marky	▲	▽	▽	▲	▽	▲		O	▽	▽	▽	▲	▽	O	▲
Patsy	▽	▲	▽	O	▽	▲	▽		▽	▽	▽	▽	▲	O	▽
Pete	▲	▽	▽	▲	▽	▽	▽	O		▽	▽	▽	▽	O	▽
Vic	▲	▲	▲	▲	▽	▲	▽	O	▲		▽	▲	▽	O	▲
Basil	▽	▲	▲	▽	▲	▲	▽	O	▲	▲		▲	▲	O	▲
Bobby	▲	▽	▲	▲	▲	▲	▽	O	▽	▽	▲		▲	O	▽
Freddy	O	▲	▽	▽	▲	▽	▲	O	▲	▽	▽	▲		O	▽
Paulie	▽	▽	O	▽	▲	▽	▽	O	▽	▽	▲	▽	▽		▽
Tommy	▲	▲	▽	▽	▲	▲	▽	O	▽	▽	▽	▽	▽	O	

High ▲ Low ▽ Did not rate O

short, respect is the most important single dimension for differentiating members hierarchically within the family. Once we had noted how important it was as a means of stratifying the family, we decided to try to assess it in some systematic way.

One third of the way through the study, we asked family members how much respect other members had within the group. Their responses are presented in Figure 4 as "high respect" and "low respect." The nature of the group being studied and the field conditions simply did not allow a more precise measurement. I tried to be as consistent as possible in asking about respect, but since I wanted to introduce it naturally into the conversation, the questions were not always asked in the same way. Furthermore, the interviews of necessity covered a period of fifteen months; I would have preferred, of course, to ask the questions of each member at the same time, since one assumes that respect, like prestige, does differ from time to time. From two members I was completely unable to get any response. I never felt close enough to Patsy Lupollo to ask the question, and Paulie Lupollo insisted that he "respected" everybody in the family the same. Finally, we had to be fairly arbitrary in ranking the responses. "High" includes such responses as "a lot," "the most," and "more than X," if X was rated low. In spite of these limitations, however, we think that the data allow some assessment of how prestige-respect is allocated in the Lupollo family. We also talked with seven people outside of the family—three first-generation residents of the Brooklyn area where the family operates, a police officer from the same area, Nick Miraglia of the East Harlem De Maio family, Nunzio Passalaqua from the New Jersey family, and James Parone, who is Phil Alcamo's nephew. Here again the nature of the study made it impossible to use a consistent approach or any sorting technique, so that the data from each respondent are only roughly comparable with those from others. Generally, however, there was congruence in the following ratings:

1. Joe Lupollo was rated highest by all respondents except James Parone, who rated him second.
2. Charley Lupollo: rated second highest by all respondents except James Parone, who rated him first.
3. Phil Alcamo: rated third highest by four respondents, fourth by two respondents, and fifth by one respondent.
4. Joey Lupollo: rated fourth highest by four respondents, third highest by three respondents.
5. Patsy Lupollo: rated fifth highest by four respondents, third highest by one respondent (James Parone), and not rated by two respondents.
6. Tony Lupollo: rated sixth highest by four respondents, fifth highest by two respondents, and not rated by one.
7. Marky Lupollo: rated seventh highest by three respondents, sixth highest by one respondent, and not rated by three.
8. Basil Alcamo: rated sixth highest by one respondent, seventh highest by two respondents, and not rated by four.

The remaining family members were either not rated or were mentioned by only one respondent.

Considering all rankings by family members and outsiders, we found that three rules emerged. First, respect is highest where power and authority are linked in one person. Not only does Joe Lupollo have the highest estimates of respect, some of the comments made by family members and others indicate that this respect is associated more with his position than with any personal attribute. The police officer we interviewed, for example, presented a less than impressive description of Joe:

> I've seen him make a jackass out of himself a couple of times. Once when he was in Brooklyn to see one of his *paesans* buried, he got his car stuck behind a big trailer truck and sent his chauffeur up to raise hell with the driver. The truck driver either didn't know or didn't give a shit about his being a big man and told the chauffer to get off his back and he would move the truck as soon as he could. Joe got wild and had the chauffeur try to go around the truck and

smashed hell out of his fender. Joe got out of the car and started raising hell with the chauffeur, but didn't say beans to the truck driver. He treats the people who work for him like dirt, but they're all afraid of him because he's boss and they respect that position.

In several of the interviews inside and outside the family, it was pointed out that old Giuseppe had had the highest respect of anyone in the family, because he controlled everything himself. He was a "man of respect" because he combined traditional authority with utilitarian power in a way his successors can no longer manage.

The second rule of ranking is that, where authority and power are not associated with the same role, the role with the higher power wins the most respect. Thus within the family Phil Alcamo is given more respect than Charley, despite the fact that Charley has more authority as second in command. Comments such as "Phil knows Senator X" or "Phil is connected in Washington" suggest that his access to national politics endows him with greater power in the eyes of family members than is true of Charley. Outside the family, however, Charley's traditional authority gives him higher prestige. (He is a Lupollo; Phil is not.)

Finally, the more recent the generation, the higher the respect given to power rather than authority. The defections from Joe as the most respected are most consistent in the younger members of the family, just as this generation's highest respect is reserved for Phil and Charley and especially Joey. It could be argued that at least some of the respect for Joey comes from his authority as heir apparent, but once again the comments made by these younger members indicate also that it is his "connections" and ability to "get things done" which lead to his high ranking.

Authority, Power, and Respect: The Interplay of Control Systems

An important function of social structure is to provide everyone with a personal community in which he can interact with other community members with some certainty of reciprocity. Thus, within a social system, each role is connected with one or more others in patterned ways which define their methods of interaction. In the Lupollo family we found three behavioral structures which relate roles to one another; the structure of authority roles, the network of alliances for power, and the ranking system through which respect (and so prestige) is awarded to various roles and so to role players. The authority structure is based on the traditional, legitimated system of role relationships which fixes power in the head of the family. Since old Giuseppe named Joe as head of the family, the values of the southern Italian culture which still illuminate the Lupollos' behavior imply that Joe should have undisputed power in the group. But as the relationship between the family and the larger society changes, it is the utilitarian power of access to establishments in that society which defines the new power centers in the family. There is inevitable conflict between authority and power, which represents a value conflict in the family as well, because Joe's traditional coercive power comes from conservative, southern Italian, kinship-oriented, *Mafia*-like values, while the new power for Charley and Phil grows out of progressive American, bureaucratic, efficiency-oriented values. Thus Joe's authority is traditional and comes from the articulation of generations in a vertical structure based on kinship, while Charley and Phil are part of a horizontal, contemporary set of power alliances which keeps them "tied in" with power establishments in the larger society.

The congruence between the vertical, kinship-oriented authority structure and the horizontal, utilitarian network of power alliances is the surest sign of group cohesion and control we found. The rules regarding this congruence seem to be two: First, where there is integration of the authority and power roles, there is a high degree of cohesion and solidarity in the family. Second, where there is not integration of authority and power roles, there is conflict. In this context, conflict is generated by the separation of authority and power as Joe becomes more dependent upon the power of Charley and Phil. Joe's source of power is his contacts in the Italian-American community and in alliances with other families in organized crime, and as the family moves toward complete legitimation, the balance of power is shifting towards Charley and Phil and their associations in the larger society. And a new factor is added to the power equation. Authority in the family is based on traditional values of kinship-oriented relationships with Italian-American culture and Italian-American syndicates in organized crime, while the new power grows out of utilitarian values associated with legitimate American power establishments.

Within the family as within Italian and Italian-American culture, the social ranking of individual members is based upon the amount of respect accorded to their role in the family. Respect is highest when a role combines traditional authority with utilitarian power, but when the two are not joined it is power which commands the greatest respect. In each new generation of the family there is more respect awarded to power, and the younger members of the family look up to Charley and Phil because they identify their own values and tastes with the life styles and power alliances which Charley and Phil have developed. Of all the family members, Joey Lupollo seems in the most secure position, for his role as heir apparent to the traditional authority of his father coincides with the power he enjoys from alliances with the younger members of the family and from his own contacts in power establishments. Today, he is a boundary runner, connecting the authority and power systems skillfully, and avoiding the creation of obvious antagonisms. Unless there is some violent upheaval in the family from internal or external sources, his ascension to power and authority seem assured.

Recruitment into Family Roles

In our exposure to the Lupollo family, our experience with recruiting was limited to the process by which family members in the various lineages were selected for inclusion or exclusion from the family business. Ever since Joe Lupollo took over control of the family, the process has been one of assigning members of the various lineages to one of three roles; (1) direct involvement in the family business, (2) involvement in one of the family-related businesses, and (3) complete exclusion from any involvement in the family business enterprise. How deliberate and conscious this process has been is difficult to assess. If, however, one traces the various lineages back to the days of old Giuseppe, two factors seem to emerge. With each succeeding generation the proportion of male members of the various lineages who become directly involved in the family business has diminished. Thus, while both of Giuseppe's sons remained in the family business, and most of their sons did as well, fewer than one-third of the fourth-generation males are involved in the family business. A second factor is that while in the first three generations members of the various lineages tended to maintain some physical proximity to one another, the Lupollo lineage, the Tuccis, and to a lesser extent the Alcamos are now dispersed throughout the country. These factors are, of course, not unrelated. As the social status of the family and its constituent lineages increases, the process of recruiting becomes essentially a negative one. The children become progressively better educated, and strike out on their own in a variety of professions. This becomes most obvious in the fourth or most recent generation; not only have few of the members remained in the New York City area, but of those who have, some have retained no obvious connection with the family business. As a result, relatives by blood and marriage of the four lineages are increasingly coming into the family business to replace direct descendants who are opting out.[5]

There is within the family a constant process of assessment of relatives who might be valuable adjuncts in the business. Here the process seems to work virtually unchanged from what we described earlier as a pattern of recruitment in Sicily. A member of the family mentions a relative who is doing well in school or who seems to have a sharp eye for business. The relative is

---

[5] It is an interesting question whether those direct descendants who have chosen not to be involved are aware of the nature of the family business. Pete Tucci once remarked in an offhand fashion that his children (none of whom is involved in the family business) couldn't care less about his business activities and that his grandchildren did not have any sense of family or feel any relationship to their Italian ancestry. Basil Alcamo also once commented that the Lupollo lineage was becoming much more conscious of its social image and that some of the younger members of the fourth generation "would like to forget how old Giuseppe made the money which put them through college and paid for their high style of living now."

given some minor supervisory position in one of the family businesses, or, if he is a specialist, is given a role in his specialty. If he does well, he can expect to move ahead in the organization under the protection of his kin-sponsor. It also seems fairly certain that relatives by blood and marriage still petition for positions in the family business enterprise. No member was added to the fifteen-man central executive group during the three years I spent with the family, but some new faces—always relatives—did appear from time to time as new executives in one or another of the companies. Whether the relatives had been selected earlier and sent on to college or law school with the direct purpose of moving them into the family business is unclear, but it was not uncommon to hear a member of one of the lineages comment that some youngster in his lineage had a real head on his shoulders and would some day be valuable to the business.

Recruiting for lower-level personnel in the illegal sectors of the family business is a process on which we have some admittedly spotty evidence, but certainly not enough to establish any rules. We did learn that there is a process by which boys are gradually brought into the operation and moved to positions of some importance. In ghetto neighborhoods kids still hang around in loosely formed gangs, looking for "action" or a chance to make some money. The local "hoods" send them on little errands—buying coffee or carrying messages —and as they get older, trust them with more important tasks, such as picking up numbers or delivering number slips. Gradually some youngsters establish increasing degrees of trustworthiness with the "hoods." It seems that the advancement of trust stops at different points with different boys and young men. When we talked to one controller of a numbers wheel in Brooklyn he expressed this sense of trust and its relationship to recruiting as follows:

> These kids in the neighborhood all want to do things and after a while you began to learn what they can do and what they can't do. They are all different. Some of them would do anything you asked them because they are tough kids but smart and they are looking for a way to get ahead. Some of the others you can trust with little things, but as soon as they get a couple of hundred bucks in their hands they go crazy and they start stealing from you. The worst ones though are the kids who are on dope and will rob you blind if they get a chance. I watch all these kids and I know their families. I know their fathers, their uncles, and their cousins and I can tell you who has good blood and who has got bad blood, and who you can trust and who you can't.

How much recruitment at lower levels still continues in this community-oriented, family-centered tradition we do not know. Certainly, as the gambling operations are increasingly turned over to Blacks and Puerto Ricans it will diminish. Neither do we know whether there is any trade-off of personnel between the legal and illegal business enterprises. Since the mid-1920's the general pattern has been to separate the legal and illegal activities in terms of personnel, which would seem to suggest that it does not. Neither do we have any evidence which would support the position that the Lupollo family is part of a larger confederation or national syndicate (*Cosa Nostra* or otherwise) in which they hold membership. If they are (and we cannot say with any certainty that they are not), their "recruiting" would be recruiting for the national organization, rather than for the family. The Lupollos do maintain contacts with other reputed "*Cosa Nostra* families" in the New York area and in other parts of the country. There is no question, however, that as far as the Lupollo family is concerned membership in the organizational hierarchy is determined by blood and marriage and is not an option for outsiders.

7 / Rules of Conduct

We began our study of the Lupollo family with two basic questions in mind: How is the family organized to achieve shared goals? What are the techniques of social control used to motivate members in that pursuit? In the last two chapters, we have described the family's organization as we saw it. Now we turn to the code of rules which not only shapes the behavior of family members but also distinguishes the "good" or successful member from the less-successful one. In the sense we use it here, control within social systems begins with values which establish preferential guides to action. Ultimately, it comes to take the form of specific rules which attempt to apply those values to everyday situations. Thus, while values direct behavior, it is the rule which states which actions will be approved and which forbidden. Rules also carry with them sets of sanctions to be applied when they are broken.

Before we describe the Lupollo family's code of conduct, the manner in which it is enforced, and the way in which new members are recruited into adherence to that code, it may be worthwhile to look at the code of rules which other investigators have found applicable to Italian-American criminal syndicates. Like the popularly known pattern of organization and roles we discussed earlier, these rules of conduct have usually been derived by analogy. That is, rather than looking directly at the behavior of criminal-syndicate members and extrapolating a code from their words and actions, investigators have tried to apply to syndicates codes drawn from observations of other groups.

Codes of Rules Derived by Analogy

"The Mafia Code." One favorite analogy for the code of conduct in Italian-American criminal syndicates is the "code of the Mafia." The report of the Task Force on organized crime, for example, reasons that since "there is great similarity between the structure of the Italian-Sicilian *Mafia* and the structure of the American confederation of criminals it should not be surprising to find great similarity in the values, norms, and other behavior patterns of the two organizations."[1] Continuing with this reasoning, the report then

---

[1] The President's Commission on Law Enforcement and Administration of Justice, *Task Force Report-Organized Crime; Annotations and Consultant's Papers,* Washington, D.C.: Government Printing Office, 1967, p. 47.

goes on to present two summaries of "the *Mafia* code"; one statement was made in 1892, the other in 1900.

> 1. Reciprocal aid in case of any need whatever. 2. Absolute obedience to the chief. 3. An offense received by one of the members to be considered an offense against all and avenged at any cost. 4. No appeal to the state's authorities for justice. 5. No revelation of the names of members or any secrets of the association.

> 1. To help one another and avenge every injury of a fellow member. 2. To work with all means for the defense and freeing of any fellow member who has fallen into the hands of the judiciary. 3. To divide the proceeds of thievery, robbery and extortion with certain consideration for the needy as determined by the *capo*. 4. To keep the oath and maintain secrecy on pain of death within twenty-four hours.[2]

The report notes that "the *Mafia* code" is quite similar to the tenets of American organized criminals—loyalty, honor, secrecy, honesty, and consent to be governed, which may mean "consent to be executed." As the report freely admits, "the *Mafia* code" is similar to the code of any secret organization, from Mau Mau to the Irish Republican Army, and even to public organizations opposed to existing authority and seeking to overthrow it.

Unless the premise of direct descent of Italian-American criminal syndicates from the *Mafia* is accepted, there seems to be no more reason for attributing these reported similarities in behavioral code to *Mafia* origins than to the general behavioral needs of all secret organizations opposed to existing power. The antiquity of the reports used to reconstruct the *Mafia* code also reduces the utility of the analogy. Again, unless it is assumed that the early immigrants to the United States brought the code from Sicily and that it remains largely unaffected by American culture, then it would seem more sensible to compare the current codes of behavior in Sicilian *Mafia* and Italian-American crime syndicates.[3]

The Code of American Prisoners. The Task Force Report and more recently both Donald Cressy and Ralph Salerno also find striking similarities between the behavioral code of organized-crime syndicates and the code of prisoners in American penal institutions.[4] Both Salerno and Cressey recognize

---

[2] *Ibid.*, p. 47; The first summary was taken from Ed Reid, *Mafia*, New York: New American Library, 1964, p. 31, and the second from A. Cutrera, *La Mafia ed i Mafiosi*, Palermo, 1900.

[3] Cf. Francis A. J. Ianni, "Time and Place as Variables in Acculturation Research," *American Anthropologist*, Vol. 60, No. 1, February 1958, pp. 39–45.

[4] Donald Cressey, *Theft of the Nation*, New York: Harper and Row, 1969; Ralph Salerno and J. S. Tomkins, *The Crime Confederation*, New York: Doubleday and Co., 1969.

the similarity of the prisoners' code to that of underground organizations in general, and see the similiarity as growing out of similar needs to control behavior.

The Code of Organized-Crime Families. While each of the major sources admits the absence of any codified set of rules in organized-crime families, all present descriptive lists drawn either from analogies with the codes we have just described or from the experience of the writers in observing organized criminals. Cressey holds that the "thieves' code" is essentially the conduct code for organized-crime families:

1. Be loyal to members of the organization. Do not interfere with each other's interest. Do not be an informer. . . .
2. Be rational. Be a member of the team. Don't engage in battle if you can't win. . . . The directive extends to personal life.
3. Be a man of honor. Respect womanhood and your elders. Don't rock the boat. . . .
4. Be a stand-up guy. Keep your eyes and ears open and your mouth shut. Don't sell out. . . . The "stand-up guy" shows courage and "heart." He does not whine or complain in the face of adversity, including punishment, because "If you can't pay, don't play."
5. Have class. Be independent. Know your way around the world. . . .

Ralph Salerno derives his list from study of organized crime during a career with the New York City Police Department:

1. Secrecy. Most members reveal as little as possible to the police, but the silence of the "Cosa Nostra" segment of organized crime has been so complete that until the famous Apalachin meeting in November 1965, many law-enforcement officials doubted its very existence.
2. The organization before the individual. As in the case of secrecy, this rule is one that many in the outside world subscribe to. In military service the individual is expected to put the good of the organization ahead of his own, even if his life depends on it. Our gallery of national heroes is made up of people who made such a choice; the heroes of organized crime are those who went to the death house with their mouths shut.
3. Other members' families are sacred. In most social groups it would be considered unnecessary to specifically prohibit members from making seductive approaches to their associates' wives and daughters. But "Cosa Nostra" is an organization of Italian-Americans and as Luigi Barzini has observed, all Italian males, married and unmarried, are in a constant state of courtship. The rule helps protect the organization from vendettas over such "matters of honor." It makes it possible for a member to be inattentive to the female relatives of another member without this lack of interest being considered unmanly. This sense of chivalry does not, of course, extend to the families of strangers. They can, and often are, taken advantage of.

4. Reveal nothing to your wife. There are three reasons for this rule. In the first place, a member might become estranged from his wife and since "Hell hath no fury . . ."—it is important that she not know anything that she could use to hurt him. Keeping wives in the dark about illegal activities diverts law enforcement attention from them and the rest of one's family. The overall policy that business is not discussed with one's wife is part of a general desire to dissociate the home and family from criminal activities.

5. No kidnapping. The rule against kidnapping [of other members] for ransom is probably a holdover from Sicily where this form of coercion and extortion was widespread.

6. You don't strike another member. This is another rule designed to avoid internal vendettas that could easily arise if an argument were allowed to turn physical. The restraint of often fiery temperaments that it demands is a graphic demonstration of the authority that the code carries.

7. Orders cannot be disobeyed. While self-explanatory, this rule is much broader than similar injunctions found in military or religious organizations. Orders must not only be obeyed, they must be properly carried out. Going through the motions, or hewing to the letter of one's instructions is not enough. This is true even though orders are not detailed or explicit.

8. Promotions and Demotions. Members are promoted in rank—soldier to *capo* to underboss etc.—to fill vacancies created by death, illness, and retirement. The rank of a member who is in prison, however, is kept by him, though his job may be performed by a substitute until he is paroled. At the same time, all members of the same rank are not necessarily equal. A highly successful soldier, for example, may operate a number of different businesses or rackets and have many people working for him. His economic power and influence will tend to make him more important than his technical rank would indicate.

9. Transfers. The majority of members spend their lives within the same family or group. The rules and traditions encourage this loyalty. Under special circumstances, though, there can be a transfer to a family in another jurisdiction.

10. All arguments to higher authority. Most of the disputes that are important enough to go to higher authority involve business practices, sales territories, new operations and the like.

11. Always be a stand-up guy. A "stand-up guy" is by definition, a man who lives by the rules and, if necessary, will die for them. He keeps his mouth shut to the police, he puts the organization ahead of himself, he respects the families of others. He is a man of honor who can be relied on. In the parlance of those in the Confederation he "has character," he is true to the code. In other words, the injunction, be a stand-up guy epitomizes what the code says a real man should be.

12. Justice. The law is the basis for the administration of justice, which is handled within each family. The authority for judgments comes down from the boss in the same way that it might from the village chief of a primitive tribe. The boss, however, does not personally preside except in very serious cases.[5]

---

[5] Salerno and Tompkins, 1969, pp. 111–128.

All these attempts to define the "code of the *Mafia*" are based on a fundamental, unproven assumption—for there to be a single "code" which covers *all* Italian-American criminal syndicates, there must be a single national organization. Any code of rules must be derived from some shared set of values; the only way *the* "code of the *Mafia*" could exist would be in the context of a unified organization. Cressey, Salerno, and the others assume that such an organization exists. We found no evidence for it in our study of the Lupollo family and our data are limited to what we were able to see and hear. Thus we have investigated the code of the Lupollos, *not* the code of the *Mafia*. Our method was to observe and record behavior and then to seek regularities that had enough frequency to suggest that the behavior resulted from the pressures of the shared social system rather than from idiosyncratic behavior. We also questioned family members and others about rules, usually by asking why some member of the family behaved in a particular way. Thus, our reconstruction of rules of conduct comes both from our own observations and from the explanations of observed behavior given by the people living under those rules.

In the Lupollo family as in the card game of bridge, there are two levels of the rules. There are game or ground rules, which structure the game, and then there are informal rules for playing the game intelligently. Similarly, in the Lupollo family there are those basic rules which structure the framework of acceptable conduct, and those supplementary rules which define who plays the game well and who plays it poorly. We found three basic ground rules for behavior in the Lupollo family: (1) primary loyalty is vested in "family" rather than in individual lineages or nuclear families, (2) each member of the family must "act like a man" and do nothing which brings disgrace on the family, and (3) family business is privileged matter and must not be reported or discussed outside the group. These three rules are basic for maintaining membership within the group, but each subsumes a number of informal rules which explain why some members are more successful at the game than others.

The Lupollo Code of Conduct

Rule 1. Loyalty to the Family. Several studies of family structure among Italians both in the United States and overseas have reported that what seems at first an *extended family*—a unit which extends horizontally and vertically to include all kin in a socially and economically self-sufficient unit—is actually an *expanded family,* nuclear families in separate households who maintain close social relationships but do not function as an integrated economic unit.[6]

---

[6] Cf. Donald Pitkin, "Land Tenure and Farm Organization in an Italian Village," Unpublished Ph.D. Dissertation, Harvard University, 1954, p. 114; Herbert Gans, *The*

Among the impoverished peasants in the south of Italy, this has always been a matter of necessity rather than choice. Poverty and the scarcity of land precluded any holdings large enough to sustain extended families except among the nobility or land-owning classes. When the peasant migrated, the new conditions of his life also precluded common residence or joint economic enterprise for the vast majority. The Lupollo family, however, while they live as separate households, are an integrated extended family in every sense. They are economically and socially self-sufficient and do not venture far outside the family group. Friends of individual members either become part of the family circle or are seen only occasionally.

It is to the extended Lupollo family (which includes the Alcamo, Salemi, and Tucci lineages) that primary loyalty is given. On the surface, at least, this loyalty supercedes loyalty to lineage and even to individual nuclear families, and is expressed in a number of ways. Members speak of the family as a unit; they are almost completely dependent on friendship, business, and social relations within the family circle; they tend to settle in physical proximity to other family members. Most fundamentally, however, this loyalty finds expression in the closeness that members feel for the family and for one another.

Once Bobby Lupollo and I talked about how close members of the family were with one another. Bobby had remarked that he thought running was better exercise than basketball, that he was going to mention this to his cousin Freddy, and that perhaps Freddy and Bobby could then get Tommy and Paulie to start jogging in a "running club." I asked Bobby why it was that he usually thought of his relatives whenever he mentioned starting some new social or business venture:

> Our family is very close like all Italian families, but ours is even closer than most. Ever since I could remember everything we did was done together. If I decided that I wanted to go to the circus, my father [Joey Lupollo] would get Tommy or Freddy to go with us, too. Even when we were dating we used to go to the same places together. I was Tommy's best man when he was married and he was mine. When I was in college I was a pledge in a fraternity —no, two different fraternities—but never became a brother because I didn't have anything in common with the other fellows. Even now that we are married we go out together, not because our wives get along together so well— they don't and Linda [Bobby's wife] is always after me to make new friends. It's because we were raised more like brothers than like cousins. Look, I can stand naked in front of you [we were in the dressing room at an athletic club] and I can stand naked in front of my wife but I can't stand naked in front of the two of you, not without all of us feeling ashamed or my wife saying that

Urban Villagers, Glencoe: The Free Press, 1962, pp. 45–46; and Philip Garigue and Raymond Firth, "Kinship Organization of Italianates in London," in Raymond Firth (ed.), *Two Studies in Kinship in London,* London: Athlone Press, 1956, p. 74.

I'm some kind of a crude guinea bastard. It's something like that with my cousins. I can say and do things in front of them that I wouldn't say or do even in front of my wife, because we're close. If I find a good business deal or see a movie that I like I always think about how they would like it too. We're a family that believes in sticking together. All Italians are that way but when it comes to business we're more like Jews than like Italians. I know that if I tell Tommy about a good deal he'll remember me when he finds a good one. Even my father is that way with Pete Tucci and he doesn't like him too much.

As Bobby's remarks indicate, the bonds which we normally associate with the nuclear family are, among the Lupollos, generalized beyond, into the extended family relationship which has been produced by the merger of personal and social interests with economic interests. This comforting sense of family is accepted by all of the fifteen members of the central family. Basil Alcamo—with Paulie, the most alienated from the family—often explains business or social arrangements which run counter to his own idea of good practice by the phrase "it's in the family." He resents Joe's old-fashioned business ideas, but he never expresses any thought of striking out on his own, nor does he refuse to go along with what he considers bad deals arranged by Joe. He protests, but only toward his "brothers" in his same age-grade rather than to Joe and his peers or to the younger family members, and he eventually accepts the decision like any dutiful "son." How much he complains to his father, Phil, and whether Phil is responsive to his complaints has not been determined; but publicly he submits to the family authority structure just as other members do. Paulie, on the other hand, never protests openly. In private conversation, however, he complained to me of the favoritism shown the Lupollo and Alcamo lineages at the expense of the Salemis.

One revealing deviation from the injunction to maintain family loyalty occurred when Freddy married Monica, a woman of Irish descent, against his parents' wishes. Soon after their marriage in 1967, they began socializing with her friends and their husbands. By 1968, the "defection" had become a problem in the family. The family's reaction included harsh and biting comments about Monica, her ancestry, and Freddy's lack of masculinity in letting her "lead him around by the balls." Their extra-familial friendships were frowned upon. Phil Alcamo commented that whenever the women of the family gathered they talked of Monica and her airs. According to Phil, who got the information secondhand from his wife (who is also non-Italian), the women's comments ranged from "she thinks we're not good enough for her" to speculation that Monica was not interested in her friends, but in their husbands. Freddy's mother bore the brunt of the collective displeasure. Finally, in exasperation and embarrassment, she would join in the chorus of disapproval and her most caustic comment was always ". . . she says she wants to give me respect, I don't need respect from her, I'm not her mother." This pressure had its effect. Freddy and Monica began turning more toward the family and gradually dropped their outside associations. After that, Phil thought Monica was not so bad "for an Irish."

The rule of loyalty to the family includes a number of subsidiaries. The most important among these is "no outside business interests which might conflict with the family." Here are two situations exemplifying this rule and its application.

In early 1968, Tony Lupollo bought a tract of land on the Toms River in New Jersey, and planned to build a motel-marina. Although the land had been purchased through Brooklyn Eagle Realty, Tony's business venture was a private one. By early 1969, ground had been broken for the motel and some of the marina piers had already been built. Then, in the summer of 1969, trouble developed over the township's zoning ordinances. News of the difficulty reached Joe Lupollo. Joe was furious at Tony both because his own interests in New Jersey would be jeopardized by any dispute involving a member of the family, and because, according to Phil, "Tony never had the balls or the head to tell his father he was doing it." Later in 1969, Phil said that Tony had sold the land at a loss and that a good way "to get his ass up" would be to ask him when the motel would be finished.

The second incident took place in early 1970, and involved Joe's son Marky, who is considered to be a poor judge of business. Marky decided that since New York was without an Italian discotheque, whoever started one would make a killing. For weeks he talked of nothing but how he would set it up, with Italian singing stars and rock groups coming over to play, and how people of all ages would flock to it. One night at dinner, Marky commented on the possibility of getting a well-known Italian singer to come over for the opening of the club, which he had already named "The Villa." Joe turned to him and said (in Italian), "I don't want to hear anymore about the club, now or ever again." Later, Phil Alcamo explained that "anyone with any sense should realize that a nightclub is the one sure way of getting into trouble, since all kinds of bums go to nightclubs and just like Joe Namath you can find yourself associated with people you don't know and who don't owe you anything." His mother (Phil said) had always told him that "if you go around with a cripple you learn to limp." Marky never mentioned "The Villa" again.

A second subsidiary to the rule of family loyalty calls for mutual aid to other family members. There are no status differences in who can call upon whom for aid. In the two years of this study, there were situations in which a member with high prestige called upon a lower-prestige member for help, as well as those in which a high-prestige member helped a person with lower prestige. The explanation is always given in terms of family. For example,

Phil gave several thousand dollars to Tony after the motel-marina fiasco. When his son Basil took him to task, pointing out that Tony could have gotten it from his father and that gratitude was not one of Tony's outstanding virtues, Phil answered simply, "he's family, Basil, how can I say no?"

A third subsidiary rule says, "Don't interfere in the business of another family member." It is an expression of the security which comes with family membership. In its most basic form, it is the insurance which goes with knowing that others will not interfere in one's best interest so long as you do not give them cause to distrust you. The rule is expressed in many ways. Pete Tucci is the best example within the family of the importance of "playing the game" properly in this area. He has no base of power other than his relationship with his father-in-law, Joe Lupollo. Since none of his children have gone into the family business, he has no paternal relationship which would allow him to call on others for support, and yet the vulnerability of his position obviously does not worry him. His role in managing the food-processing sector of the family business is an important and lucrative one, which would be profitable to any other member—better connected—who craved it. Yet, so long as Pete does not try to move into someone else's area, he is secure. No one really thinks very highly of him—he is considered little more than "Joe's boy" in the business—but he does not have the role of isolate. He is *a member of the family,* and as long as he gives it his first loyalty he enjoys its collective security.

The basic rule of loyalty to the family over all else and the subsidiary rules which define the way to use the rule to one's best advantage give the family a group solidarity against anyone or anything outside the family. While the younger members of the family do not seem to show it as belligerently as their parents and grandparents, it is still an important behavior guide for them. They are known in the Italian-American community as members of the family, and without exception they see the future of that organization as their own.

The rule of loyalty does not ensure smooth social relationships within the family. There are squabbles, and rivalries, and cliques, and the various lineages do stick together; but the family as a unit absorbs these differences and continues to function. When there are attacks from outside the group, the force of family cohesion comes into play and the divisions disappear.

Not all members of the family use the rules equally well. Those with high respect or prestige show more awareness of and conformity to the subsidiary rules than those with low respect or prestige. Only when someone seems to be ignoring the rule of loyalty itself, as when Freddy began finding new friends and when Tony got involved in the potentially troublesome motel-marina, is the question of loyalty raised. Marky's desire to start the Italian nightclub was simply considered foolish and everyone could laugh at it; Freddy and Tony actually lost some respect as a result of their actions, and group pressure was exerted to bring them back into line.

Rule 2. *"Act Like a Man."* The concept of "being a man" goes by many names in the Lupollo family. At various times it is expressed as "being a stand-up guy," or "having balls." At the same time, however, the notion of being a man carries with it a distinct sense of humility and willingness to accept decisions, even when they are troublesome to ego, without resort to complaints, whines, or other unmanly actions. In fact, the rule of being a man seems so close to the concept of *omertà* found in the south of Italy that it is tempting to assume that *omertà* is its origin. To one who has watched both systems in operation, however, it is logical to conclude that both *omertà* and the injunction to be a man are part of the social contract created when a group of men bond themselves together in a secret society. In such bonding, the alliance demands that each man depend on the others in the group to pro-tect their common interest, and to act like a man in the company of other men.

The importance of being a man within the Lupollo family is part of the code for each generation, and no one escapes its demands. But the demands differ according to one's status in the family. Generally, the higher the status the more important it is to present a public image of self-control, willingness to accept decisions, and interpersonal power which demands respect from others. Being a man is also mediated in non-"business" relationships. Joe Lupollo, for example, is stern and authoritarian even with his grandchildren in all matters related to the family business, but he is permitted to show grandfatherly concern for them in social and personal relationships even in public. The younger members of the family have learned to read the particular role he is playing and to react accordingly. Freddy, for example, will actually tease his grandfather about his old-fashioned suits and shoes in front of other members of the Lupollo lineage, but whenever members of other lineages or persons outside the family are present he is respectful and correct in relations with Joe. This same pattern of situational determination of the content of the requirement to be a man is true throughout the family between father and son, godfather and godson, and brothers.

In many ways, the behavior involved is similar to the Chinese or Oriental concept of "face." That is, just as "losing face" is a much more obvious and observable social and behavioral feature than gaining it, so those behaviors and group reactions which appear when someone is *not* being a man are more obvious in the Lupollo family than the behaviors and reactions appear-ing when someone *is*. In this negative aspect, it appears that being a man has two different dimensions, one primarily social and one primarily personal. The social aspect of being a man is part of the awarding of respect within the family and, while it does characterize family members to outsiders, it is much more obvious and important within the group itself. It is the *groups'* valuation of the individual member in terms of how they define him as a man worthy of trust and so respect. Since group functioning depends on mutual trust and confidence that other family members will perform in ways appropriate to being a man, behaviors which are not so defined can cause serious problems for the individual and the group. During this study, only one incident occurred which approached a loss of respect and consequent loss of status for a family member. Early in 1969, Joe's son Marky evidently entered into a business arrangement with Albert Cuccio, who is a cousin of Dominick Maisano of the East Harlem De Maio family. Marky kept it from his father and other members of the family. In the spring of that year Marky left for Florida and did not return until late June. One of the younger members of the family told me that Marky had gone away for a while because his father was so furious with him that it was best to "keep out of the old man's sight" for a while. Joe was particularly upset because Cuccio was reputedly involved in the drug trade, and thus Marky had possibly compromised the family by being seen with Cuccio. What made matters worse for Marky was that he had behaved badly when confronted by his father and his Uncle Charley. Marky apparently tried to implicate his brother Joey and refused to take responsibility for his own actions. Evidently just being seen with Cuccio was sufficiently dangerous that his subsequent refusal to admit his error was viewed as cowardly and disruptive of family discipline. Marky's son Tommy was particularly upset, because some of the criticism spilled over to him.

While we have little information on even this case of loss of status within the group as a result of behavior contrary to the requirement to be a man, we venture to suggest these rules: (1) loss of respect within the group can come from behavior defined as contrary to the requirement to "be a man" and (2) such loss reaches beyond the individual to affect his closest relatives and associates. Being a man in this collective sense means earning and keeping the respect and trust of one's associates. In the case just described, Marky violated the first rule of family loyalty by endangering the group through association with a reputed drug baron and then, having been discovered, did not accept the responsibility for his actions and lost the respect of his fellows for not acting like a man.

There is a second dimension to being a man which is personal in that it is part of an individual's "reputation." While the social aspect of being a man is essentially internal to the group and suggests that the individual can be depended upon to behave in a fashion which will not bring danger or disgrace to the group, the reputational aspect of being a man is much more a matter of his image outside the family. In earlier chapters some of these external "reputations" were described—Freddy's being a "ladies' man" and

Phil Alcamo's being an "astute political animal." Such reputational aspects of "being a man" can change without any great effect on the person's role within the family, for they are part of the individual's role in the *external* environment. They can be enhanced or diminished, changed by personal effort or clever maneuvering, and even borrowed through association with the right people. The social aspect of being a man, however, is not only defined within the group, it is maintained or lost as a whole. After Marky returned from Florida, his position within the group seemed to have diminished to the point that it created serious personal and social difficulties for him.

The reputational aspect of the injunction to be a man is supported in family legendry by numerous oft-told tales of family members or their associates who have shown that peculiar combination of personal courage mixed with humility which is defined as being a man. In one such story, the protagonist, a relative of the Salemi lineage who was known as *"Don Cece,"* was picked up by the police in front of one of the storefront social clubs in Greenwich Village for questioning. One of the police officers, a detective inspector, knew enough about the importance of respect in the world of the families that he decided to shame *Don Cece* (who was then in his early sixties) by having two patrolmen beat him to the ground and handcuff his hands behind his back. When they lifted him to his feet, his face was bloody and his glasses had been knocked off onto the sidewalk. One of the patrolmen, somewhat abashed by what he had done, picked up the glasses and started to put them back on *Don Cece's* nose, but *Don Cece* turned his head aside and said (in Italian for the benefit of his audience), "I have seen and remembered all I need to this morning." The Lupollos always tell the story in the same manner that second- and third-generation Italian-Americans tell tales of their immigrant forebears' courage, endurance, and simplicity in face of the adversity of the ghetto. Here, however, the moral is very obviously not the stoic perseverance of the peasant immigrant but the refusal of someone in a family to allow himself and so his family to be publicly shamed.

Rule 3. The Rule of Secrecy. The third set of conduct rules fit under the basic rule that family business matters are privileged and are not to be reported or discussed outside the group. An obvious reason for secrecy in the Lupollo family is their involvement in illegal activities. But even in the legitimate business enterprises the degree of secrecy goes beyond that found in other business organizations. This could be explained by the linkages between the illegal and legal activities, except that secrecy extends even beyond legitimate business activities, to include the social and personal behavior of individual members of the family. This extension of secrecy is manifest in a number of characteristic behaviors among family members. The most obvious is that family members use a jargon made up of words and phrases which have meaning only to family members. Some of the "code" refers to business activities. The family-controlled Absford Linen Service, for example, is always called "the Long Island place" or "Vince's place" (Vincent Corallo is the owner of record) in conversation. The same approach is used with personnel; Vincent Corallo is referred to as "the fellow in Long Island" or "Patsy's brother-in-law." But the jargon carries over into all conversation, and even when social or kinship relations are being discussed the same descriptive terms are used. In addition, in the second and third generations (but less so in the fourth generation), Italian and Sicilian words and phrases are used in their original meanings as part of a conversation in English. Marky, for example, might say to Patsy, "I know that guy from meeting him a couple of years ago and he is a real *cafone* (idiot)." The use of Italian and Sicilian terms in English sentences is not an uncommon practice among other Italian-Americans of the same generations, but here it combines with the use of jargon to provide a shared language which serves to protect the conversation from those not part of the group.

There is another function of secrecy in the Lupollo family beyond concealing or obscuring information. In Sicilian *Mafie,* the differentiation of individuals as members or outsiders is one of the purposes of secrecy. Those individuals who share the secrets are fellow members; those who do not are outsiders. Secrecy in this sense serves as a bonding mechanism among the members of the group. Not only does it assign individuals to a membership or outsider status, it establishes a comaraderie among group members. In the Lupollo family, this shared sense of membership excludes those members of the various lineages who are not part of the family business and all female members of the lineages as well. Rosa Parone, who is Phil Alcamo's sister and operates the family-related Melrose Cigarette Company, is the only woman who has any contact with any of the family businesses, and most of the actual business operation is actually handled by her son James. Even the brothers and sisters of members are excluded. Usually, where one part of a group joins together and agrees to hold certain secrets in common, the action invites hostility from those who are not members. In the Lupollo family, however, this does not seem to be so.

Finally, secrecy serves as a means of establishing and maintaining dominance and social distance not only between family members and nonmembers but within the family as well. Some secrets are more secret than others, and are shared by only some members of the group. In part this circumstance relates to the structure of authority in the family. Joe Lupollo and his brother Charley have access to all family information; some they share with other members, but some they do not. In part the differentiation is an outgrowth of the relationship between the respect-rating structure of the group and secrecy. There are some members of the family who enjoy low respect and do not have access to as many secrets. But in part it is also the natural result of the various power networks, which make for greater confidentiality among some members than others. In the Lupollo family, despite the cardinal importance of the basic rule that loyalty to the family comes before loyalty to lineage, there seems little question that, for example, Phil Alcamo and his son Basil share a father–son confidentiality, as do Joe Lupollo and his favorite son Joey.

Every business organization has secrets of some kind. Business practices, tactics, and strategy to some degree are always private and privileged information. A difference in the Lupollo family business, however, is that the rule of secrecy is more inclusive than in most business operations, and violations are considered independent acts against the collective welfare of the group. The injunction against disclosure of information is not specific to the illegal sectors of the business operations, but cover virtually all areas of the family operations. The preferred behavior is not just reluctance to disclose business secrets which might aid competitors, but complete silence in the face of any inquiries, formal or informal, official or private, about business affairs. In a sense, then, this rule reflects not only the businessman's reluctance to make business matters public, but also the strength of the bond among family members which defines all others as "outsiders." Here again it is the kinship bond, both real and fictive, which effectively serves as the basis of enforcement; to violate the injunctions against disclosure of information is not a bad business practice, it is an act of disloyalty to the family. And family in this context excludes wives, those members of the various lineages who are not directly involved in the family business, and all others.

Enforcing Rules of Conduct

Rules of conduct are meant to be enforced, and a system of sanctions always has to be established. Previous studies of organized crime have stressed the coercive sanctions or the allocation of punishments, including death, as the principal means of control in Italian-American criminal syndicates. It would be naïve to suggest that such sanctions do not exist in the Lupollo family, but this study did not produce any evidence of them. Within the family, the canon of reciprocity forms the motive force behind rules of conduct. Individuals within the group have obligations toward others and, in turn, have expectations concerning how others will relate to them. Because the group is small and close primary relationships exist within the group, violations of the rules of conduct are not frequent. Where they do occur, they tend to be idiosyncratic behaviors rather than outright disobedience. This shared understanding of what is right and what is wrong in terms of behavior keeps conflict over rules at a minimum. And, since in groups of this type rules tend to be enforced only when something provokes enforcement, it is usually sufficient for the offending behavior to become public within the group for behavior to become appropriate once again. Thus in the examples of rule violation we described earlier—Freddy's turning outside the family for friendship and the actions of Patsy and Marky that jeopardized the welfare of the group—it was sufficient for group attention to be focused on the violations. There are, however, some members of the family who blow the whistle on infractions of rules with some consistency. Joe Lupollo, as head of the family, seldom intervenes except when his anger is aroused—as when he felt Marky was behaving foolishly in attempting to open a nightclub—or where an infraction is of such magnitude that his authority is questioned. Generally, Charley Lupollo questions the behavior of other family members. Usually this is done publicly without much rancor, as any uncle or father might do in a traditional Italian-American family. What is different is that Charley takes the initiative for citing rule infractions in every area of behavior, from business practices to social protocol, and he acts in the name of his brother Joe. This surrogate position is obvious both in his approach to the erring family member and in the reaction of the miscreant. Charley will, for example, chide Patsy for being late to some gathering and suggest that Joe expected everyone to be there on time. Patsy's response will differ depending on whether Joe is scheduled to be there or not; in neither case, however, will Charley pursue the point. He lets his suggestion that Joe will be offended serve as warning enough.

In addition to Charley, Phil Alcamo and Joey Lupollo are also frequent critics of rule violators. Phil usually cites rule violations on the part of members of the next lower generation in the family—Patsy, Marky, Basil and so on—while Joey reserves his criticism for the younger members of the group, who are also his next-generation relatives. Our limited experience with rule violation and consequent enforcement makes it difficult to differentiate rule enforcers in the family with any certainty, but it seems that Charley's role as Joe's surrogate is a fairly formal one, while Phil is acting as an informal rule enforcer as a result of his age and respect ranking in the group. Joey, on the other hand, acts both in his role as heir-apparent and as the role model for his younger relatives within the family.

8 / Familialism and the Organization and Control of Italian-American Crime Families

When we undertook this study we were interested in looking at an organized-crime family as a social system, to see whether we could discover some system of order or code of rules that described organization and social control within such groups. In this chapter we pull together the code of rules we constructed by observing behavior in the Lupollo family, and from this code we draw some conclusions about how this family is organized and controlled. But we also go beyond the specific data on the Lupollo family and attempt to relate these rules back to the cultural patterns they share with south Italians here and abroad, and offer some speculations about the nature and structure of similar crime families. We will be arguing throughout this chapter that it is the bonds of kinship—not crime or some network of conspiracy— which tie the Lupollos and other Italian-American crime families together, and to one another. By now the reader has had many opportunities, both in looking at *Mafie* in Sicily and in watching the Lupollos at work and leisure, to draw this conclusion himself. We will, however, offer some additional data on other Italian-American crime families in support of this position.

Italian-American Crime Families as Formal Organizations

As a formal organization, the Lupollo family is a business empire made up of a number of legal and illegal enterprises which mesh into a structure of business corporations, investments, tactics, and personnel like any other corporate enterprise. The only difference is that unlike other business organizations, the Lupollo family earns a portion of its income from illegal activities.

Like all organizations, the Lupollo family is structured to facilitate those goals which its members hold in common. And like all organizations, its structure can seem very different depending on what one is looking for and what one manages to see. Most students of Italian-American criminal syndicates have viewed them as formal organizations and so have studied them as if they were business or governmental organizations. The result, we think, has been to distort the nature of Italian-American criminal syndicates and the way they operate. The formal-organization approach provides insight into only a part of the whole.

In current social science usage, a formal organization is defined as a social unit which has been deliberately designed and constructed to achieve a set of specified goals.[1] It has certain characteristics such as a division of labor, a distribution of power, and a network of communications, but these are also found in other human groupings such as tribes, social classes, and families. What makes it a distinctive unit in society is that it is rationally designed and constructed rather than randomly or traditionally patterned, and it has the ability to reconstruct itself—repattern its structure, transfer or substitute personnel, and reorder its priorities—to increase its efficiency in realizing its goal. Actually, tribes and even families can do all of these things too, but these capabilities are consciously designed into the formal organization; it is this ability to plan and control its own destiny which defines the formal organization and sets it apart in the scheme of human groupings.

Government law enforcement agencies and their consultants have insisted that Italian-Americans have, in part, created just such a formal organization. Donald Cressey, for example, writes:[2]

> When there are specialized but integrated positions for a board of directors, presidents, vice-presidents, staff specialists, work managers, foremen and workers, there is an economic organization. When there are judges, and administrators of criminal justice, there is a political organization. Like the large legitimate corporations which it resembles, *Cosa Nostra* has both kinds of positions, making it both a business organization and a government. Further, *Cosa Nostra* exists independently of its current personnel occupying the various positions making up the organization. If a president, vice-president or some other functionary dies or resigns, another person is recruited to fill the vacant position. No man is indispensable. Organization, or "structure," not persons, gives *Cosa Nostra* its self-perpetuating character.

Fitting the available data about Italian-American crime families into this "formal organization" framework, however, has given a bureaucratic characterization to descriptions of how Italian-American criminal syndicates are organized. The model that is described is a parody of the American corporate organization. Cressey's *Cosa Nostra* seems not much different from the Bell Telephone System, except that the services of *Cosa Nostra* are described as "illicit" and its ultimate aim as the corruption of "the basic economic and political traditions and institutions" of the country.

Like the Bell System, *Cosa Nostra* is described as "a nationwide . . . cartel . . . dedicated to amassing millions of dollars" through the provisions of serv-

---

[1] Talcott Parsons, *The Social System,* Glencoe, Ill.: The Free Press, 1951, p. 17.
[2] Donald R. Cressey, *Theft of the Nation,* New York: Harper and Row, 1969, p. 110.

ices to the public. It is described by the President's Commission on Law Enforcement and the Administration of Justice[3] as a confederation of local syndicates or "companies" which function with some independence at the local level, but are subject to corporate policy decisions by a "national Commission" which, structurally, at least, sounds like a board of directors. Just as "Ma" Bell rules over a family of local companies all of which provide the same service to their communities, so *Cosa Nostra* is said to be made up of local units differentiated only by territoriality, for each can "participate in the full range of activities of organized crime." Like any large corporation, this organization "continues to function regardless of personnel changes" because *Cosa Nostra*'s local organizations are "rationally designed with an integrated set of positions geared to maximize profits." The descriptions of the local units or families continue the analogy in terms of positions, functions, and authority structure. The position of *caporegime* in the *Cosa Nostra*, for example, "is analogous to plant supervisor or sales manager" in a business organization and the "underboss" is "the vice-president or deputy director." And the Bell System, *Cosa Nostra* is said to maintain contacts with its counterparts overseas.

Secret societies such as the *Mafia*, however, are not really formal organizations in the sense that the President's commission describes them. They are not rationally designed and consciously constructed; they are responsive to culture and are patterned by tradition. They are not hierarchies of organizational positions which can be diagrammed and then changed by recasting the organization chart; they are patterns of relationship among individuals which have the force of kinship, and so they can only be changed by drastic, often fatal, action. Secret criminal groups such as *Mafia* and *Camorra* are not formal organizations; they are traditional social systems. We do not mean that they are disorganized or even unstructured; our point is that they are structured by action rather than by a series of statuses and that like any social system, they have no structure apart from their functioning.

Kinship and Social Organization in the Lupollo Family

From our field data on the Lupollo family's business and social structure, we have developed two sets of rules which present a somewhat different perspective on the organization of crime families. One set of rules has to do with the family's increasing movement, over a seventy-year period, into legitimate business—a movement accompanied by substantial changes in the organization of the family's legitimate and illegitimate enterprises. Old Giuseppe seems

---

[3] All exemplary quotations in this paragraph are taken from The President's Commission on Law Enforcement and Administration of Justice, *Task Force Report: Organized Crime,* Washington, D.C.: Government Printing Office, 1967.

to have started the process as soon as he arrived. To accomplish it, he established one paramount rule—he relied only on kinsmen, relatives whose loyalty to the family was assured through blood or marriage.

We were also able to trace historically, as well as to observe in action, a second set of rules which regulate the organizational structure of the family, and assign individuals within the organization:

1. The family operates as a social unit with social organization and business functions merged.
2. All leadership positions, down to the "middle management" level are assigned on the basis of kinship.
3. The higher the position in the organization, the closer the kinship relationship.
4. Leadership positions in the family are assigned to a central group of fifteen family members, all of whom have close consanguineal or affinal relationships which are reinforced by fictive godparental relationships as well.
5. Members of this leadership group are assigned primarily to either legal or illegal enterprises, but not both.
6. Transfer of monies from illegal to legal and back into illegal activities takes place through individuals rather than companies and is part of the close kin-organization of the family.

The first four of these rules are the most important in organizing the family as a social system. Considered as a set of guides to behavior, they summarize the pattern of relatedness among members which holds the system together and gives it a distinctive character. They tie individuals to each other and to the family in a mutuality of rights and obligations which arises out of a pattern of social relationships, and not a formal organization of statuses. Each of these rules also confirms the assumption we made earlier, and the major implication of our study of the Lupollo family: kinship and the pattern of rights and obligations associated with kinship relations are the bases of the social order of this system. Not only is kinship the basis for organization, it also serves as the most important factor in differentiating roles within the family, and it establishes the hierarchical relationships among these roles as well. As one indication of the effectiveness of this kinship bond in welding the Lupollo business empire into a familial social system, it is important to note again that not only are all members of the fifteen-member core group cognates or affines, they have bound themselves together even more closely by establishing new bonds of godparenthood which are then sealed by a sacred act. Numerous other indications of the kin-centered character of the Lupollo family have emerged throughout our account of the behavior and social relationships of the members as individuals, as members of a group and as part of a larger network of real and ritual kinsmen.

The family is a quasi-corporate being, and the individual must always subjugate his desires, plans, and ambitions to it. For the fifteen members of the core group, there is no loyalty save to the family; the individual does not exist except as part of the group. Even among the supervisory personnel—those who report directly to the core members—kinship plays a major role. In the legal businesses of the family empire, relatives near and distant are always given preference for positions and promotion in this supervisory circle. The relative who does well moves up rapidly in the organization and those who do not are at least always assured a job. There seems to be less nepotism in the illegal aspects of the business, but this is a more recent development. The various lineages which make up the family have begun to shun crime as a career. In old Giuseppe's day, this area of the family's interests was operated by relatives, and at present the central management is still in the hands of the kindred Salemis. In the third level of the family, the lower-level supervisory or specialist positions, kinship is also important and recruitment usually comes about by knowing some member of one of the lineages or, even better, being related to one no matter how distantly. The Lupollo family organization *feels* like a kinship-structured group; familialism founded it and is still its stock in trade. One senses immediately not only the strength of the bond, but the inability of members to see any morality or social order larger than their own.

The origins of this familialism are Italian and not American. In the south of Italy, as we have seen, the family is the basis of the social order. The primary value there is honor, which, like the individual, is inseparable from the family. To be honorable means that no member of one's family has brought disgrace to the family; any blot on the honor of an individual is a stain on the corporate honor of the family. For the Lupollos, southern Italian familialism seems to have had a particular importance in establishing and shaping the business and gambling empire which marks them as an organized-crime family.

Extending the Family. Every commentator on the culture of the *Mezzogiorno* agrees that the family is the basic core of its social structure, that it reaches out to include in an arc of relationships the full range of affinal and consanguineal relatives (*i parenti*), and that nuclear families and lineages within this bounded network are tied to each other in a web of honor. Within this network of mutual responsibility, however, it is still the nuclear family which is the basic social unit, and the network of extended kin is really a ceremonial and customary association of *economically* independent groups of parents and their children.[4] The extended family in the south of Italy is an

---

[4] See, for example, the reports of Donald Pitkin, "Land Tenure and Farm Organization in an Italian Village," Unpublished Ph.D. Dissertation, Harvard University, 1954, p. 119.

ideal, a dream of a widespread clan of mutually helpful and protective relatives who work together for the common good and who are held together in a
oneness of feeling and organization by the blood relationship which alone can
be trusted. Like so many of the dreams of the *Mezzorgiorno,* however, it has
always been kept out of the reach of the poor by the harsh social and economic
realities of the region. For some, the aristocracy and landed classes, it was
possible; but for most, the nuclear, neolocal family oriented to a wider, loosely
associated system of kindred lineages was the best that could be realized.

This dream of the cohesive extended family survived emigration, and in
fact, like so many imported values, it gained through nostalgia. Virtually every student of first- and second-generation Italian American life points out
that the immigrant family was extended to include those kindred here and,
to a lesser extent, those who remained behind.[5] Here, the added threats of a
strange and alien land reinforced the recognition of a formal code of rights
and obligations among kin and newly arrived migrants sought out their kinsmen for jobs and homes. But even in America, the ideal of the closely knit,
socially and economically integrated extended family remained illusory. Virtually all the peasant immigrants joined the urban proletariat, and each nuclear family barely eked out its own existence. As in Italy, the kindred remained at best a ceremonial network of associated relatives who exchanged
visits, gathered together at all important rites of passage such as births,
marriages and funerals, provided hospitality and help when it was needed, but
still worked and lived as independent nuclear families. But for some families—
and the Lupollos are one—success in business, whether legal, illegal, or both,
allowed the realization of the peasant dream: they used their wealth and
power to build a family business patterned on the extended family.

The inability of the peasants of the *Mezzogiorno* to extend their nuclear
families for mutual protection had been one of the primary factors leading to

---

[5] See for example Leonard Covello, "Social Background of the Italo-American
School Child," Ph.D. Dissertation, New York University, 1944, p. 243; Lawrence Pisani,
The Italian in America, A Social Study and History, New York: Exposition Press, 1959,
p. 53; Francis A. J. Ianni, "Residential and Occupational Mobility as Indices of the Acculturation of an Ethnic Group," *Social Forces,* Vol. 36, October 1957, p. 66; and Rudolph
Vecoli, "Contadino in Chicago: A Critique of the Uprooted," *American Journal of History,* Vol. 51, 1964, p. 409.

For a summary of reports on the relationship between the nuclear and extended
family in Italian culture see Constance Cronin, *The Sting of Change,* Chicago: University
of Chicago Press, 1970, pp. 24–27. This same emphasis on the extended family was observed in England in a study of kinship patterns among Italian immigrants: "Among
Italianates, the domestic family of husband-wife, while considered as the basic unit, as in
English kinship, is frequently also part of an extended family or an economic group com-
posed of kin." Philip Garigue and Raymond Firth, *Two Studies of Kinship in London,*
London: Athlone Press, 1956, p. 92.

the development of *mafia*. *Mafia* and other secret criminal societies in the south are in reality attempts to bring a familial order and stability to a chaotic and repressive society. If the social structure of the south of Italy is the family in macrocosm, the *Mafie* are that social structure in microcosm. There was no dissonance between the values of *mafia* and the values of the people, at least not until recently, and it is only as the old values of the south begin to erode that there is any resistance to the control of social and economic life by the *Mafie*. But all this did not begin to happen in Sicily until after the Lupollos, the Alcamos and the Salemis left. For them, the ideal of the extension of the family to include all kin was still paramount in the lexicon of values. By shrewd management of both legal and illegal enterprises, old Giuseppe and his heirs were able to obtain the ideal. Their success has reinforced the value and acted as a cushion between them and the greater society.

Eventually, all four of the basic rules which govern the organization of the Lupollo family—the merging of social and business functions into one kin-centered enterprise; the assignment of leadership positions on the basis of kinship; the correlation between closeness of kin relationship and the hierarchy of positions; and the requirement of close consanguineal or affinal relationship for inclusion in the core group—can be traced back to south Italian culture. When the Lupollo family left Sicily, not only the *Mafie,* but the entire society operated on the basis of these same rules of organization. Old Giuseppe applied them to his business enterprises because they were the only rules he knew, and when they worked here as they had in Sicily, his children and grandchildren found it hard to tell him—and perhaps even to tell themselves—that they were ill conceived for the new American venture. So long as Giuseppe could operate within the protected and protective environment of the ghetto, he could depend on the acceptance of these same values by other Italian-Americans to insure his success. It was not until his success plunged him into the greater society that he had to add new rules (to supplement, not replace, the old ones) to answer to a new set of values and requirements. The Italian-American community was characterized by collective amorality toward extra-familial authority structures; but the outside world defined some parts of his activities as illegal. In kinship and family Giuseppe found his new rules. If the ghetto could no longer contain the Lupollo business enterprise, the extended family could and did. As new enterprises were added, the staffing and necessary transfer of monies was structured by kinship; monies flowed from illegal to legal and back into illegal activities through individuals related by close ties of blood and marriage, who could always be trusted.

We have enough reliable information on the Lupollos to name them a *clan,* an associated group of lineages that have become intricately bound to one another through a network of marriage ties and ritual kin associations, so that they form a social system structured and regulated by the mutual obligations and rights of kindred. When one traces their heritage and history back to Sicily, it seems obvious that things could not have been otherwise. In their world, everyone's status and security is dependent on power, and power is a function of family and kin. It is the family and not the individual that is recognized, dealt with, allied with, and remembered. Even those who are not related see the family-clan model as the only basis for organization; its inner cohesion and its characteristic ability to take on the rest of the world are based upon a kinship model which embraces even those who are not in the true genealogy of the family.

Social Control and Behavioral Systems in the Lupollo Family: A Summary

In studying the Lupollos, we also found three clan-based structures which determine behavior and relate roles to each other: the structure of authority roles, the network of alliances for power, and the ranking system through which respect (prestige) is awarded to various roles and role players. Most obvious of these was the hierarchical structure which defined roles according to how much authority, or legitimate power, the role player was accorded. Among the Lupollos, we found that the assignment of authority roles is largely governed by traditional southern Italian values, such as *generation* and *kinship,* although (as we pointed out earlier) there is also an informal rule regulating authority ranking, not based on traditional values, through which the possession of expertise valuable to the clan's survival increases a member's authority. To summarize our findings:

- The earlier the generation, the higher the rank.
- Within generations, the Lupollo lineage takes precedence over others.
- Specialists (those with valuable expertise) are ranked higher than generalists.

Throughout the Italian-American community, Joe Lupollo is known as the family's undisputed head. The southern Italian values which underlie his authority not only give him the power to command deference and other "following" behaviors from family members, but also make him responsible for holding the clan together as a tightly integrated social-business unit. The tradition-based, kinship-oriented sources for Joe's authority, his ultraconservatism in business and politics, and the fact that he operates entirely within the Italian-American community naturally gives his leadership a highly conservative basis.

Second to Joe in the authority structure is his brother Charley. Within the family, we observed that he functions as the traditional head when Joe is absent, and acts as a go-between on behalf of younger or less powerful members who are afraid to approach Joe directly. Phil Alcamo and Joey Luppollo also occupy high positions in the family's authority ranking. Their authority, based partly on age and kinship, is further enhanced by their specialist qualifications. Charley and Phil serve as the family's political contacts; Joey Lupollo, Phil, and Phil's son Basil are the family's business brains.

The southern Italian cultural values which make Joe the head of the family's authority structure also imply that he should have undisputed *power* within the family's executive group. And he does have the greatest power there. Because of the submissiveness that family members feel for him as traditional, legitimate family head, he is by far the most influential in deciding such power-based matters as the allocation of resources, the selection of goals, and the ordering of business and social life. But while Joe enjoys the greatest control over family decision making, we noticed that his leadership is being eroded by the growth of new sources of power. Joe's power, we saw, lies in the strength of conservative, kinship-oriented, *Mafia*-like values. But these values are no longer vital to the survival of the family, at least not in terms of the family businesses. Rather, as the family moves more and more into the mainstream of American enterprise, it becomes increasingly important for the family to have leaders who are well connected in the political and business "establishments" of the larger society. During the period of study, we noted that Joe's authority—which comes from the articulation of generations in a *vertical,* kinship-based structure—was increasingly challenged by a new set of *horizontal* power alliances which connect certain family members with the "American" power structures.

These new power connections are represented most prominently in the family by Charley and Phil. Without their contacts, the family could not continue to function successfully either in its legitimate or in its illegitimate activities. By providing the vital connections, Charley and Phil amass increasing influence in the family councils, and their influence inevitably challenges the supremacy of Joe's authority. More educated, more "American," more progressive in outlook, they also compete with Joe as role models in the eyes of younger members.

Although the challenge to traditional values and traditional sources of power is still latent, it is becoming more and more obvious, and it brings with it the potential for disruption. We found that two rules were in operation here:

- Where authority and power roles in the family are integrated, a high degree of cohesion and solidarity is produced.
- Where authority and power roles are not integrated (where for example, an individual's power rank exceeds his authority position) there is friction and occasionally conflict.

One result of the conflict between old and new sources of power has been the growth of a network of alliances for power in the family which exists alongside the legitimate authority structure. One of the networks we traced revolved around Joe. Faced with the implicit challenge from Charley and Phil, he seems to have turned to others in the family's executive group—Vito Salemi and Pete Tucci—for support. Both share his orientation to the Italian-American community and his conservative social values; both look to him to preserve the traditional unity of control within the family. With these allies, and with the support of his sons Tony and Marky, and of Vito's son Vic, Joe fortifies his power position in the family.

But if Joe has his power network, Charley and Phil have theirs. Basil Alcamo is closely allied with his father; Patsy Lupollo with his. We noted that in the fourth generation, all the family members save one line up with Charley and Phil, whose life style and power connections they respect more than Joe's tradition-based authoritarianism.

A third power network was also evident—a private network surrounding Joey Lupollo. Though his values would logically lead to an alliance with his uncles Charley and Phil, he offers his allegiance to his father, Joe, whose chosen successor he is. The affiliation with Joe then permits him to offer special favors to younger family members, gaining for himself a network of loyal supporters. Resembling Joey in attitudes and tastes, all four of the fourth-generation family members relate to him easily, and whatever their other affiliations, they are also allied with him.

From the different ways in which Joe, Charley and Phil, and Joey recruit their supporters, we extrapolated these rules of the Lupollo power networks:

- Kinship, real or ritual, remains the most important basis for power alliances, and also forms the basis for legitimating power into authority.
- Mutuality of interests and a common outlook on the family's future also provide motivations for new alliances.
- A system of reciprocal obligations within the family also operates to link individuals to each other and into power alliances.

Given these rules, we feel that Joey Lupollo is in the best position to benefit from the shifting balance of power within the family. Like Charley and Phil, he relates well to the power establishments of the larger socity; unlike them, he is deliberately working to build a network of supporters based on reciprocal obligations. And finally, he is also allied with Joe, whose traditional authority as head of the clan he is slated to inherit.

We found some confirmation of our views on power and authority when we surveyed the family to discover the rules behind the third behavioral structure that determines role relationships—the ranking system which awards different degrees of respect (prestige) to family members. In Italian-American society, as in Italy, respect has traditionally been mediated through age, kinship, authority, and power. Within the Lupollo family, as within Italian-American society in general, we have seen that authority, and to an even greater degree, power, are beginning to outweigh the other standards by which respect is awarded to members of the group. In interviewing members of the family's core group and outsiders who know the family well, we found that most gave Joe Lupollo the highest respect rating. Translated into the terms we have used, their explanation was that Joe, as family head, has greater authority and greater power than any other family member. Phil Alcamo was rated second by most family members, despite the fact that as Joe's surrogate and second in command Charley stands higher in the family's authority structure. Comments made by the raters suggest that Phil's access to national politics outweighs Charley's involvement in city politics in the eyes of family members; because of his connections in Washington, Phil is seen as more powerful.

While outsiders and the older members of the family consistently give Joe the highest respect rating, *younger* members of the family usually reserved the highest respect for Phil, Charley, or Joey. Their explanations—that these men were well connected and able to "get things done"—testify that younger family members are giving increasing weight to utilitarian power as against tradition-based authority. Our findings about how respect is awarded may be summarized as follows:

• Respect is highest where power and authority are linked in one person.
• Where authority and power are not associated with the same role, the role with the greatest power wins the most respect.
• The more recent the generation, the more respect given to power rather than to authority.

Kinship and Social Control in the Lupollo Family. We believe that members of the Lupollo family are sustained in action by the force of kinship rather than driven by fear or motivated by crime. Every one of the rules we learned about how authority, power, and prestige are distributed and behavior is controlled within the family can, we think, be traced ultimately to the clan organization pattern which holds it together. The authority structure which organizes the family vertically is legitimated by tradition and kinship; it is this sense of kin-based legitimacy which allows Joe Lupollo to commit resources to the pursuit of goals in the name of the family. Joe's authority is legitimated by his role as "boss" of the family and business interests of the clan. It is his incumbency in the office assigned him by old Giuseppe that is the basis of this legitimation.

While the new utilitarian power relationships seem non-kinship based to some extent, they are a function of kinship within the family. Among the Lupollos as elsewhere, power within the system is dependent in large measure on developing a network of supporters, followers, and allies who aid the individual in gaining and maintaining followers. Followers are obtained through an alliance system, a network of reciprocal relationships whose members extend and expect to receive mutual assistance and loyalty. In the Lupollo family, the basic social relationships which structure alliance networks are always kinship centered. Each member of a power alliance—and recall that the alliances usually follow lineages—acknowledges his obligation to give some favors to others and to receive them over time. Some individuals in the family are mediators of linkages between the various power alliances, because they link lineages and generations together.

It is true that the new, utilitarian power alliance between Charley Lupollo and Phil Alcamo and their favorable positions in the establishment are in conflict with the kinship structure and authority of the family, but even that alliance is in part the result of kinship. Charley and Phil are brothers-in-law and Phil's lineage connection is through Charley. Their power alliance has led Joe Lupollo to depend increasingly on Vito Salemi, whose real kinship ties are with Joe's son Tony. Vito is important to Joe because his lineage has the strongest kinship ties with other crime families in the New York–New Jersey–Pennsylvania area. As the movement into legitimate business continues and the balance of power shifts more and more toward Charley and Phil, kinship may lose some of its authority. For now, however, Joe Lupollo is firmly in control.

When power and authority are not integrated, there is conflict in any clan-type organization. Here again, the Lupollos behave like any clan. The structure of authority is kinship-based, and challenges to that structure are keenly felt. It is then that the power alliances become obvious, because the underlying obligations are brought to light. When alliances and obligations are integrated, as they are now among the Lupollos, the stable composition and cohesion of the group is greatest and the mutual obligations, while they exist, are less obvious because they have not been called into service in the conflict.

The assignment of respect within the family is also a function of kinship, at least to the extent that for the Lupollos and for the Italian-American community in which they operate, prestige is power based upon reputation rather than reputation based upon power. We found that where authority and power were centered in one individual, prestige ratings were the highest; in the patri-centered Lupollo clan, this is so only when kinship rules are followed in selecting leadership. It is significant that even the role of age as an avenue for gaining prestige in the Lupollo family cannot be separated from the continuation of the kinship-based authority structure. A number of field studies of peasant family structure in Italy have cited the rather hollow respect which is accorded to the aging male in south Italian families and communities.[6]

---

[6] See, for example, Pitkin, 1954, p. 185; and Joseph Lopreato, "Effects of Emmigration on the Social Structure of a Calabrian Community," Ph.D. Dissertation, Yale University, 1960, p. 72. (Later published as *Peasants No More,* San Francisco: Chandler, 1967.)

Constance Cronin, who presents a summary of some of these findings, con-
.cludes from them that:

> The prestige of a working-class man is based on his ability to support a family,
> and when this activity ceases so does his prestige . . . the ebbing of his strength
> presages the diminution of his male role.[7]

A recent article by a writer who has lived for twenty years in Italy also
supports this view of the aged both in Italy and among Italian-Americans:

> The longer I lived among the Italians, the more I saw that their large families
> treat their old like those insects that paralyze grubs with a sting and then store
> them up in their nests. The old are cared for, but they are not allowed to do
> anything. . . . The old have no golf; they have no tennis, not even the pen-
> sioner's pat-ball version. They may be allowed a dip in the sea at the highest
> of high summer, but should they strike out beyond the rollers, the family will
> line up on the beach and start shouting desperately.[8]

Given this attitude toward aging males in south Italian culture, the respect shown for older men in the Lupollo family is probably a function of their
ability to maintain power rather than any veneration for the old. We found
ample evidence that this is true. The somewhat contemptuous attitude of the
youngest members of the family for Joe does not lead them to revolt against
his authority. In part this fact results from Joe's strength and power alliances
with Vito Salemi and Pete Tucci. But to some extent it must also be associated
with the kinship bonds within the clan; someday Joe will pass on his authority
to another relative in the Lupollo lineage, to which all of the younger members belong.

The roles we found within the organization also seem to be a function of
kin relationship. Joe Lupollo occupies the one position we are certain of in
the clan-business enterprise, that of *capo famiglia* or what has been called
boss in organized-crime terminology. Charley Lupollo, we think, because
he is Joe's younger brother, occupies the position of mediator between Joe
and other members of the family, again a role which seems somewhat similar
in function to the positions of underboss and *consigliere* in the classical
descriptions of *Cosa Nostra* organization. The other role we identified was
that of heir apparent, which Joe Lupollo's son Joey enjoys and which gives
him a special place as a mediator, somewhat like his Uncle Charley. All other
roles in the family are specialist roles such as the corrupter (Phil and Char-

---

[7] Constance Cronin, *The Sting of Change,* Chicago: University of Chicago Press,
1970, p. 82.

[8] Aubrey Menen, "The Italian Family is a Commune," *New York Times Magazine,*
March 1, 1970, p. 78.

ley) and buffer (Charley) roles which Donald Cressey identified in organized crime. Even these positions, at least in the Lupollo family, seem a function of kinship for they are entrusted only to close kindred.

Finally, but most fundamentally, the Lupollo family seems to form for these kinsmen the widest public within which law and order can be enacted and enforced. It is not just that they, like most south Italian peasants and immigrants, exhibit what Edward Banfield[9] has called " 'amoral familialism'— an inability to concert activity beyond the immediate family—" they have also managed to extend their familialism to include a wide range of relatives, employees, and clients within their behavioral expectations and have insulated themselves against the rest of society. This tradition of ignoring the laws of the state and attending to family business goes back to the *Mezzogiorno*, where society was controlled by customary sanctions which, in the small villages at least, meant the bounded network of related nuclear families. Social control in such systems requires that acts against any member of the system activate all other members to right the wrong or avenge the misdeed before the system can return to equilibrium. It also requires that members of the system keep faith with each other and not take outsiders into their confidence. So strong is this rejection of non-kinship-based social relationships that Danilo Dolci reports that in Sicily the word "association" usually stands for "criminal association," since the people do not realize the potentially positive aspects of association.[10] Thus it is that *Mafia* originated within families and grew into a new extended family for the protection of its members, in return for which they took on the formal ties of kinship implying rights and obligations. It is the certainty of what George Simmel called "the reciprocity of service and return service" in the kinship bond that holds the Lupollos together as a clan. When consanguineal or affinal kinship does not exist to create alliances, there may well be an effort to create it. In some of the interlocked families we have looked at in various parts of the country there seems to be continuous and conscious intermarriage which may have the same function as the alliances among European royalty: to provide solidarity. Marriage provides a new group of kindred and so new protectors. In the Roman Catholic dogma which is still potent to Italian-American crime families, all those related to one's wife become related to oneself in the same degree, and so two extended families are joined by a marriage, and the relationships consecrated by the church.

If the recognition of kinship ties and kinship obligations explains how and why consanguineal and affinal relatives in the Lupollo family learn and follow the rules of behavior we described earlier, how then can we explain

---

[9] Edward C. Banfield, *The Moral Basis of a Backward Society,* Glencoe, Ill.: The Free Press, 1958, p. 10.

[10] Danilo Dolci, *Waste,* trans. R. Monroe, New York: Monthly Review Press, 1964, p. 261.

that these same rules seem to be accepted by numbers of "family members" who are not genealogically related? We believe that the interdependence of cultural traditions and kinship which gave birth to *Mafia*-style secret criminal organizations in the south of Italy and which structure Italian-American crime families create the same bonds of interdependence and reciprocity which characterize the kinship bond. Whether the fictive bond is formal as in *compareggio* or informal, the members of the clan take on a kinship-like pattern of behavior and expectations of behavior from others. Although unrelated members freely acknowledge that they are not genealogically related, they can and do learn to take on the rights and obligations which are expected in this type of kinship link. All of the rules of conduct, the requirement to place the family before all else, the injunction to protect the family honor by being a man, and the code of silence where family matters are concerned are freely accepted in return for the security and certainty that go with clan membership. Unlike ties of biological kinship, those of ritual kinship are formed on the basis of choice.

How is it possible to create artificially the bonds which are inherent in kinship? Such bonds are not based on blood, of course, but on the social and individual recognition that reciprocal rights and obligations exist between kin. These bonds have their most extreme manifestation in the nuclear family where dependence and time allow them to be socialized most effectively in the growing child. But new kinship bonds between husband and wife or father and son can and often do surpass the bonds of the individual's family of orientation. Many of these bonds are cross-sexual (as between husband and wife) but there is no reason to assume that these must be strongest. Lionel Tiger, for example, has argued that the strength of the male–male bond can and often does form the basis of political and social organization of most societies.[11] Unisexual bonds compete actively with the family in many societies. They range in size from diadic groups, such as comrades, blood brothers, or best friends, to larger and more formal organizations such as gangs, secret societies, and fraternities. If the real function of kinship is to affiliate individuals into a system of reciprocity and exchange, there seems to be no reason why the kinship relationship cannot be artificially produced among males and why a nonbiological, extra-genealogical family unit and spirit cannot be engendered. Three features of the biological family would seem to require a place in the new family group. First, the new group must provide security for the individual and, if it is to compete with or replace the family, it must provide more security than one can expect from his family. Next, if the new group is to function properly, there must be some symbolic representation to replace the concept of blood, and to explain why they came together and why they stay

---

[11] Lionel Tiger, *Men in Groups,* New York: Random House, 1969.

together. Finally, there must be some systematic basis for recruiting new members if the group is to survive. Many groups fail to provide this third feature, and perish because they are only horizontally integrated groups of peers with no past and a foreshortened future. Gangs are representative of this class. Other groups, such as secret societies, have apprentice systems as well as ancestors so that they provide the same continuance as the biological family.

The Lupollo clan meets all three of these needs for its members, whether they are consanguineal, affinal, or ritual. It provides more security than is possible in the individual lineages because of the alliances formed within it and between it and other clans. The individual member is "connected" and can operate in his sphere without fear, even fear of the police. *Omertà,* the *mafia* code of ritual secrecy and honor, provides the symbolic representation, and so long as the member abides by it he remains "in": if he fails, he is ejected from the clan and the dishonor must be washed clean in blood. New members are recruited, often from existing lineages of the clan, adding new blood and a future to the family.

Kinship ties are, for Italian-Americans, one of the major elements influencing behavior. In this, as in so many features of their lives, the Lupollos are more Italian than most. The closer Italian-Americans are to traditional south Italian culture, the stronger will be the solidarity of the family, the exclusion of non-family members, and the preferential treatment of kin. Many of these Italian kinship values are at odds with American culture and so are the behaviors which they produce, but it is these values which produce the social control within the Lupollo family and will continue to do so until the certainty of eventual acculturation overcomes them. This is, of course, already beginning to happen. The fourth generation of Lupollos, Alcamos, Tuccis and Salemis are giving up the father-obedience and mother-respect which are essential to the preservation of the *mafia*-oriented clan organization which has produced and preserved the family as a business and social organization. The signs of internal disorder are already beginning to show in the power-vs.-authority clash described earlier. The family can continue as a composite clan only while the kinship bond remains strong, and that strength depends on adhesion to the authority structure. In one more generation the authority structure will have disappeared, and the clan with it.

Other Italian-American Crime Families

If all of this is so for the Lupollos, what of other Italian-American crime families? Are they as responsive to the heritage of kinship and *mafia* as this clan? No one will know until more studies like ours are done. But from government reports, charts showing membership in various families throughout the country, and similar data, we are convinced that they are.

Figure 1. East Harlem De Maio Family

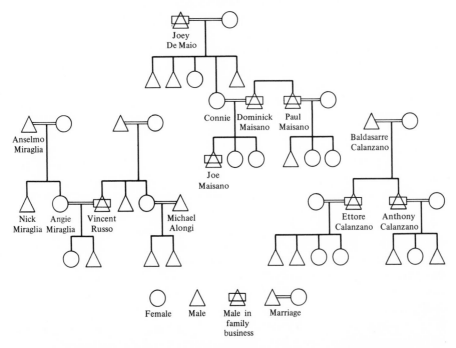

When we first became aware of the importance of kinship as an organ-
izer in the Lupollo family, we decided to look for some comparative data on
other Italian-American families identified as involved in organized crime. We
already had some partial data on the East Harlem De Maio family and some
scattered bits and pieces on the New Jersey group mentioned earlier. These
data were not as complete and detailed as what we had gathered on the Lupollos, but they did show the role of kinship in these groupings. (See Figure
1). In East Harlem, Joey De Maio's son-in-law, Dominick Maisano, and the
other members of the Maisano lineage run a nunber of gambling enterprises as
part of the De Maio family organization, which is paramount in that area. Paul
Maisano, whose street name is "Polly Mason," works for his brother Dominick in the policy game and also operates a luncheonette which serves as the
collection point for the family numbers enterprise. Dominick's son, Joe
Maisano, began working with his father in 1968, after returning from two
years in the U.S. Marine Corps. Vincent Russo and his brothers-in-law, Mi-
chael Alongi and Nicholas Miraglia, operate a garbage-hauling and disposal
company headquartered in East Harlem. Nick Miraglia is a cousin of Marky
Lupollo's wife, but the Miraglia–Alongi–Russo group are part of the De Maio
family, not the Lupollo group.

Antony and Ettore Calanzano are both Sicilian immigrants who came to the United States in the 1920's and settled in East Harlem. In the 1930's they worked with their father, who was a bodyguard for the organizers in the International Ladies Garment Workers Union. Today they run a profitable loan-shark business and are reputedly involved in the sale of narcotics. We wanted to look beyond these groups since they are allied through kinship with the Lupollos. It was, of course, impossible to gather any in-depth data on families in other parts of the country, but we did have available the extensive data released by the Justice Department, various governmental commissions and committees, and newspaper accounts listing the reputed membership of various families throughout the country. Where data on kin relationship were provided we checked them; where they were not, we went to specific cities to look for relationships. Our findings—still preliminary, but accurate as far as they go—indicate that the role of kinship in integrating individual families and creating alliances among them is not peculiar to the Lupollos.

Several interesting points emerge from these data. Even today, virtually every Italian-American who has been identified as involved in organized crime is of southern Italian peasant origin, and Sicilians predominate among them. As one reads the governmental and newspaper accounts of *Cosa Nostra* indictments, a second salient factor emerges: these are old men, in their sixties and seventies, almost all of whom immigrated from the south of Italy as children or young men. Only in a few cases are they American-born children of immigrants. We also found that the families are usually made up of a number of lineages, and frequently the leadership roles are assigned within one or two of the lineages.[12] The families seem to share some common business interests as well.

The basic pattern of kinship organization occurs in families we looked at not only in New York City, but in Philadelphia, Pennsylvania; Buffalo and Utica, New York; Kansas City, Missouri; New Orleans, Louisiana; Tampa, Florida; and Detroit, Michigan. Not only are individuals within families related, but there is widespread intermarriage among families throughout the country. Of the more than sixty *Mafia* bosses identified as participants at the famous Apalachin meeting in November 1957, almost half were related by blood or marriage, and many of the others were related by *compareggio*. At one point, two of the five bosses of New York's families—Carlo Gambino and Thomas Lucchese—had children who were intermarried.[13] We believe that

---

[12] These data are scattered throughout various government reports. The primary sources, however, are: Special Committee to Investigate Organized Crime in Interstate Commerce, 81st Congress, *Third Interim Report,* Washington, D.C.: Government Printing Office, 1951; and Select Committee on Improper Activities in the Labor or Management Field, 85th Congress, 2nd Session, *Hearings,* Washington, D.C.: Government Printing Office, 1957–59.

[13] We are indebted to Ralph Salerno for these data.

these relationships are actually a series of complex alliances binding lineages within the same family and allying families into what we have called clans, for the purpose of systematic exchange of services. As an example of the complexity of these alliances, Figure 2 traces relationships among the twenty Italian-American families identified by various senate committees as the leaders in organized crime in Detroit, Michigan. After extracting these data from the committee hearings and making a kinship chart, we checked the data in Detroit and other parts of the country.

Not only are all twenty families intermarried, they have also formed alliances through marriages with families identified by government sources as involved in organized crime in Buffalo, New York City, and New Orleans. This intricately woven web of kinship ties families in various parts of the country together. Consider just one alliance, that between the Tocco and Zerilli lineages. William Tocco married Rosalie Zerilli, who is the sister of Joseph Zerilli. Joseph Zerilli's daughter Rosalie is married to Dominic Licavoli. Dominic Licavoli's brother Pete married Grace Bommarito. William and Rosalie (Berilli) Tocco's son Anthony is married to Carmela Profaci, daughter of Joseph Profaci, who was the boss of a family in New York City. Carmela Profaci's cousin is married to the son of Joseph Bonanno, a now-deposed former boss of another New York family. Profaci's other daughter, Rosalie, married the son of Joseph Zerilli (the brother of Rosalie Zerilli, who is married to William Tocco). William and Rosalie Tocco's son Jack Tocco married Antoinette Meli, who is the daughter of Angelo Meli. Antoinette's brother Salvatore Meli married Dolores Livorsi, the daughter of Frank Livorsi, who is a functionary in another New York family. Dolores' sister Rose is married to Tom Dio, a member of a New York family reputedly involved in labor racketeering. Antoinette (Meli) Tocco's cousin Marie is married to William Bufalino, reputedly a leading member of an upstate New York family. Antoinette (Meli) Tocco's brother Vincent Meli married Pauline Perrone, daughter of Santo Perrone. One of Pauline's sisters is married to Agostino Orlando; another is married to Carl Renda. This network of alliances intersects with several others which reach into families all over the country and is strengthened by an equally complex pattern of godparent-godchild relationships.

Italian-American criminal syndicates are rightly called families because the relationships established within them produce kinship-like ties among members, ties which become even stronger when they are legitimated through marriage or godparenthood. Every family member knows that every other member has some duties toward him and some claims on him. Whether the relationships are based on blood or marriage as they often are, or are fictive as in the intricate pattern of *compareggio,* it is also kinship which ties generations together and allies lineages and families.

Membership in a family is not like membership in a gang or a formal or-

Figure 2. Marriage and Kinship Lines

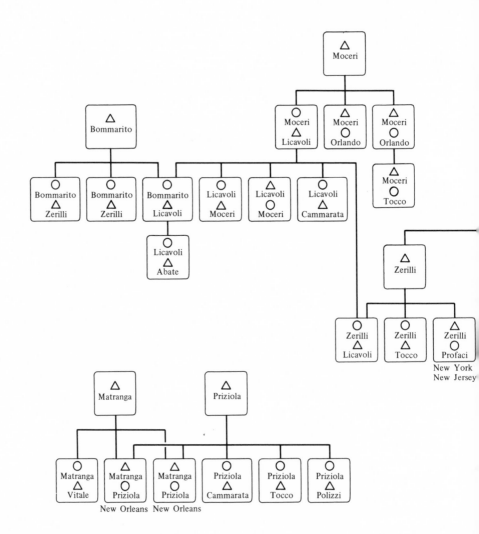

Among 20 Families in Detroit

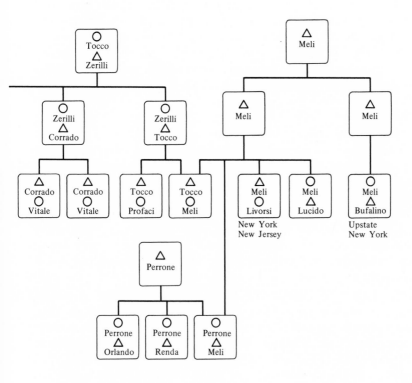

ganization. A member does not receive a salary. He is usually engaged in his own activities. Members of families may even be competitive with each other. Nor does a family member necessarily give a share of his earnings to the head of the family. The closest analogy is the feudal system—a member swears fealty, receives protection, and provides his services to protect others when it is asked.

It is this feature which sets Italian-American crime families off from the organized-crime gangs of previous ethnic groups. Every government report, after the *de rigeur* disclaimer that "of course, the vast majority of Italians in this country are god-fearing and hardworking" goes on to marvel at how tightly knit Italian-American crime families are, and how closely structured the network among families is. The most frequently used term is "clannishness." One report describes this clannishness as "the cement that helps to bind the Costello–Adonis–Lansky Syndicate"; another comments that among Italian-American crime families, "a certain clannishness contributed to the retention of the custom of clannishness." The term is apt.

Italian-American crime families are actually a number of lineages linked together into a composite clan. Like clans everywhere, these crime families enter into exchange relations with one another and form alliances which are perpetuated. Like clansmen everywhere, members treat each other as brothers and acknowledge mutual rights and obligations on a kinship pattern, however remote they may be genealogically. Each clan has its own territory. Because of its kinship base and its territoriality, the clan can establish and maintain its own rigid code of familial law and pass authority from one generation to another. As in the great *Mafia* families of Sicily, the "descendants" intermarry continuously, for the clan defines who may and who may not marry whom. As in clans everywhere, the relationship between the intermarrying pair is defined as strengthening the social structure.[14]

This clan pattern of organization also provides a common system of roles, norms, and values which not only regulate the behavior within the family but also structure relationships among families. Some clans obviously form compact, interlocked regional groups with frequent intermarriages cementing the alliances; all are related by some common business interests.

The primacy of kinship was strikingly obvious in the Lupollo family, but we cannot warrant its centrality in other Italian-American crime families. Certainly it seemed to be an important organizational basis in every Italian-American crime group we had any access to or were told about. Yet it remains to be seen whether the Lupollos are typical of other families or whether they are

---

[14] Cf. Claude Levi-Strauss, *Elementary Structures of Kinship,* trans. James Herle Bell; John Richard Von Sturmer and Rodney Needham (eds.), Boston: Beacon Press, 1969.

somehow unique. Certainly the transfer of power from old Giuseppe to his son Joe, and the probable transfer to Joey, is not typical. From the evidence supplied by government sources, there seem to have been only a few cases where a son succeeded his father in power and authority. Neither are we certain that the rules of conduct and the techniques of social control observed among the Lupollos are valid for other Italian-American crime families. It may well be that the Lupollos are much more kin-oriented than other families and that their behavior reflects this bias. These questions and numerous others left unanswered by our study will only be answered when the proper theoretical and methodological perspective is applied to the study of other Italian-American crime families. Whether such studies can ever be done is questionable, but until they are, the data and the rules we extracted from them must be viewed as descriptive of how one family is organized and operates and, at best, suggestive of the logic that may apply in similar groups. We are certain, however, of the ancestry of these rules and techniques, and of the clan model of organization which gives rise to them. They are part of the heritage of southern Italians in this country and they could, and we think do, serve other Italian-American crime families as well as the Lupollos.

We believe that it is the universality of this clan organization and the strength of its shared behavior system which makes Italian-American criminal syndicates seem so similar. And we believe that it is this similarity which has inclined observers to maintain that the different crime families constitute some sort of highly organized national or even international crime conspiracy.

9 / On the Methods Used in This Study

Since the basic technique used in the study of the Lupollo family was that of participant observation, it is important that the reader know who and what I am.

Personal Background of Francis A. J. Ianni

Both of my parents came to this country from the Italian province of the Abruzzi during the mass migrations in the early part of the century. My mother was about two years old when her father settled in Wilmington, Delaware, just before the First World War. My father was nineteen when he left the Abruzzi in 1920. He settled briefly in New York City, but then moved to Wilmington to join an older brother who had lived there since 1910.

Wilmington's Italian colony was small compared to those in New York or Philadelphia; it was really several small transplanted southern Italian villages. The men left the colony early every day to work in the mills and factories or in construction work, just as they had left for the fields in Italy, and at night they returned to the social world of the colony. Everyone saw himself as somehow different from the surrounding Americans. We had our own values and expectations, our own gossip and problems.

Wilmington's Little Italy had grown around its Italian-language church, which dominated the colony culturally as well as architecturally. The founder and first pastor of St. Anthony's was the Most Reverend J. Francis Tucker, who later became the chaplain of Prince Rainier of Monaco and who (according to Wilmington's Italian-Americans) arranged the Prince's marriage to an Irish-American girl, Grace Kelly, from the neighboring city of Philadelphia. Father Tucker had been educated in Italy, spoke fluent Italian, and ruled the parish and, therefore, the whole Italian colony, with all of the force and love of a benevolent despot. Like Father Tucker, all of the younger priests were Irish-American; however, they did not speak Italian.

Most of the Italians in Wilmington were Neapolitans or Sicilians, and the few families from the Abruzzi all lived in the same neighborhood. My parents met in Wilmington and were married there. I was their first child and also the first child baptized at St. Anthony's, and so I was named Francis after Father Tucker and Anthony after the church.

I grew up in the Italian colony, and went to school there as well. All of my relatives and most of my boyhood friends still live there, and whenever I go back we talk a good deal about what life was like in the "old days." Life was regulated by the social and religious calendar of the church, and was contained within the boundaries of Little Italy. Associations were segregated by sex and age. Yet everyone knew everyone else, and a family tragedy or accomplishment was immediately known throughout the colony. Each neighborhood was a bounded network of families, and each network reached out to others through kin or village relationships in the old country.

Everyone was open about activities which are now classified as part of organized crime. In the mid-1930's, when I was growing up, former bootleggers were still well-known and respected men in the colony. When Father Tucker decided to establish a parochial school in the late 1930's, he moved the nuns who were to run the school into a house that had been the home of a well-known bootlegger. I used to go there in the morning to serve mass, and the nuns would delight in showing me the large storage tank built into the basement ceiling, and the protruding spigot from which the bootlegger had filled the bottles.

In Little Italy and in the adjoining Black ghetto, everybody played the numbers. The collectors made the rounds of the houses every day to take the numbers and the money. They were the older brothers of my friends, and after work they "hung out" with the same street gangs as everybody else. The number drops were in candy stores at Eighth and Lincoln Streets and at Sixth and Lincoln. The drop at Sixth and Lincoln was run by a Sicilian who had been a bootlegger but now was in the contracting business. The one at Eighth and Lincoln was run by Blacks; but everybody knew that "the mob" was behind both operations. I never really knew who or what "the mob" was, and I don't think I do today; I never heard the word *Mafia* or *Cammora* used. We always "knew" that the numbers game was somehow tied in with Italians in Philadelphia. But the people on the local scene who were involved were just like everybody else, and no one seemed to spend much time worrying about it. Everyone knew and accepted the fact that one of Carmine Spargo's sons was writing numbers, just as they knew that the other was going to be a priest.

While everyone knew who was involved in the numbers game, there was an element of mystery surrounding it. We heard that each of the numbers drops had a chute under the counter into which the bankers could pour the numbers slips in the event of a police raid, but I don't remember any raids. Nor was anyone killed or shot. There were men in the colony who were considered violent and dangerous, and some who went off to the "workhouse" from time to time. "The police caught them" always seemed to be a more satisfactory explanation than any of the specific acts with which they were charged.

Growing up in the Italian colony was strictly regulated by an age-grade system. All of my playmates and peers were within one or two years of my own age. Each neighborhood had its "corner," and each corner its series of age-graded gangs. Most of the other kids in my street gang were the youngest children in immigrant families in which the parents were really of my grandparents' generation. Since the younger gang always clung to the periphery of the next higher age-grade gang, I was at a disadvantage because I did not have an older brother in that next age-grade to look after my interests. As a result I moved back and forth between two separate street gangs and eventually, in about the sixth grade. I began going around with American boys from school. Then I went off to college and into the Navy, and left the colony for good.

After finishing college in 1949 with a degree in psychology, I began graduate work in sociology and anthropology. At that time Italian-Americans in anthropology were still enough of a rarity that when the time came to select the topic of my master's thesis the only question seemed to be *which* area of Italian-American acculturation to select. My adviser and I settled on a study of the rate of intermarriage with non-Italians as an index of acculturation, using my own home colony of Wilmington as the field situation. My doctoral dissertation was a field study of residential and occupational mobility as indices of acculturation among the Italian-Americans in Norristown, Pennsylvania. Norristown, which is a small industrial city just outside of Philadelphia, was my first real contact as an anthropologist with Italian-Americans in organized crime. A large proportion of the Italian-Americans there had come from the city of Sciacca on the western coast of Sicily. My chief informant and constant companion in Norristown was an old physician from northern Italy who had emigrated before the First World War. He commented in great detail and with some scorn on the habits and beginnings of the leading Sicilian-American businessmen in Norristown. All were related by blood or marriage, and he spoke darkly of blood feuds which had decimated families until marriage tied the enemies together. He traced the intricate, overlapping kinship and business relationships among them and insisted that the "mentality of the Sicilian race" made it impossible for them to think of any group larger than the family or to accept the rule of law. Therefore, each family made its own law and its men their own destiny.

Since completing the Norristown study, I have done a number of field studies of acculturation in this country and in Italy. My interest in studying Italian-American criminal syndicates, however, came only partially out of this background.

Origins of the Study

From 1958 to 1961 I taught and studied in Ethiopia, and developed a lively interest in secret societies, their internal organization, and their external functions. Since then, I have found numerous and intriguing examples of secret organizations (such as Mau Mau in Kenya) which have emerged at particular points in history, served their original function, and then disappeared as the social, political, and economic factors which gave meaning to that function disappeared. The most impressive feature of these secret societies seems to be the strong, cohesive group force which binds the members together. The question of how this force is related to the cohesive forces which bind families together is fascinating.

My interests in Italian and Italian-American culture and in secret societies rather naturally flowed into an interest in the *Mafia* in Sicily. Reviewing the Italian literature, I began to sense a relationship between Sicilian culture and the *mafia* code, and a congruence between the organizational model of the *Mafia* and the kinship structure of the Sicilian family. Turning to the literature on the *Mafia* in the United States, I was struck by the lack of research data and particularly by the glaring inaccuracies about Sicilian *Mafia* which formed the basis for the imputation of an organizational link between the Sicilian *Mafia* and Italian-Americans in organized crime. In 1966 I began to plan a field study of Italian-American crime families that would test some of my notions about kinship as the basis for structuring Italian-American involvement in organized crime. First, of course, I had to gain access to one or more "*Mafia* families" in the United States.

In a very real sense, I found the Lupollo family before I started looking for them. In 1964 I was director of research programs in the United States Office of Education in Washington. In those early days of the Johnson administration, as in the inaugural period of any new administration, most of the congressional offices I visited were bustling with hordes of lobbyists and favor-seekers jockeying for position. It was in a congressman's waiting room that I first met Phil Alcamo. Phil was introduced to me as "a business leader from New York City and an outstanding Italian-American." We spoke briefly about my role in the Office of Education, and he left for another meeting.

Two weeks later, I encountered Phil Alcamo in a Washington restaurant. Phil introduced me to his friends as "an Italian boy" who had "done big things with the Office of Education's research program." After exchanging a few pleasantries I returned to my table and finished my lunch. About three weeks later Phil invited me to dinner with a group of his friends. The dinner was a pleasant affair with Phil, his son-in-law, and a few of his friends, including two special assistants to congressmen, one of whom I had met previously. During the next two years I met Phil occasionally for dinner or lunch in Washington, and on one occasion we had lunch together in New York when I was there on business. At these meetings we usually talked about national politics, the Washington scene, and other matters of mutual interest. Phil impressed me with his knowledge of Washington. He spoke the lobbyist's language, but with a charming disdain for Washington manners and morals. He was always very good in those peculiar Washington conversations in which people try to convince each other how much they really know about what is going on in the government, because he generally did know. He would occasionally ask my advice about the education of his children or relatives, but our friendship was based principally on co-ethnicity. Phil, twenty years my senior, told fascinating Runyonesque stories of his early life in Brooklyn. He had grown up with boys like Joe Profaci, and with boys who had become Congressmen, state Supreme Court judges, and well-known civic and business leaders.

In 1965, I left the Office of Education to join the faculty at Columbia University. Shortly after my arrival in New York I got in touch with Phil and our friendship continued. We saw each other frequently. My role was that of an Italian-American professor interested in Italian-American culture and with the role of that culture in American society. I soon realized that Phil was a member of a larger family business syndicate, which was made up of four lineages, the Lupollos, the Alcamos, the Tuccis, and the Salemis. Over the next four years I gradually came to know Phil's relatives as individuals and to observe them in interaction at various gatherings, such as weddings and dinner parties.

When I first began to meet the members of this extensive family through Phil, I reacted to them first as his relatives and then as individuals. Some I liked and some I didn't; some were responsive and some weren't. I knew about their involvement in gambling long before I came to New York, because Phil had mentioned his relationship to the Lupollos, and they are known as one of the Italian-American families involved in a range of activities which spill over into organized crime. They are not, however, a notorious family; there has been little public notice of the illegal side of the Lupollo family business. Within the Italian-American community however, and to the police and federal agencies, the family is known to be involved in crime. I found them friendly and open.

Planning The Field Study

Once the formal research project was under way, my relationship with the Lupollo family changed in my own eyes if not in theirs. Before the project I had been a participant observer in the family, but the observer role was secondary to that of participant. I was there because I enjoyed their company and found them interesting. Now, because I was engaged in a systematic study of these people, the role of observer took precedence. Where I had attended only those family functions or individual meetings which suited my particular interests and needs at any given time, I now felt the need for as much interaction as possible.

Soon after the proposal was approved, I had dinner with Phil Alcamo and told him about the research project. He was neither surprised nor distressed. He had always known of my interest in Italian-American crime syndicates and accepted the new project as part of my general interest in the acculturation of Italian-Americans. I described the purpose and approach of the research and gave him some preliminary observational notes I had already developed on the Lupollo family as an example of the types of material I would be collecting. The fact that I was interested in Italian-American acculturation and his memories of growing up within Brooklyn's Italian ghetto, and fascinated by his explanations of the Lupollos' complicated business relationships, made the new project seem logical to him. Phil's advice was that I should tell each member of the family what I was about *only* when it was necessary to ask questions or seek specific pieces of information. What he was telling me, in effect, was to proceed on a "need to know" basis rather than attempting deception or announcing my intentions at a family meeting. I followed his advice and found it sound. I never asked for specifics on criminal activities, and yet because of my role with the family I rather naturally learned such things.

In this study, as in all field work, a preliminary condition for success was the reality of my role as a participant-observer. Because of the nature of this study, however, there were some additional problems. In the first place, the group I was observing was a closed system, at least part of which—the illegal activities—I could not hope to observe with any degree of regularity. I could not really immerse myself in the lives of the people I was studying and had to be content with observing whenever the opportunity presented itself. Actually I found that these restrictions on my role as participant sharpened my skill as an observer. Knowing that in this study there might well never be a chance to observe a particular piece of action a second time, I grew very careful in recording observations. In field work I usually prefer to follow the stream of behavior rather than pre-plan each encounter. In this study, because I knew the limits of my opportunities to observe, I did much more pre-planning of observation than I normally do. I drew up a chart listing thirty-seven categories of information—age, education, affinal and consanguineal relationships, etc.—I wanted to get on all family members. Before attending a wedding or having dinner with family members, I would, for example, review all of my previous field notes on the individual or individuals involved or look into my "unfinished business" file for pieces of information I still needed. I found that I was often looking *for* something as well as looking *at* what was taking place around me.

My role with individual members of the Lupollo family did not change significantly as a result of the study, or at least their reactions to me did not seem to alter. Certainly during the three-year period in which I interacted with them there were changes in their attitudes to me. At one point Phil became quite upset with me because I could not attend a political banquet with him in Washington. The reason—an academic function at the University on the same night—seemed trivial to Phil. For a week or two after that there was a strain in our relationship, and since Phil was my sponsor in the family I felt somewhat ill at ease meeting with other members. But this soon blew over, like all such squabbles among friends, and the relationship returned to normal.

Although I could never be an insider with the Lupollo family, I was able quite naturally to become part of the larger Italian-American social setting in which the family operated. The clique of Italian-American business and professional men in New York City is a fairly small and cohesive network and has its own subculture. Members discuss questions among themselves which are not shared with anyone outside the group. These men, including most of the members of the Lupollo family, are upwardly mobile and aspire to higher social positions. They are businessmen, physicians, lawyers, and builders who either came to the United States at a very early age or are second-generation children of Italian immigrants. My status as a university professor made me somewhat unusual in the network, but my background as an Italian-American made me an accepted member of the group. I moved freely and easily in this world, which centers around a few social and athletic clubs and a number of Italian restaurants. I could enter the network at any time simply by going to one of the clubs or restaurants. Thus, while I did not "go native," I had fairly easy access to the world in which the Lupollo family lives.

I observed Lupollo social interactions and behavior in a number of settings. I frequently met Phil and other members of the family at one of two social clubs to which we both belonged. We would usually spend some time together at the club, have dinner there or at one of a number of restaurants (almost always Italian), and sometimes go to a nightclub after that. I was invited to Lupollo and Alcamo family functions such as marriages and christenings, and received dinner invitations from various family members. Sometimes I encountered some family member or members at Italian-American social and religious events.

In all of these encounters, as is usually true of participant observation in field work, the relationship between me and the people I was observing was one of exchange. I was part of the group and gave freely of myself in social interaction and in interpersonal relationships. I answered questions, gave advice and information whenever it was asked for, and did favors for a number of people who did favors for me also. Obviously my presence, as is true in all participant observation studies, did have some effect upon what I was observing. I do think, however, that our shared ethnicity and my long association with the family tended to reduce this problem. At times conversation stopped when I entered a room where two members of the family were meeting. But this did not happen with any greater frequency after the study began than it had before.

The public role as participant-observer is always accompanied by a more personal, private empathy relationship which the field worker establishes with individual members of the group he is observing. Uncle Phil was my closest friend in the family, and my relationship with him was the most constant in terms of both time and depth. At the other extreme was Tony Lupollo, who did not like me, trust me, or really want me around. At first I was upset about this, both personally and because it might affect my relationship with the family. His dislike of me was a significant problem because the legitimacy of my role could be challenged at any point. But I simply avoided him, and the problem solved itself. I was not, of course, in any physical danger from Tony or any other member of the family. My colleagues at the University and at Russell Sage Foundation frequently commented—sometimes humorously— on the potential danger of working in this particular setting. At no time during the research did I sense any danger or any possibility of physical harm.

Colleagues frequently asked another question: How could the data be valid, given the very special character of the group I was studying? My training and subsequent field experience have convinced me that direct observation of human action is better than the collection of verbal statements about that action if one would understand how a social system functions. I place great reliance on observing and recording only what I have seen, and so the question of validity is really two questions: Did I see what I thought I was seeing? Did the actors perform naturally, or were they attempting to mask their behavior? The second question is answered, I think, by the fact that I spent three years in close relationship with the family and they could have ejected me at any point. Why should they bother to attempt to deceive me? It would have been much simpler to have refused to see me. The first question is common to all field work and is answerable in terms of the methodology we used and the way we organized and analyzed the data we gathered. We cross-checked all data, so that unless two or more persons gave the same information or we could use other sources for checking, we did not include the data in our summaries.

Problems and Categories in Observation

The problem of how to classify what is observed in field work is persistent and has many dimensions. Two are especially problematic. Should the categorization of behavior take place prior to going into the field or during the field experience itself? The other question has to do with how categories or units of observation are derived. Does the field worker create his own logical categories, or does he let them emerge from what he is studying?

The first question—which asks, essentially, whether categories for observation in field work are properly derived from theory and then taken into the field with the field worker or whether they arise from the observation situation itself—is one that is currently under examination in both sociology and anthropology. At the heart of the issue is the question of how theory should be generated. Under the classical logico-deductive scheme, theory is first developed, and then taken into the field and examined through the research process. In an earlier period of sociological research, the "Chicago school" of sociologists emphasized field work as the basis for discoveries about human society and the social system—letting theory emerge from what one finds in the field. Today, a number of sociologists are calling for a return to that tradition. Barney Glaser and Anselm Strauss, sociologists who have been working in the medical field, have developed a paradigm for the relationship of theory and research which they call "grounded theory." While the generation of theory should always involve a process of research, they maintain that the development of theory in the logico-deductive paradigm sometimes incorporates ideas from non-research data sources. Thus, they say, theory should be developed *in* (not before) the process of research, so that it is is "grounded" in the empirical world in which the research is being carried out.[1] We have used a similar approach, which we call "situational analysis," in some of our studies of social action in education systems. Of course, other schemes being developed elsewhere share this new—or at least newly rediscovered—approach in the field of qualitative research.

Unlike sociologists, anthropologists have always dealt with qualitative questions. But even here a "new ethnography" is developing. Sometimes called "ethnoscience," it is an attempt to "break the mold of the categorical outline of culture which most anthropologists now take with them into the field."[2] In both the "new field work" in sociology and the "new ethnography" in anthropology there is a strong emphasis on letting categories of observation emerge in the field-work experience. This does not mean that the sociologist or anthropologist goes into the field "as a camera" and records all that is to be seen. That is, of course, impossible. One always goes into the field looking *for* something and using prior knowledge and experience as a guide. In our own method of situational analysis, we took "concepts" into the field with us and used them as guidelines for observation but did not pre-plan and pre-build an elaborate conceptual framework into which we forced all of the observations we made. To say this differently, we did not build a series of theoretical and conceptual boxes, take them into the field, and fill them with appropriate pieces of action; rather, we went out and observed the social action and then

---

[1] Barney G. Glaser and Anselm Strauss, *The Discovery of Grounded Theory,* Chicago: Aldine Publishing Co., 1967.

[2] Thomas Gladwin and William G. Sturtevant, "Headnote" to a paper by Charles Frake, "The Ethnographic Study of Cognative Systems" in their *Anthropology and Human Behavior,* Washington, D.C.: Anthropological Society of Washington, 1962, pp. 72–73.

built the boxes in the field, using conceptual materials which were already a part of our repertoire. There is, of course, no utility in rediscovering concepts which are already known. We already knew, for example, a very useful concept called role-model. We took this concept with us into the field as a category for observation, and as the study progressed we discovered that each generation in the Lupollo family had a different role-model and that an adequate understanding of the family required more knowledge than we had or theory could provide. The process of "filling in" the knowledge required gathering and classifying more cultural materials to explain the origin and function of these different role-models.

Once we had derived categories into which to fit observations—either from theory and experience or *de novo* from observation—we continuously tested and refined them. We did this by constant comparison of observation reports, looking for plausible categories suggested in the data. Then we took these embryonic categories and discussed them with some of our key informants, to see whether the categories we had developed fit the logic of the group under study as well as our own logical assumptions. This technique grows out of our position on the second issue I described earlier: whose categories take precedence in the field, one's own or the natives'? In our field work we have always followed the injunction that "the native's categorization is the only correct one." Constant rechecking with key informants was necessary because we proposed as one of our most important tasks the search for the right organization of any set of observations to conform with the reality of the world we were studying.

The major themes of the research began to emerge very early in the field work, but they changed and shifted constantly. My own field notes, for example, contain four different answers, made at four different times, to the question of the existence of a national or regional "council" which oversees the activities of Italian-American criminal syndicates. But the notes also show that a process of refinement was responsible, and that the fourth answer was consistent with the finding of new data. At the same time I found that strategies and approaches in the field changed very early, and continued to do so quite frequently. In many cases our expectations for the research were not met when we finally entered the field. People we expected to be hostile were not, while people we expected to work well with sometimes proved difficult. But that usually happens in field work and we did not find it any more of a problem here than in other studies.

Role and Role Relationship—Definitions

The basic tools we used in our study of the Lupollo family structure were the concepts of "role" and "role relationship." By a role, I mean that constellation of behaviors which defines an individual's relationship with others when they interact with him in that role. Thus the role determines both how he will interact with other individuals and how they will interact with him. Within a social system, roles are social norms which define how specified categories of members will interact with each other. The focus here is on dynamic relationships rather than on static positions. This approach seems to dictate two important considerations for the empirical study of role phenomena. First, since role behavior is interactional, it has to be observed in interpersonal relationships rather than in observations of single action. Second, identifying and describing roles can come only from studying the regularities in behavior in interpersonal relationships between the role-actor and other individuals. Having observed these behaviors and the frequency with which they occur, it is then possible to describe some distinctive, integrative patterns of behavior and behavior expectations which seem to characterize a particular role. Having observed one such pattern, the field worker must then observe others having in the same role (or seek out other studies which have done so); he then attempts to identify those patterns of interpersonal relationship which seem indeed to characterize a particular role in many settings, and to factor out those which are idiosyncratic to a particular role-actor. Finally, following our general principle of looking for the rules which regulate behavior, we looked for the social norms which define roles.

The Use of Nonparticipant Data-Gathering Techniques

While participant observation was our fundamental methodology, we also employed a number of other data-gathering techniques. Important among these was the use of key informants to provide additional information and to validate data acquired by observation. During the two years of the study, we were able to interview each of the core members of the Lupollo family business at least once. The interviews were usually informal and in conjunction with other business. We kept a file of data on each of the core members of the family and reviewed it periodically to see what other data were necessary to fill out our knowledge of each member's role in the family business. Some interviews were formal, in that we specifically asked members of the family if they would discuss some particular question on which we needed additional information.

Negotiating the role of interviewer was more difficult for me than that of participant-observer, since it was not a part of my normal relationship with family members. I developed a fairly complex set of interview behaviors within the family. An example is the mundane but in this case important set of behaviors surrounding payment of the check when the interview took place at a restaurant. Since the interviewer–informant relationship is based upon an intricate pattern of exchange, I assumed at first that it was incumbent upon me as the interviewer to pay for any expenses that came up in the course of the interviewing. But with the second- and third-generation members of the Lupollo family—Charley Lupollo and Phil Alcamo, for example—this would have been considered an insult. Part of the status-assessment process within the family, and within the Italian-American business and professional group in general, is the pecking order associated with paying for checks. There is no fumbling and no debate because the person with the highest perceived status —the greatest "respect"—very naturally pays for the check. With the fourth-generation family members, however, since I was older than they and since they were in most cases more acculturated to the American social scene, I was expected to pay for lunch or dinner.

Interview behavior also differed with different generations in other areas. With the second- and third-generation members I found myself asking questions in the stylized way in which this group approaches the questioning procedure. I would not, for example, ask "Does Joey have any business dealings with his Uncle Phil?" but rather "Joey has some business dealing with his Uncle Phil, doesn't he?" The positive thrust of the question was not intended to structure the answer and I'm sure did not do so, but rather placed the question in the social form most common in that group. With fourth-generation members of the family, on the other hand, I could ask questions directly.

Elizabeth Reuss and I also interviewed many non-family members who were familiar with the family business, and some who were involved with other Italian-American families. As always we found some people more helpful than others and some people completely unwilling to speak with us. Phil Alcamo became the principal informant and was in many ways the chief expositor of the family. But over-reliance on any one informant should be avoided in field work. Although it is appealing to check all information with one individual, such reference raises the serious danger of viewing the social system only through the eyes of that individual. Individuals vary greatly in both degree of knowledge of and depth of involvement in a particular social setting, and those most willing to discuss it are not always those who know most about it. In fact, about half-way through the research I experienced the beginnings of a role exchange with Phil. Our relationship had been such that I would often discuss with him the particular reasons why some item or items were necessary and how they could be used to fill in information gaps for particular categories of behavior. Phil was interested right from the beginning. We often discussed concepts in the behavioral sciences, and he would draw examples of their operation and reality from his own experience. Later, however, he began to make a gradual role change from informant to "junior" colleague. When discussing particular aspects of the family business, for example, he would preface a story with "now here's a good example of role conflict." This is not an uncommon occurrence in field work and many of my colleagues have commented on the joys and problems which it presents. If a study involves field work over a long period of time with a small number of informants, it is possible to train informants to look for particular pieces of information. The problem, however, is that one is then never sure that he is in fact getting culturally relevant materials, since the informant may be looking for what the anthropologist wants and will surely find it. With Phil, the problem handled itself when he left for Europe, spent seven weeks there, and upon his return had completely forgotten his new role.

We also used other techniques, such as gathering life histories and developing kinship and network charts for the family. We used some of the files of the Justice Department to develop these kinship and network charts and got considerable information on relationships from a number of people who were familiar with the family. How we did this and the technique we used for getting at other data such as business portfolios, sociometric data, and data on power and prestige are described in detail in the chapters which deal with these specific topics.

Validity and Reliability in Interviewing

I have always assumed that the problem of validity is greater in interviewing than it is in participant observation, because the data are one step removed and one is "observing" through the eyes and perception of other individuals. In this study validity checks on interview information came from a process in which we measured the internal consistency of interview data through verification of information by more than one informant. And, since we were also involved in the process of observation, some of the data could also be checked against our own observations. Even so, the question of the reliability of our informants was an important one.

Problems of reliability are common to anthropological field work, but they are obviously more pronounced where one is observing deviant behavior that actors may want kept secret. Our solution was to establish a standardized system of assessing both the validity of the data which we were recording and the reliability of the individuals from whom we were gathering the data. Our problem was a dual one: how to assess the reliability of the source, and how much validity to assign to the information itself. An individual informant who has always proved reliable in the past may provide information which he is passing on from someone else and about which the analyst must make a separate judgment; an informant who is usually unreliable may pass on a piece of information which can be checked against factual data, such as ownership records of a business. Because we felt that the questions of informant reliability and data validity had to be looked at separately, we set up a two-dimensional system for assessing data.

Following our earlier assumption that the closer the field worker is to the data the more certain he is of what he is seeing and hearing, we assigned the highest validity score to those data gathered by observation where we were involved as direct participants. The second highest score went to data gathered by observation where we were not direct participants. We assigned lower validity scores to data gathered in interviews and graded interview materials according to how carefully we were able to check the data. Interview data which could be checked against standard, available documented sources—arrest records, marriage records, home and business addresses, business ownership, and so on—received the third highest rating. Data which could not be checked but which were corroborated by more than one informant, either spontaneously or as a result of our checking information from one source against later interviews with other informants, were given the fourth highest score. Where the data came from one source only, we assigned the lowest score.

Since we were constantly comparing data as they were gathered, we also began building up a profile of how reliable our major informants were. Here again we assigned the informants to categories: "always reliable" where information from that source was consistently accurate in terms of factual checks or subsequent interviewing, "usually reliable" where the data usually but not always checked out, "reliability unknown" where we had been unable to check, and "unreliable" where later checking indicated that the individual seldom seemed to provide accurate information.

Once we had assigned both a reliability score and a validity score to interview data we used only those data of the first four validity grades and the first two reliability grades. The later chapters, describing family behavior, include a few data with lower scores which I felt shed some light on a particular question. These appear as quotations on pages 84, 92, 97–98, 126, and 133.

Since our interest was in finding and describing the code of rules by which members of the Lupollo family organize their universe and behavior, our problem in analyzing the field data was to formulate rules from what we had seen and heard. Our approach was essentially that of developing a natural history of the areas of behavior in which we were interested; what was generic about the behavior of members of the family in these areas, and how did they explain this regularity? Since we were continuously coding observational and interview data into categories for analysis and constantly comparing the behaviors we sorted into a particular category, we began formulating tentative rules from the very beginning of the research. As new data came in we reexamined the code of rules and when we were satisfied that our formulation of a particular rule was sufficient to allow us to make the judgments and perform the acts in the way which members of the family would consider appropriate, we added the rule to our code of rules along with any exceptions we noted.

In the two years in which we studied the Lupollo family, we gathered a substantial quantity of data. As is so frequently true in field studies, selecting those data for eventual analysis and writing up was not an easy task. Confidentiality was, of course, a major problem. Our relationship with the Lupollo family has been such that we did acquire information which could be potentially harmful to them. Since our major interest in the study was in social organization, rather than criminal behavior, many of the potentially harmful data were not really pertinent to our interests anyway. Some of it, however, is important to understanding how the family functions. Nonetheless, we have not included any information which is not directly pertinent to the study and so we have honored the bargain we struck with the family when we started the study.

10 / Epilogue

Now that the study is over, I still see the Lupollos—particularly Uncle Phil—occasionally, although not as often as I did. I justify this by imagining that my need to take time from other things to be with them is not as strong now that I am not trying to collect pieces of information. But I still feel guilty that I do not seek them out any longer simply because I do not need them any more. There is, however, another reason I do not see them as much, one which I began to sense in mid-1970, when I first recognized the conflict developing within the family between the traditional old-country authority of Joe and his cronies and the newer, utilitarian power relationships which Charley, Phil, and the younger members of the family are seeking in the world outside.

When I first talked to members of the staff at Russell Sage Foundation about this study in 1968 one of the senior sociologists caught me off guard with a question I had not anticipated. As we talked about the history of the *Mafia*, its origins, and the heritage it has provided for the development of Italian-American criminal syndicates, he turned to me and asked: "You *do* think the *Mafia* should be destroyed, don't you?" I said that of course I did. Now, four years later, I would probably answer the question in the same way; but I must confess to some feelings of closeness and admiration for the old-style *mafioso* who was humble, taciturn, scrupulously moral in his living habits, and a man of honor. Whatever else he was—a killer, a manipulator, a despot—he did seek to provide justice and order for a people who knew neither. Danilo Dolci was once told by a village *mafioso* in the mountains of Sicily:

> This is the way I was born, Signor Danilo. Whenever somebody asks me to do him a favour, I do it, because nature made me that way . . . A man comes and says: "I have a quarrel with Tizio. Could you please help me settle it?" I call the person mentioned, or I go to see him, according to the case, and make the two men come to an agreement. It is a power I have. I am neither vain nor ambitious. I open my arms wide to all kinds of men. I cannot say no to anybody . . . Often, of course, one gains people's gratitude, one makes friends, many friends, and opportunities arise when one can demand some favour in return . . . Things follow each other, one after the other, in life . . . Tomorrow, for instance, I must leave the threshing, my cattle, all my things,

in order to go to Agrigento. I have been asked to recommend a student to his teachers, so that he may surely pass his examinations. You see how things are?[1]

Some of this spirit is part of the heritage which shaped Italian-American criminal syndicates, and it can be found in some of the nostalgic stories about old Giuseppe. There are even some traces of it in Joe. I share that same cultural heritage, and I was taught in childhood that many of the manly characteristics of the *mafioso*—his sense of honor and humility—are virtues, and that some of his ancient arts of guile are necessary for getting on in life. The lessons of childhood are hard to forget, and it is sad to see the traditions and the values disappear. And yet they must, and they should. What is left of the tradition in the families is not worth saving, and internal dissension as well as the changing times will soon dissolve the families anyway.

The Future of the Lupollo Family Business

The successful blend of illegal and legal enterprises which constitutes the Lupollo family business empire has been seventy years in the making. Its constantly increasing prosperity has enabled the heads of the family's various lineages to provide their relatives—from children and grandchildren to distant cousins—with jobs and financial security; even with a lavish life style. The kinship-based clan organization of the Lupollo family empire has enabled family members to preserve and even embellish a type of extended-family system which the counterpressures of American life could have easily destroyed.

Yet while the family business is flourishing today, a number of sociocultural developments cast a shadow over its future. Most important of these is the decline in saliency of the kinship model on which it is based. After three generations of acculturation, this compelling pattern of organization is finally losing its hold on Italian-Americans generally—and on the crime families as well. In the Lupollo clan, the change can be seen in many ways. The old authority structure in which generational position, the closeness of kinship relations, and a traditional set of personal qualities (ruthlessness, a high sense of honor, etc.) determined a man's role in the family is being challenged by new conditions. What the younger men admire in Charley and Phil is their political influence and their ability to work outside the Italian-American community—qualities the ghetto-oriented Joe lacks. As the Lupollo family's legitimate businesses continue to move into the American mainstream, these qualities will become even more important for the continued success of the family empire. So too will efficiency and technical expertise. Ultimately, the Lupollo family's businesses will become more bureaucratic and more like other American business corporations; status will be achieved rather than ascribed. When

---

[1] Danilo Dolci, *Waste,* trans. R. Monroe, New York: Monthly Review Press, 1964.

this transformation is completed, ability rather than kinship will be the primary criterion for determining positions and rewards, and the Lupollo family business structure will no longer be coterminous with the family's social organization.

The effect of acculturation on the Lupollo family can be seen in another, more direct way: the younger generation is increasingly disengaging itself from the family business. Currently, top leadership positions within the family's legitimate and illegitimate enterprises are still held by the core group of fifteen members of the Lupollo, Salemi, Alcamo, and Tucci families. The group still includes the directorate of Joe and Charley Lupollo and Phil Alcamo; and at various lower levels, Vito Salemi and his son; Pete Tucci; Joe's sons Joey, Tony, and Marky; Charley's son Patsy; Phil's son Basil; and four of Charley's and Joe's grandsons. Today, however, the group does not take in all male members of the four lineages, for with each generation, more children have made independent careers. In the third generation, both Joe and Charley have sons who do not seem to participate directly in the family business. In the fourth generation, only four out of twenty-seven males are involved in the family business organization. The rest are doctors, lawyers, college teachers, or run their own businesses.

The movement of the younger generation of the four lineages out of the family business seems to support the thesis that for Italian-Americans, as for other ethnic groups, organized crime has been a way station on the road to ultimately respectable roles in American society. If the Lupollo family is a fair example, it is predictable that fewer and fewer young Italian-Americans will be recruited into criminal syndicates of the future. Instead, like the Irish and the Jews before them, they will continue to advance into legitimate politics, professions, and corporate businesses. Only one obstacle seems to stand in the way of this trend: with public interest in organized-crime infiltration of business and politics at its height, the *Mafia* stigma will act, temporarily at least, as a brake on this natural movement.

As American culture continues to erode the strength of family and kinship in Italian-American culture, the families must, however, weaken and give way to the next wave of aspiring ethnics, just as the Jews and the Irish did before them. The evidence of this displacement is already apparent. In New York City, for example, Blacks, Puerto Ricans, and Cubans are now displacing Italian-Americans in the policy or numbers rackets. In some cases, particularly in East Harlem and in Brooklyn, this is a peaceful succession as the Italian-American families literally lease the rackets on a concession basis. The family supplies the money and the protection, the Blacks or Puerto Ricans run the operation. In other cases we know of in Central and West Harlem, however, the transition is not so peaceful, and the Italian syndicate members are actually being pushed out. Current estimates are that upwards of one-fourth of the control and operation of the policy racket in New York has already changed hands.

The outlook for the Italian crime families is not promising. Ethnic succession in organized crime will force them out, but their movement into legitimate business areas, whether as families or as individuals, is blocked by current interest in organized crime infiltration of business. They might, of course, go underground as the *Mafie* did in Sicily under Mussolini. But even if they do, there seems little chance they will reemerge, for Italian-American culture will not sustain them.

The future of the popular belief in an American *Mafia* and in its conspiracy to corrupt our way of life is less certain. A Harris Poll in 1971 indicated that "a majority of Americans"—a decisive 78 to 17 per cent of the sample Harris chose—believe "there is a secret organization engaged in organized crime in this country which is called the *Mafia*."[2] Then, at the annual rally of the Italian-American Civil Rights League, Joseph A. Colombo, Sr., the founder and president of the League and a reputed leader of a New York City *Cosa Nostra,* family was shot by a Black man. The police announced three theories on the attack—it was a gang shooting, it was the work of Black revolutionaries, or it was the work of a psychotic assassin—but finally said it was a gang shooting. Some observers, most notably the officers of the League itself and the head of the federal organized-crime strike force in New York insisted that it was the work of a lone "nut." In any case, the incident reinforced the official and public belief in the existence and power of *Cosa Nostra*. More realistically, whichever theory one accepts, it underscored the certainty of ethnic succession in organized crime in America.

An era of Italian crime seems to be passing in large measure because of the changing nature of the Italian community which resides in American culture and its inclusion in the society. To that extent, the pattern of Italian crime seems to be following that of previous ethnic groups. But what is distinctive about Italian crime is the myth that went with it. a myth that arose more out of the need of Americans, nourished in a populist politics, to believe in formidable conspiracies as a means of explaining reality. If the Lupollos provide any clues, the cultural ingredients of a *Mafia* still exist; but they are compounded of a cultural attitude and a web of kinships which are attributes peculiar to the Italian scene, rather than the "big business" pattern which is a projection of the American imagination. What remains to be seen is whether the specter of the *Mafia*—the image of a nationwide conspiracy to control all organized crime, and to subvert legitimate business and political life—will die out too, for the notion is a haunting one.

---

[2] *The Chicago Tribune,* May 17, 1971.

Index